FRANK LLOYD WRIGHT'S MARTIN HOUSE

ARCHITECTURE AS PORTRAITURE

Jack Quinan

PRINCETON ARCHITECTURAL PRESS

An Architect has had a rare chance to read the souls of man and woman when he has finished building a home. What they are, what they hope to be, is all there in highlight to be easily read.

—Frank Lloyd Wright, 1896

Published by
Princeton Architectural Press
37 East Seventh Street
New York, New York 10003

For a free catalog of books, call 1.800.722.6657.
Visit our web site at www.papress.com.

The cost of photographs and drawings used in this publication was underwritten
by the College of Arts and Sciences, the University at Buffalo.

To maintain the authentic style of the correspondence quoted herein, quirks of
spelling and grammar remain unchanged from their original state.

Editing: Nancy Eklund Later
Copyediting: Elizabeth S. G. Nicholson
Design: Jan Haux

Special thanks to: Nettie Aljian, Nicola Bednarek, Janet Behning, Megan Carey,
Penny (Yuen Pik) Chu, Russell Fernandez, Clare Jacobson, John King, Mark
Lamster, Linda Lee, Katharine Myers, Jane Sheinman, Scott Tennent, Jennifer
Thompson, Joseph Weston, and Deb Wood of Princeton Architectural Press
—Kevin C. Lippert, publisher

Library of Congress Cataloging-in-Publication Data

Quinan, Jack.
Frank Lloyd Wright's Martin House : architecture as portraiture / Jack Quinan.
    p.   cm.
Includes index.
ISBN 1–56898–419–7 (alk. paper)
1. Darwin D. Martin House (Buffalo, N.Y.) 2. Wright, Frank Lloyd,
1867–1959—Criticism and interpretation. 3. Prairie school (Architecture)—
New York (State)—Buffalo. 4. Buffalo (N.Y.)—Buildings, structures, etc.
I. Title.

NA7238.B9Q56 2004
728'.37'092—dc22
                                                            2004010362

Contents

ACKNOWLEDGMENTS

This book began, with a grant from the National Endowment for the Humanities (NEH), as a more ambitious project that was to encompass the entire thirty-two-year relationship of Frank Lloyd Wright and Darwin D. Martin. In that form, it was read and criticized by Victoria Newhouse and Karen Banks just as the illustrious years of the Architectural History Foundation were drawing to a close. With the formation of the Martin House Restoration Corporation in the early 1990s and my designation as curator of the project, I came to realize the need for a book focused specifically on the Martin House; hence this book was extracted from the original project. During the time I have spent in its preparation, and as the realm of scholarship has overlapped and merged with an ambitious historic preservation effort, I have incurred debts to many individuals and institutions.

I owe a special debt of gratitude to Leonard K. Eaton, the first scholar to write about Wright's clients, for his support in my quest for the NEH grant. During my thirty-year involvement with the Martin House, I have been the beneficiary of discussions and interpretations of the house by numerous visiting scholars, critics, architects, and incisive others including H. Allen Brooks, Donna Butler, Robert Campbell, Elizabeth Cromley, John Eifler, Bruno Freschi, Robert Furhoff, Wilbert Hasbrouck, Donald Hoffmann, Donald Kalec, Carla Lind, Robert McCarter, Patrick Mahoney, Toshiko Mori, the late Senator Daniel Patrick Moynihan, John O'Hern, Cheryl Robertson, Werner Seligmann, Julie L. Sloan, Edgar Tafel, and John Vinci. Neil Levine has been a particularly strong influence through his writings, his lectures, and his visits to the house. Many other scholars, including Jason Aronoff, James Bono, David De Long, Alice Friedman, Donald Hallmark, David Hanks, Mark Heyman, Kathryn Smith, and Carol Zemel, have variously assisted, encouraged, and enlightened me over the years. John C. Blew helped to orient me to Chicago's suburban neighborhoods. Daniel I. Larkin, Martin A. Berger, Jean Lamarche, Sandra Firmin, and Judy Caraotta each read portions of the manuscript and provided useful suggestions. Nancy Knechtel was most helpful in the early stages of the project. James Ulrich has done the bulk of the photographic work for the book, and I am especially grateful to Michael O'Hara and Bhavna Sharma for their respective drawings.

I wish to express my special appreciation to Carolyn Mann Brackett and the late Everett K. Martin, descendants of William E. Martin; and Dorothy Martin Foster, Darwin R.

Martin, Darwin Foster, and Margaret Foster, descendants of Darwin D. Martin, for sharing family memories and documents with me. Mr. and Mrs. Richard Talaske kindly gave me access to the William E. Martin House in Oak Park, Illinois, a visit that was significantly informed by Jack Lesniak's excellent tour script.

Bruce Brooks Pfeiffer, director of the Archives of the Frank Lloyd Wright Foundation, and his assistants Oskar Muñoz and Margot Stipe have assisted me with research and the acquisition of illustrations. At the Archives of the University at Buffalo I have been ably assisted and encouraged by Shonnie Finnegan and her successors, Christopher Desmore, Kathleen Delaney, and John Edens; and their assistants, Rodney Obien and Dan Di Landro. Mosette Broderick, keeper of the Henry-Russell Hitchcock Archives at New York University; Mary Woolever, of the Ryerson Library of the Chicago Art Institute; and Pierre Richard Bernier and Louise Désy of the Canadian Centre for Architecture have each graciously provided illustrations from their institutions. The acquisition of the Wright-Martin Papers, from which so much of this book has been drawn, depended upon the generosity of Edgar Kaufmann, Jr., Victoria Newhouse, Adolph Placzek, Phyllis Lambert, the University at Buffalo Foundation, the Landmark Society of the Niagara Frontier, the Baird Foundation, Robert and Lorelei Z. Ketter, and Paul and Jean Hanna.

Ted Lownie of Hamilton Houston Lownie, Architects, P.C., the architect charged with restoring the Martin House, continues to reveal new and exciting aspects of the Martin House to me as the project unfolds. Jamie Robideau of the Hamilton Houston Lownie office has answered innumerable questions about the buildings' construction. Jim Gold and the staff of the Bureau of Historic Sites of the New York State Office of Parks, Recreation, and Historic Preservation at Peebles Island, New York—our partners in the restoration of the Martin House—have contributed substantially to my understanding of the furniture and the interior created by Wright. John Courtin, the executive director of the Martin House Restoration Corporation, Eric Jackson-Forsberg, associate curator, and Margaret Stehlik, the director of the Martin House Volunteers, have each become astute students of the house and have informed and challenged me frequently during the past decade. My gratitude to Robert J. Kresse, chairman, Howard Zemsky, president, and the Board of Directors of the Martin House Restoration Corporation for undertaking to return this great prairie-house complex to its original splendor is immeasurable. Finally, I wish to thank Colleen Mullaney for her patience and understanding.

This book is dedicated to John Quinan.

| fig. 1
Darwin D. Martin House.
First floor plan

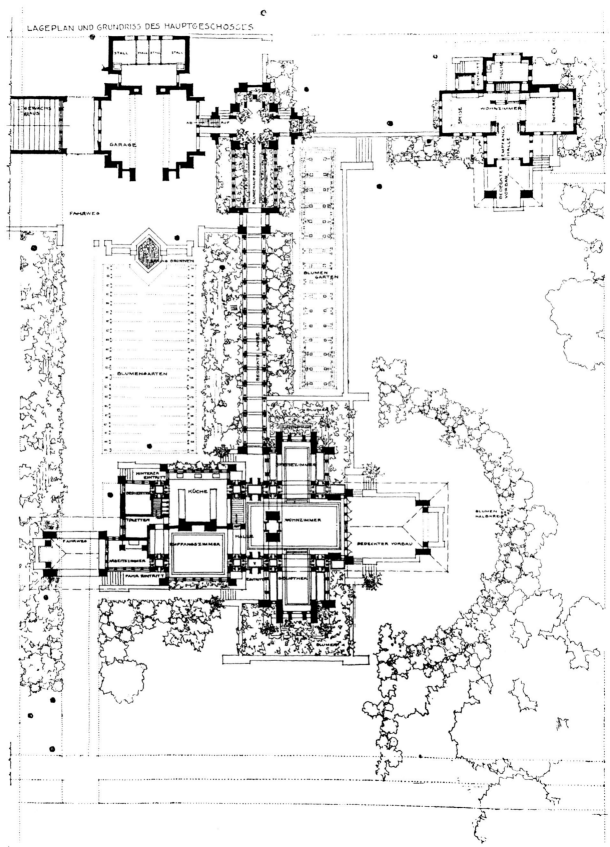

fig. I

INTRODUCTION

FRANK LLOYD WRIGHT'S Darwin D. Martin House (1903–06) | *fig. 1* is a complex of six prairie-style buildings that occupies a 1.5-acre site at the corner of Jewett Parkway and Summit Avenue in the Parkside neighborhood of Buffalo, New York. It is one of three large-scale, multiple-building complexes among more than sixty houses designed and built to Wright's specifications during the architect's prairie period. The principal structure of the complex, the sixteen-room Martin residence, stretches 167 feet along the north side of Jewett Parkway, spanning the equivalent of five (or six) typical neighborhood house lots. Many of the salient characteristics of Wright's prairie style—cruciform plan, low profile, layered roofs, broad eaves, massive chimneys, pier and cantilever construction, and art glass windows—take the design of the Martin House to an unprecedented level of skeletal openness and abstraction. Rendered in a warm, yellow-brown Roman brick and a russet-colored roof tile; bound together by long, horizontal cheek walls, concrete copings, and extruded foundations; and generously festooned with ivy-filled planters and urns, the Martin House sets the tone, texture, and rhythm for the entire complex.

Immediately behind the main house a long, pergolated walkway reaches northward to the conservatory, a cruciform plant-growing space constructed of brick piers supporting a metal and glass roof and housing a full-scale replica of the Nike of Samothrace (ca. 200–190 B.C.). To the east of the conservatory and connected to it by a single brick wall stands the George Barton House, a two-story, eight-room prairie house built for Darwin Martin's sister, Delta Barton, and her husband. Just west of the conservatory is the "barn," an imposing structure containing a garage for the Martins' automobile, a stable and paddock, a heating plant, and (on the second floor) a chauffeur's apartment and loft. A commercially designed greenhouse extends farther west from the barn toward Woodward Avenue, the site of the Martin gardener's house, a small wood-frame and stucco cottage built two years after the completion of the rest of the complex.

Despite its quiet profile and easy integration with the natural features of its site, the Martin House contrasts dramatically in scale and appearance with the rest of the houses in the neighborhood. Parkside is a picturesque suburban district designed in the 1870s by Frederick Law Olmsted, with gently curving tree-lined streets populated by evenly spaced middle-to-upper-middle-class Victorian and colonial revival homes. Amid these lofty, multigabled testaments to romantic nostalgia, Wright laid out his grids, piers, and layered roofs with the force of a new set of laws. During construction a bemused newspaper reporter described the Martin House as "a Jules Verne House,"[1] and today, a century later, it still appears strikingly at odds with the houses around it. One wonders, who designed these buildings, who commissioned them, and what were they thinking?

That this is one of Wright's renowned prairie houses offers a partial explanation, but much remains to be said about this particular commission. Frank Lloyd Wright (1867–1959) | *fig. 2* was thirty-five when he first encountered Darwin Martin late in 1902, but despite his youth he had already spent nearly five years working in the offices of Adler & Sullivan, the leading tall-office-building design firm in Chicago, and nine additional years in independent practice. The latter period encompassed an intense search for a personal idiom that was finally resolved with the creation of the first prairie-house design in 1901. By 1902 Wright had designed approximately 120 buildings, mostly houses, 75 of which were realized.[2] This extraordinary output was concentrated primarily in the greater Chicago area and in southern Wisconsin.

Darwin D. Martin (1865–1935) | *fig. 3*, Wright's client, was a high-ranking executive of the Larkin Company, a successful soap manufacturing and mail-order business based in Buffalo. Martin became wealthy as the company grew, and he invested shrewdly in real estate and other business ventures. He and Isabelle, his wife, moved into a modest Queen Anne house in the Parkside neighborhood in 1888. Their initial encounter with Wright resulted from the Larkin Company's need for a new administrative office building, which Wright was eventually commissioned to design in 1904. Upon meeting Wright, Darwin Martin was immediately captivated by the architect's radical ideas and mesmerizing personality. Isabelle Martin remained somewhat more skeptical.

Wright traveled to Buffalo in November 1902 to meet with potential clients among the Larkin executives and their families. The Martins commissioned the George Barton House in March 1903, and Wright began to design the rest of the Martin residential complex, including the main house, a few months later. Ground was broken for the conservatory, pergola, garage/stable, and main house in mid-May 1904; the complex was framed up and roofed by December 1904; and the Martins moved into their house in November 1905, although work on the main house was not completed for another full year.

| *fig. 2*
Frank Lloyd Wright

| *fig. 3*
Darwin D. Martin

| *fig. 2*　　　　　| *fig. 3*

The importance of the Martin House, widely acknowledged today, was promoted by Wright himself in 1908, when he featured more photographs of the house than any other project in the March issue of the *Architectural Record*. This unprecedented retrospective included eighty-seven illustrations of Wright's work and his essay "In the Cause of Architecture." For the issue, the architect created an idealized version of the plan of the Martin House that would subsequently appear, with slight alterations, in two publications by the German publisher Ernst Wasmuth—*Ausgeführte Bauten und Entwürfe von Frank Lloyd Wright* (Berlin, 1910) and the smaller *Frank Lloyd Wright: Ausgeführte Bauten* (Berlin, 1911)—and in countless publications on Wright and on modern architecture thereafter.[3]

Many others followed Wright's lead by recognizing the significance of the Martin House in their writings and making liberal use of the photographs commissioned for the March 1908 publication from Clarence Fuermann, principal photographer, Henry Fuermann and Sons, Chicago.[4] The distribution, however, of the six modestly scaled Martin buildings over their large site makes the complex difficult to capture in a single, all-encompassing image, so that even in the sixteen photographs published in the *Architectural Record* it is seen piecemeal, in fragments, and remains elusive. Hence it is the redrawn Martin plan, with its spatial transparencies, pier construction, powerful axes, and intricate weave of space and structure, that makes the Martin complex comprehensible and has imprinted itself so indelibly on the collective consciousness of architectural historians and critics.

The scholarly and critical discussions of the Martin House that have taken place for nearly a century fall well within the parameters of the larger dialogue on modernism in architecture. These writings have centered on the abstract nature of the building, particularly its fragmented plan. This emphasis on formalism reached its apogee when William J. R. Curtis juxtaposed Wright's Martin plan with Piet Mondrian's *Composition in Blue* of 1917.[5] While the power of abstraction in Wright's work is as undeniable as it is compelling, such a viewpoint fails to consider in the Martin House any manifestation of the relationship between Frank Lloyd Wright and Darwin D. Martin. Nor does it support any analysis of the building as a functioning home or as a composition that bears symbolic content.

What follows is a chronological narrative of the design, construction, completion, and subsequent alteration of the Martin House and an interpretation of the house as the site of a unique architect–client relationship, as a major work in the history of architecture, and as a functioning home. This endeavor was made possible when, in the 1980s, the Wright-Martin Papers came on the market and were purchased in a joint arrangement between the University at Buffalo and Stanford University. These archival documents supplemented gifts of drawings, blueprints, and related materials to the Archives of the University at Buffalo by Darwin R. Martin, the son of Wright's client, two decades prior to the auction of the Wright-Martin Papers. Subsequent to the acquisition of the papers, the Archives of the University at Buffalo received quantities of supplementary materials, chiefly Martin family letters, photographs, and artifacts. Altogether these holdings constitute a unique and comprehensive record of the interaction between Wright and Martin during the three years in which the Martin House was built, as well as during the thirty additional years following the project's completion, when the two men continued to correspond. A wealth of diaries, notebooks, autobiographical manuscripts, and similar papers extensively document the life and personality of Darwin Martin and his family.

The unusual richness and depth of these materials—to which there is nothing comparable for any other Wright commission executed between 1887 and 1910, the early and prairie periods—suggested additional opportunities within this study. The correspondence between Wright and Martin and between them and others involved in the project (such as Darwin Martin's brother William, Wright's office superintendent, Walter Burley Griffin, and the building contractor, Oscar S. Lang) provides invaluable insights into Wright's working methods during what Grant Manson characterized as Wright's "First Golden Age."[6]

A third avenue of exploration presented itself around the individual personalities and the relationship of these two men. Despite the extensiveness of the Wright bibliography and the ample attention that has been devoted to the architect's personal life, he is nowhere else revealed as a person—humorous, manipulative, imperious, charming, elusive, utterly and disarmingly confident—as he is in his correspondence with Darwin Martin. Little known beyond his status as one of hundreds of clients of Wright, Darwin Martin was an important figure in the history of American business and an interesting character in his own right—brilliant in his way, insecure, exacting, and drawn mothlike to Wright's flame. In the end, it is the interaction of these two dynamic personalities that elucidates the history of the Martin House.

Also revealed in this rich archive of papers and correspondence is the significant role of Isabelle Martin in the design and construction of the Martin House. Her influence resulted not from creative input but from her marginalization during the process and her subsequent reaction to its results. There is an unusually wide gulf between the Martin House as a major work in the history of architecture and the Martin House as a home, a gulf in which Isabelle Martin was left to function in her daily life and against which she rebelled. In her dilemma lies the first serious critique of the Martin House.

The Wright-Martin correspondence, for all of the insights it provides into the design and construction of the house and the personalities and practices of the architect and his client, is devoid of any sustained discussion of the symbolic nature of the Martin House. It is possible that Wright discussed the meaningful content of the design with Darwin Martin during his many visits to Buffalo; but in the absence of any concrete documentation to that effect, Wright's frequently repeated claim that his buildings were portraits of his clients may prove to be the best indication of the architect's deeper aesthetic intentions.

Wright stated this claim prior to and during the prairie period in seven documented instances—not many in view of the hundred-odd commissions he obtained during those years but significant when one considers that most of his interactions with clients took place in the Greater Chicago area viva voce and hence were lost to posterity. Wright first stated the claim in a tentative way in 1894, in a public presentation to the University Guild in Evanston, Illinois, entitled "The Architect and the Machine." "There should be as many types of homes as there are types of people, for it is the individuality of the occupants that should give character and color to the buildings and furnishings."[7] He reiterated the idea in additional presentations in 1896 and 1897,[8] and in 1900 he embellished the concept by comparing the work of the artist John Singer Sargent to his own:

> A Sargent might paint a hundred portraits without a signature, and
> the moment we see the work we might recognize it as Sargent's. But
> no less, for all that, each portrait [would] be a revelation of the indi-
> vidual soul of the subject, and this revelation would be accomplished
> through the medium of pigments, colors, and canvas instead of sound

put together with Sargent's brains and feelings, and insofar he was true to the limitations imposed upon him by his pigments and canvas and to the degree he made his arrangement of colors and lines express the nature of the sitter, the result would be a work of art. The directions his interpretation took, the materials he found in that human soul to portray, he might merely characterize and possess little more than the insight of the great craftsman, or he might idealize them with the insight of the true poet, according to his own fiber, and be truly great as an Artist.[9]

Wright reiterated the portrait idea, including the reference to Sargent, in a letter to prospective clients, the Avery Coonleys, on September 24, 1906:

> I try to make each home characteristic of its owner and an interpretation when possible. I think all of the buildings are entitled to a certain family resemblance in so far as they concern each other, but I feel that I have failed if I do not fix the character of the building and the atmosphere of the environment, where it belongs, with the client?
>
> Sargent is a good portrait painter and the individuality of his subject suffers no less, I think, because it is apparent to the observing that "Sargent" painted the portrait. Of course I don't profess to build as well as Sargent paints, but I would like to.
>
> Those who invite Sargent to fix their characters on canvas for them do so because they sympathize with his work, and he succeeds because of that sympathy. An architect is similarly placed at an advantage or at a disadvantage. When his client seeks him naturally there should be something in common to begin with.
>
> I think that with Mr. and Mrs. Avery Coonley I have a splendid opportunity and if I fail to make the most of it it will be entirely my own fault. [10]

The importance that Wright attached to the portrait idea is manifested in its inclusion in the first national publication of the architect's work in a professional venue, the afore-mentioned "In the Cause of Architecture" article, published in the *Architectural Record* of March 1908. The repeated reference to Sargent suggests that this may have become a routine approach to clients on Wright's part, and certainly one that he took very seriously:

> The individuality of an owner is first manifest in his choice of his architect, the individual to whom he entrusts his characterization. He sympathizes with his work; its expression suits him and this furnishes the common ground upon which client and architect may come together. Then, if the architect is what he ought to be, with his ready technique he consciously works for the client, idealizes the client's character and his client's tastes and makes him feel that the building is his as it really is to such an extent that he can truly say that he would rather have his own house than any other he has ever seen. Is a portrait, say by Sargent, any less a revelation of the character of the subject because it bears his stamp and is easily recognized by anyone as a Sargent? Does one lose his individuality when it is interpreted sympathetically by one of his own race and time who can know him and his needs intimately and idealize them; or does he gain it only by having adopted or adapted to his condition a ready-made historic style which is the fruit of a seed-time other than his, whatever that style may be?[11]

It is impossible to determine with certainty that Wright made such a statement to Darwin Martin in the early stages of their relationship, but it is clear that Martin absorbed the idea either from Wright himself or from some of Wright's clients in Oak Park just before he wrote to his employer, John Larkin, in March 1903:

> We were inside of five and talked to owners of four of Wright's houses. You never witnessed such enthusiasm. Not one will admit

a fault in their house. They will admit faults in other of Wright's
houses but not in theirs. That, Mr. Wright says is because he
studies his client and builds the house to fit him, so his different
houses do not fit his clients who live in other houses. [12]

Although Wright embraced the idea of architecture as portraiture and made it his own,
there were important precedents for it at the end of the nineteenth century. A pervasive
tendency toward the expression of individuality in the home occurred as a by-product of the
industrial revolution, the rapid expansion of the city, the increase in the size and wealth of the
middle-class population, and the development of suburbs. It was manifested architecturally
and socially in the Victorian cult of domesticity and in the enthusiasm for *Gesamtkunstwerk*
(total work of art) of the art nouveau, in the work of Charles Rennie Mackintosh and the
Glasgow school, and in the Jugenstil movement. John Ruskin and Louis Sullivan, two figures
who were especially important to Wright's development, each addressed the idea of the building as portrait. [13] Ruskin wrote, "I would have, then, our ordinary dwelling-house built to last,
and built to be lovely...at all events, with such differences as might suit and express each man's
character and occupation, and partly his history." [14] Sullivan, who did not involve himself much
in domestic architecture, aimed his remarks more broadly toward the American people. "As you
are, so are your buildings; and, as are your buildings, so are you. You and your architecture are
the same. Each is a faithful portrait of the other." [15] Hermann Bahr, a client of Josef Hoffmann,
sounded a similar note in the German-speaking world in 1901. "The architect...should strive to
express the personality of his client both in the house as a whole and in all its details. The ideal
house should be a *Gesamtkunstwerk* that would reveal the inner truth of its inhabitant." [16]

Both Wright's portrait strategy and the vogue for individualized homes are indicators
of the growing interest in human psychology in Western culture during the nineteenth century. The work of psychologists throughout the century culminated in the cluster of writings
around 1900 by Sigmund Freud that propelled human psychology, and especially Freud's
notion of the ego/self, into the forefront of twentieth-century thought. [17] The American
phrenologist Orson Squire Fowler was no Freud, but his cranial readings of his thousands of
subjects—William and Darwin Martin among them—are further evidence of the preoccupation with the inner self common at the end of the nineteenth century. [18]

Whatever its sources, Wright's portrait idea raises numerous provocative questions. How can a building portray someone? Who would the building portray: the husband, the wife, both of them, the entire family? What does Wright's portrait idea tell us about him, and why has this aspect of Wright's work been ignored by historians? The radicalness of Wright's departure from the conventions of American domestic architecture is addressed in the opening paragraph of his "In the Cause of Architecture":

> Radical though it be, the work here illustrated is dedicated to a cause conservative in the best sense of the word. At no point does it involve denial of the elemental law and order inherent in all great architecture; rather, is it a declaration of love for the spirit of that law and order, and a reverential recognition of the elements that made its ancient letter in its time vital and beautiful.[19]

Wright's portrait concept might be interpreted, then, as a strategy for closing the gap between his radical new house type and the expectations of the tentative, tradition-bound client. It is more than that, however. It is a logical extension of the notion of an organic architecture grounded in Wright's Unitarian-Transcendentalist training.[20] Just as the pier and cantilever construction of his prairie houses broke down the barriers between interior and exterior, so his attempts at personal portrayal were a way to dissolve the barriers between the house and its client, thereby enhancing the overall continuity of client, house, and nature. In its promise of an unprecedented personal dimension in architecture, Wright's philosophy could not be matched by his more conventional contemporaries in whose work the specter of historicism intervened between the architect and the client and functioned as the principal "subject" of the work. Wright saw his own work as essentially astylistic, a perspective that enabled him to draw aside the scrim of historicism and to confront the issues of personality directly. Consequently he wrote, "There should be as many kinds (styles) of houses as there are kinds (styles) of people and as many differentiations as there are different individuals. A man who has individuality (and what man lacks it?) has a right to its expression in his own environment."[21]

Historians of architecture have largely ignored Wright's portrait philosophy, for some obvious reasons: Wright's work has such a powerful integrity of principle that it is difficult to look beyond the obvious typological similarities and formal characteristics shared by all of the prairie houses, and beyond questions of Wright's development as an architect, of the proper attribution of his work, and even of quality within the work, to engage the possibility that his houses are in some significant way individualized. The impact of European modernism, with its emphasis on abstraction and universality, further detracted from the individuality of Wright's prairie houses. Moreover, Wright's well-known egocentricity has made it difficult to accept that he had genuine concern for the personalities of his clients. Pronouncements such as "You see, early in life I had to choose between honest arrogance and hypocritical humility. I chose honest arrogance, and have seen no occasion to change—even now"[22] have led historians like Norris Kelly Smith to conclude,

> although Wright professed concern for the character of each of his clients, he did not feel obliged to give his clients what they wanted. All of his houses reflect the style and thought of their creator as clearly as do the portraits of Rembrandt [but] one feels that each commission presented him with an opportunity for solving afresh a problem that was essentially his own.[23]

Finally, a paucity of deep documentation concerning the biographies and personalities of Wright's prairie clients (most of whom died in the 1930s, 1940s, and 1950s) makes it extremely difficult to verify that any of the buildings were individualized to a significant extent. The emergence of Darwin Martin's unique archive presents the first significant opportunity for client-based interpretation.

Smith, the only architectural historian to address Wright's portrait philosophy, flatly denied its validity and argued that only a lesser architect would seek "to merely please his clients rather than to express his convictions and to be 'true to himself.'"[24] In 1966 Smith wrote:

> But to think that any configuration of architectural elements might constitute a "portrait" of a living man or woman must surely seem farfetched. The stylistic variations that differentiate Wright's houses cannot, in fact, be clearly related to those qualities of temperament and predisposition that the words "personality" and "character" suggest

to us, nor can we deduce by looking at those houses anything at all about the natures of their commissioners. Moreover, if Wright really believed, with Emerson, that "what is true for you in your private heart is true for all men," there would have been no reason for him to take serious account of the personal peculiarities of his clients, most of whom he probably could not have known at all well, anyway.[25]

The intention of this book is not to prove Smith wrong, although his contention that Wright hardly knew most of his clients (many of whom were his friends and neighbors in Oak Park and River Forest) is unsubstantiated and indeed, dead wrong in the case of Darwin Martin, whom he came to know intimately. The goal is rather to discover to what degree Wright's portrait philosophy can be brought usefully to bear on an understanding and inter-pretation of the Martin House and to test that analysis by making comparisons with sever-al other prairie commissions and their clients.

The Martin commission contains some strong portraitlike qualities, but several issues bearing on their assessment warrant clarification. First, the Barton House was commissioned by Darwin Martin for his sister and brother-in-law, Delta and George Barton, who, it is safe to surmise, would not have chosen to live in a Wright house on their own and could not have afforded to do so without assistance from Darwin.[26] Moreover, the Barton House was a reworking of a design made for another client—hardly the stuff of portraiture. Second, owing to Darwin's cautious, tentative approach to Wright's architecture, the full Martin complex was commissioned piecemeal, in three stages: first the Barton House (in 1903 and 1904); next the stable, pergola, conservatory, and Martin House (in 1904, 1905, and 1906); and finally, the gardener's cottage (in 1905 and 1908). This irregular process is difficult to recon-cile with the composition of a portrait. Third, there is the question, raised directly by Norris Kelly Smith, as to whom is being portrayed. Was it Darwin? Darwin and Isabelle? Darwin's entire family, including the Bartons? Finally, there is Smith's contention that the idea "that any configuration of architectural elements might constitute a 'portrait' of a living man or woman [is] farfetched."[27] Each of these issues deserves consideration.

The fact that the Barton House was a second-hand design commissioned for an unin-terested party effectively removes the possibility that the house was in any sense a portrait of

George and/or Delta Barton, but it does not negate the possibility that the house contributed to the portrait element in the commission as a whole.

Smith's contention that the notion of a building bearing a physical resemblance to a living person is far-fetched has some validity. If one adopts a less literal interpretation of "resemblance," however, it could be argued that all serious architecture is involved to some degree in embodying ideas and aspects of personality, both individual and collective, and that domestic architecture in particular has always been concerned with issues of a personal nature, with accommodating the lifestyle of a person or family and with presenting some kind of chosen public face to the exterior world. In that sense, Wright, in proffering his claim of portraiture, took the common concerns of all domestic architectural clients a step further, that is, from accommodation to portrayal.

Smith raised a thornier question when he wrote, "What the notion of the 'architectural portrait' leaves out of account altogether is the fact that a house is not built for a single person but for a family group, the members of which will not possess the same traits of character and will themselves change with the passage of time."[28] The question as to whom is being portrayed is both interesting and challenging with regard to Wright's work, and the Martin House provides an ideal forum for examining this issue in depth. Indeed, insofar as the Martin complex was a portrait at all, it was a portrait of Darwin Martin. The considerable evidence of Darwin's letters, diaries, autobiography, and other papers dating back to the mid-1880s, when he first met Isabelle Reidpath, indicates that the demanding, success-driven businessman was the dominant personality in his marital relationship as well. Moreover, it was Darwin who discovered Wright, invited him to Buffalo, commissioned the Martin and Barton houses, assisted the architect in obtaining the Larkin Office Building commission, corresponded with him tirelessly, defended him (even to his brother William), and eventually became his friend and patron for life. In short, Darwin was ideally positioned to be the principal subject of Wright's architectural portrayal.[29]

Isabelle Reidpath Martin (1869–1945) | *fig. 4* , on the other hand, appears to have been shy and retiring, a person of quiet strength who, like so many middle- and upper-middle-class women of that period, got along by working through her husband in subtle and circuitous ways. Note Darwin's comment to Wright: "She [Isabelle] is quite accustomed to

| *fig.* 4
Isabelle Reidpath Martin,
circa 1895

changing my mind. Strange how any good wife can change a man's mind."[30] That Darwin confided in Isabelle on many matters pertaining to the Martin complex and that he respected her opinions is apparent in the letters written in the early design stages of the Barton and Martin houses, but Isabelle's involvement in these designs was otherwise confined principally to issues of decoration and to spaces like the kitchen and sewing room.[31] Conclusive evidence of Darwin's role as the portrayed "subject" of the Martin building complex exists in two letters written by Darwin to Wright in 1926 regarding the design of a summer house (Graycliff) for the Martins, in which the writer takes pains to remind Wright that for this commission, "Mrs. Martin is your client."[32]

While the piecemeal development of the Martin complex over a period of two years might appear to have been an impediment to Wright's effort to characterize his client, this was not a problem in actuality. Darwin discussed a multiple-building complex—one that included the Martin and Barton houses, a stable or barn, and a greenhouse—at his initial meeting with Wright in November 1902, thus providing Wright with a large commission to contemplate at the very outset.[33] Furthermore, the evolution that took place from November 1902 to the final plan as it was executed during 1905 and 1906 was informed by a constant interaction between the architect and his client. Wright visited Buffalo approximately thirty times between the end of 1902 and 1906, and Darwin visited Chicago and Oak Park to see Wright on a few occasions as well. The more than three hundred letters they exchanged during the design and construction of the Barton and Martin houses all bear witness to a thorough familiarity and steadily deepening friendship between Martin and Wright. The plan matured along with the maturation of Wright's acquaintance with Darwin Martin over time; the "portrait" thus resembled Darwin more and more closely, and, in fact, the house was shaped to a significant degree by Darwin Martin's relentless fussing over every detail. The analogy of a portrait painted during repeated sittings is apt.

Having cleared away some potential obstacles to analysis and interpretation, the question remains, just how did the Martin House and its related buildings actually portray or characterize Darwin Martin?

Chapter One

FRANK LLOYD WRIGHT AND
DARWIN D. MARTIN

ON THE EVENING of September 11, 1902, Darwin D. Martin | see *fig. 3*, secretary of the Larkin soap and mail-order company in Buffalo, New York, boarded a train bound for Chicago, where he was to spend the following day, Friday, at Sears, Roebuck & Company. On Monday and Tuesday he would visit the western headquarters of the Larkin Company in Peoria, before returning to Buffalo.[1] The schedule left him free to see his brother, William E. Martin, in Chicago, over the weekend. Darwin relished the prospect. Separated as children from their three older siblings, Darwin and William Martin had been through some difficult times together on the western frontier in the 1870s. Although they eventually went their separate ways, becoming successful industrialists in their respective cities, the bond between them remained strong. Indeed, Darwin wished that William would move to Buffalo and had asked him to do so on numerous occasions.

Darwin's visit to William was not just a social call, however. In the previous month the Martin brothers had exchanged a number of letters regarding William's intention to move his family out of Chicago to one of the newly developing suburbs.[2] In September Darwin finally traveled to Chicago to assist William in his search for a new home. Although William was two years older than Darwin and the owner of a successful stove- and shoe-polish manufacturing firm, he regularly sought advice and financial assistance from his younger brother, whose incisive mind, encyclopedic knowledge of business, and considerable wealth lent him a special authority.[3]

On Saturday morning, September 13, despite William's explicitly stated preference for a north shore location (such as Winnetka or Lake Forest), the Martin brothers rode directly to suburban Oak Park, about ten miles west of downtown Chicago, to look at real estate. Why Oak Park rather than Winnetka or Lake Forest? It seems that William R. Heath, a Chicago attorney who had joined the Larkin Company in Buffalo in 1899 as personnel manager, was the brother-in-law of Elmer E. Andrews, an Oak Park contractor who was then completing the Frank Lloyd Wright-designed J. J. Walser House in Austin, the Chicago neighborhood that borders Oak Park.[4] Since Heath and Darwin Martin worked closely together at the Larkin Company and Heath would certainly have been aware of Darwin's trip to Chicago, it is likely that Heath urged Darwin to visit Oak Park in order to see Wright's work.[5]

Once the Martin brothers arrived in Oak Park, their attention was immediately captured by a few buildings of unusual serenity and distinction amid the otherwise Victorian streetscape. These were the recently completed houses designed by Wright for Frank Thomas (1901), William Fricke (1901), and Arthur Heurtley (1902). The Thomas House | *fig.* 5 shares the multiple roofs, exaggerated eaves, window sequences, and horizontal accents characteristic of all of Wright's prairie houses, but it is also individualized in terms of its materials, structure, art-glass window patterns, and spatial arrangement.

The Martin brothers soon found their way to Wright's home and studio at the corner of Forest Avenue and Chicago Street | *fig.* 6 . What transpired there is described in a letter written by Darwin Martin to Elbert Hubbard, Darwin's former supervisor at the Larkin Company. Although Hubbard had left the Larkin business in 1893 in order to write and found the Roycroft Arts and Crafts community in East Aurora, New York, he maintained a warm, somewhat paternalistic friendship with his former protégé. In Oak Park, Darwin immediately recognized an affinity between Wright's work and that of Hubbard's Roycrofters. The Martin brothers did not meet Wright that day, but they talked at some length to his office superintendent, Walter Burley Griffin (a redhead like Darwin), about Wright's work and his architectural principles.[6] In his letter to Hubbard, Darwin wrote,

> To my uncultivated mind Mr. Wright's houses, of which there are many examples in Oak Park and vicinity, seemed very fancy, but after I had a talk with Mr. Wright's Red One I was convinced that the style is simplicity itself, and the startling thing about his architecture is that notwithstanding he charges 7 1/2% instead of the conventional 5%, he makes $8,000 look like $15,000 in a house.[7]

Darwin urged Hubbard to commission a Wright building for the Roycroft campus: "The Wright studio," he wrote, "is very Roycroftie." He relayed the comments of a woman he and his brother had met by chance in Oak Park: "Wright is a queer fellow, like Hubbard you know...he sometimes noses around his houses in silk knickerbocker breeches, etc." Having said that, Martin concluded his letter to Hubbard by maintaining, "Yet he is no

| *fig.* 5
Frank Lloyd Wright,
Frank Thomas House,
Oak Park, Illinois, 1901

Oscar Wilde. He must be a man, every inch: accepting nothing from anybody but the good, and knowing him to supply the good in every instance."[8] Hubbard replied in his medievalizing way, "Dear Brother Martin:…I am glad to say that I know of Brother Wright of Oak Park. He is certainly a genius in his line, and no man admires him more than I."[9]

One month after Darwin's visit to Chicago, William Martin met Frank Lloyd Wright. He immediately wrote a highly enthusiastic account of the event to his brother in Buffalo:

> Dear Dar—I have been—seen—talked to, admired, one of nature's noblemen—Frank Lloyd Wright. He is an athletic looking young man of medium build, black hair (bushy, not long), about 32 years old. A splendid type of manhood. He is not a fraud, nor a "crank" —highly educated and polished but no dude —a straightforward business-like man—with high ideals.[10]

William's letter indicated that he had talked to Wright about an office building for the Larkin Company, a house for himself, and a house for Darwin. Wright, sensing grandiose possibilities, cautioned against building on Darwin's recently acquired 75-foot front lot on fashionable Oakland Place in Buffalo. The possibility of an office building commission prompted Wright to tell William that he was educated as a civil engineer, had gained experience in large office buildings with Adler & Sullivan, and was head man at the firm, where he stood next to Mr. Sullivan. Wright also told William that it was strange that he was only known as a residential architect when his best and greatest experience was in large buildings.[11]

Based upon previous conversations with Darwin, who sometimes chafed at John Larkin's reticence, William ventured to write further:

> I suppose that if you discover this man that Mr. L[arkin] would never consent to his drawing the plans, yet I am sure he is the man you want, and if some way could be devised so that Mr. L[arkin] would first discover him that he would be tickled to death with his find. Mr. Wright says he doesn't want any man to accept his ideas

|*fig.* 6
Frank Lloyd Wright's
Home and Studio, Oak
Park, Illinois, 1889–1909

first because they are his—he proposes to furnish a reason for his
ideas and wants judgments made solely on the merits.

You will fall in love with him in ten min[utes] conversation. He
will build you the finest, most sensible house in Buffalo. You will be
the envy of every rich man in Buffalo. It will be talked about all over
the east. You will never grow tired of his work, and what more can
you ask? When will you come and see him?

Can you not manage to have him first discovered by Mr.
L[arkin]? An office such as Wright can build will be talked about all
over this country. It will be an ad that money spent in any other way
cannot buy. I am not too enthusiastic in this—he is pure gold.[12]

Darwin replied to William a week later, enclosing a letter addressed to Wright inviting
him to Buffalo at the sender's expense. Darwin informed his brother that Mr. Larkin, who
had previously expressed an interest in having Louis Sullivan design the administration
building, was "quite willing to consider him as the architect for our office building."[13] He
concluded the letter, "Incidently, if he obtains business here it might make him a little
more mellow in his dealings with you,"[14] an indication that William was also considering
commissioning a house from Wright.

As a result of Darwin Martin's letter, Wright traveled to Buffalo on November 18, 1902,
and remained until the evening of the following day. Darwin's only record of the visit is suc-
cinct: "Nov. 18, 1902: Frank Lloyd Wright of Oak Park, Ill., Architect (aged 35) our guest
overnight. Nov 19: Darwin to Niagara [Falls] with Mr. W[right]."[15] Nevertheless, from
subsequent letters and documents and from the resulting commissions, it is apparent that
Wright met with Larkin Company executives and their families and discussed possible
projects. William R. Heath commissioned a substantial brick house almost immediately, but
Darwin Martin and John Larkin proceeded more cautiously. Wright was offered the commission for the Larkin Administration Building on a provisional basis, and Darwin Martin
apparently discussed a modest house for his sister, Delta, and her husband, the success of
which would determine whether or not Wright would be given the commissions for the rest
of the Martin complex and the Larkin Administration Building.[16]

The tentative nature of the Larkin and Martin commissions was vexing to Wright.[17] In the long run, however, his visit to Buffalo proved exceptionally fortuitous, as it led to more than forty commissions, eleven of which were built. It also led to a warm and enduring friendship with Darwin Martin, from whom the architect derived more than thirty years of financial and moral support that sustained him through some of the most difficult stretches of his career. Indeed, the Wright–Martin relationship was sufficiently important to Wright's overall development as an architect, and to both men on a personal level, that a brief review of their lives up to the time of their meeting in 1902 is in order.

FRANK LLOYD WRIGHT, TO 1902

The life and work of Frank Lloyd Wright have been the subject of extensive study and warrant only cursory discussion here.[18] Wright was born in Richland Center, Wisconsin, in 1867, the son of William Cary Wright, a Baptist minister and music teacher, and Anna Lloyd Jones Wright, a former school teacher who is said to have doted on her son and encouraged him to become an architect from his earliest years.[19] Owing to his father's restless temperament, Wright and his family lived for brief periods in Iowa, Rhode Island, and Massachusetts. In 1885 his parents divorced, and his mother returned with the three children (Frank, Maginel, and Jane) to live among her relatives on a farm in Spring Green, Wisconsin. Wright attended high school in Madison and briefly attended the University of Wisconsin before setting off for Chicago in 1887 in search of architectural employment. He first obtained work in the office of Joseph Lyman Silsbee, a specialist in Queen Anne-style houses, but he soon moved to the prestigious tall-building firm of Adler & Sullivan, where he remained for about five years. Wright's rapid rise to the position of chief draftsman in the office is one of the earliest indications of his prodigious abilities.

In 1893 Wright left Adler & Sullivan and established an independent practice in suburban Oak Park, where he specialized in domestic architecture. Over the ensuing seven years, Wright's practice flourished. His domestic work exhibited a marked preoccupation with linear plans, attached octagonal spaces, and an articulative system derived from a melding of classical precedent with Louis Sullivan's system of decoration and Wright's own burgeoning vision. Gradually, however, cumulative influences from the Froebel kindergarten method, Japanese art and architecture, nature, the arts and crafts movement, tall-building engineering, and Sullivan's decorative style began to coalesce; a layered horizontality entered, walls gave way to piers and glass in-fill, and interior spaces increasingly opened to the surrounding landscape. The moment of crystallization occurred early in 1901, when Wright created the first prairie-style house.

The Martin brothers' visit to Oak Park occurred about a year and a half after Wright produced his initial cluster of prairie-house designs, which included the "Home in a Prairie Town" and "A Small House with 'Lots of Room in It'" | *figs. 7, 8* (featured in the *Ladies' Home Journal* in February and July 1901, respectively) and houses for Warren Hickox and Harley Bradley in Kankakee, Illinois | *figs. 9, 10*. These were soon followed by the Heurtley, Fricke, and Thomas houses in Oak Park and the Winslow, Williams, and Davenport houses in nearby River Forest. Wright's prairie house constituted a powerful critique of the eclectic styles that had prevailed in American domestic architecture throughout the nineteenth century | *fig. 11*. Eschewing historicism, Wright disassembled the conventional house into its principal constituent elements—foundation, structural components, roof, chimney, and living spaces—giving each an emphatic, articulate form. An extruded foundation anchors the building to its site; structural piers support low-pitched roofs with broad sheltering eaves, beneath which the traditional boundaries between interior and exterior are only discreetly suggested by the rhythmic occurrence of piers and mullions interspersed with screenlike art-glass windows. Within the house Wright reestablished the hearth as the epicenter of the American home, making it a massive masonry core from which living spaces extend outward along the four cardinal directions in a progressive engagement with nature. A proliferation of horizontal accents in the form of eaves, copings, deeply raked joints (in the brick houses), and window sequences convey an impression of the house as a pavilion of floating planes, at one with the prevailing horizontal line of the prairie landscape yet somehow enhancing it.

The significance of the prairie house is manifold: in its reverence for nature and its natural use of materials, its skeletal openness, its pragmatism, its functionalism, and in its rejection of European precedent, the prairie house was quintessentially American. In its spatial–temporal conflation of inside and outside, in the analytical processes of its creation, in the transparency of its spaces, and in its derivation from machine-inspired thought, the prairie house was truly modern. The prairie house also represented the initial crystallization of

| *fig. 7*
Frank Lloyd Wright,
"Home in a Prairie
Town," *Ladies' Home
Journal*, February 1901.
Elevation

Wright's organic architectural theory; it transformed the American conception of domesticity and, on a popular level, it became the progenitor of the ubiquitous American ranch house. The prairie house was not, however, merely a new domestic building prototype to be doled out to waiting customers as so many variations on a theme. Instead, Wright considered it something personal and intimate, like an article of clothing. Driven by a deep attachment to Unitarian and Transcendentalist thought,[20] a belief in the oneness of all things in nature, Wright strove to integrate the building as much with the client as with the surrounding landscape, a fact that has been largely ignored in the scholarship on Wright.

The complex of buildings that Wright designed for Darwin Martin is one of six major prairie-style projects among the sixty-odd domestic commissions designed and built to the architect's specifications between 1900 and 1910—the others being the Susan Dana House in Springfield, Illinois (1902–04), the Avery Coonley House in Riverside, Illinois (1906–09), the Ward Willits House in Highland Park, Illinois (1902–03), the Frederick C. Robie House in Chicago (1908–10), and the Francis V. Little House in Wayzata, Minnesota (1912–14). Each of these commissions was the product of a large budget, each was extensively furnished by the architect, and each is highly distinctive within the common bond of Wright's architectural idiom. The Martin House is unique among these prairie masterpieces in the elegance of its detailing, in its pavilion-like spatial freedom, and in the unusual coherence and equipoise of its plan. Even today, the hovering planes and nimble geometries of the Martin House seem to mock and defy its more traditional neighbors.

If the Martin House is truly a portrait of its owner, then who was this man? How did Wright come to see him? And what was his role in the creation of the Martin House?

DARWIN MARTIN TO 1902

The youngest of five children of Hiram Martin, a cobbler and farmer, and Ann Martin, a housewife, Darwin Martin was born on October 25, 1865, in Bouckville, a village in central New York State.[21] In 1867 the Martins moved to a small hilltop farm in nearby Clayville, where Hiram and Ann were better able to provide for the family. Years later Darwin would recall that life on the Clayville farm seemed idyllic—that is, until the sudden and untimely death of his mother on September 4, 1871.[22]

| *fig.* 8
Frank Lloyd Wright, "A Small House with 'Lots of Room in It,'" *Ladies' Home Journal,* July 1901. Elevation

fig. 9

Frank Lloyd Wright,
Warren Hickox House,
Kankakee, Illinois, 1901.
Elevation

|fig. 10

|fig. 11

|fig. 10
Frank Lloyd Wright,
Harley Bradley House,
Kankakee, Illinois, 1901.
Elevation

|fig. 11
Arthur B. Jennings, S.
Bayard Dod Residence,
East Orange, New
Jersey, 1885. Elevation

Unable to farm, operate a cobbler shop, and raise five children by himself, Hiram Martin arranged to marry Ann Winyard, a widow living with her four daughters on a farm in southeastern Nebraska.[23] Hiram placed his three oldest children, Frank, Alta, and Delta, with relatives and friends,[24] and set out in August 1872 by train for Nebraska with eight-year-old William and six-year-old Darwin in tow. Upon arriving in Nebraska City, the Martins moved into the crowded Winyard farmhouse, where Darwin and William shared an unfinished, loftlike second floor with their four stepsisters. It was the first of many unsatisfactory living arrangements that Darwin would endure during his boyhood.

Farm life was arduous in Nebraska in the mid-1870s, but it was especially difficult for Darwin Martin, who was small for his age, sickly, depressed, and deeply resentful toward his new stepmother.[25] He gamely tried to hold his own, but the physical demands of farming on the frontier and the unfamiliar nature of the environment only compounded his misery.[26] The opportunity to escape from Nebraska came in August 1878, when his oldest brother, Frank, a salesman for the Larkin soap company, invited twelve-year-old Darwin to come east to "sling" soap in the New York City area.[27] Armed with a $40 advance from Frank and a few books and sandwiches, Darwin crossed the country by train in a week and arrived in Newark, New Jersey, on August 31, 1878.[28]

During the ensuing year Darwin and Frank worked the streets of Greater New York City and Boston, selling soap from a horse-drawn wagon and living in boardinghouses that cost Darwin $2.50 of his $3.00 weekly salary. The pay was meager and the quality of life in the boardinghouses was marginal.[29] Darwin made the most of it, however, by visiting the principal sites in each city, attending services and Sunday School at a variety of churches, borrowing twenty-four books from Boston libraries in seven months, and enrolling in one of the city's pioneering night schools. He also managed to pay off his debt to Frank and save an additional $27 within the year.[30]

Word of Darwin's exceptional character reached John D. Larkin (1845–1926), president of the Larkin Company | *fig.* 12, who visited Boston, promoted Frank Martin to the rank of traveling salesman in the Midwest, and invited Darwin to work as a bookkeeper in the main office in Buffalo, New York. Thus, at the age of thirteen, Darwin Martin found himself alone in an unfamiliar city, living in a boardinghouse with neither friends nor relatives nearby, with nothing to do but work | *fig.* 13.

| *fig.* 12
John D. Larkin, in 1890

| *fig.* 13
Darwin Martin, in about 1879 at age 14

| *fig.* 14
Elbert Hubbard, in 1885

| *fig.* 12

| *fig.* 13

fig. 14

John D. Larkin and his brother-in-law, Elbert Hubbard | *fig.* 14, founded the Larkin soap company in a two-story, 15,000-square-foot brick building in 1875 | *fig.* 15.[31] Larkin supervised soap production and the bookkeeping department while the more personable, extroverted Hubbard was in charge of marketing and sales. In 1877 the vigorous promotion and sales of Larkin's Sweet Home laundry soap enabled the company to move to a larger building, at 659–663 Seneca Street, to which a three-story brick office was added the following year | *fig.* 16. Larkin soap sales rose steadily during the early 1880s, thanks to the development of new products and to creative marketing strategies devised by Hubbard.[32] The addition of new factory buildings in 1882 and 1885 | *fig.* 17 provides a measure of the rapid development of the business—a remarkable combination of innovation and growth that would continue unabated into the early twentieth century.

The workday at the Larkin Company ran from 7:30 A.M. to 6:00 P.M. six days per week, but Darwin Martin often found himself working until 10:00 P.M. on weeknights and midnight on many Saturdays.[33] He frequently returned to the office on Sundays to clean up the bookkeeping department and write letters to his family. His salary remained at $3 per week and he was not given a week's vacation for two years. Despite the long hours and low pay, however, Darwin genuinely liked his work as a bookkeeper,[34] and he soon began to demonstrate a precocious grasp of the larger aspects of the business.

Initially, Darwin worked under the direct supervision of John Larkin, whose concerns for the welfare of his young employee were masked by a formidable personal reticence.[35] The office atmosphere brightened considerably for young Darwin when Elbert Hubbard withdrew from his travels as sales supervisor and began to spend more time in Buffalo. Handsome, charismatic, and flamboyant, Hubbard gave Darwin gifts such as extra theater tickets as bonuses, lent him his library card, and occasionally took him on outings.[36] Still, Darwin's personal life was utterly dismal. He lived near the Larkin factory in a boardinghouse populated chiefly by rowdy railroad men. Many a night's sleep was interrupted by drunken brawls and noisy card games,[37] and Darwin endured a variety of illnesses there without the benefit of a caring hand. To combat his isolation and loneliness, Darwin wrote frequently to his father and siblings, and he maintained a diary from 1882 to 1892 in which he expressed his deepest personal concerns. "Oh! How I hated to say goodbye to my darling sister," he wrote shortly after

| *fig.* 15
Larkin Company,
Buffalo, New York, 1875

| *fig.* 15

a visit to Delta in 1883, "I wish we had a home together."[38] In October 1883 Darwin wrote about his brother Frank, whom he had not seen in four years. "Wrote a long letter to Frank. I wish he were here today. After dinner I went down to see Mr. and Mrs. Charles Gray, married just two weeks and have a cozy home and seem so happy. I only wish I had a home like it."[39] An entry on September 4, 1883, the anniversary of his mother's death, is especially revealing: "Twelve years ago this morning our darling mother died. Oh! what I would give to have her back and a bright home of our own. The sweetest song on earth is 'Home, Sweet Home.'"[40]

Driven by the need to communicate with his dispersed family (Hiram remained in Nebraska; William and Frank worked as soap salesmen in the Midwest and West; Delta lived in Auburn, New York; and Alta lived in Orange, New Jersey), Darwin read and wrote himself into an advanced state of literacy by the time he was fifteen, and by sixteen he had made himself the conduit of all family information. While William and Frank were Larkin salesmen, Darwin also wielded power as a source of information about company activities. This was a decisive step in gaining control of his own destiny, and with it, he began to formulate a desire to reassemble his family around him in Buffalo.

The quality of Darwin's life began to improve during 1882. He grew from 4' 11" to 5' 4 1/2" in less than a year.[41] He developed friendships with George Korn, his assistant bookkeeper, and Dan Robins, a young railroad brakeman assigned to room with him because the landlady considered Robins "our nicest boarder."[42] Darwin later wrote, "I learned to love [Robins] like a brother."[43] Darwin and his two friends spent most of their evenings together scheming about ways to make a fortune, until Korn left the Larkin company in April 1882 for a position in a railroad office in Leadville, Colorado. Early in January 1883, Robins was crushed to death between two train cars at Niagara Falls. Darwin was devastated by the loss of his friend.[44]

In his renewed loneliness, Darwin plunged further into work at the Larkin Company. Owing to the success of their Creme Oatmeal soap, the Larkin factory had begun in 1881 to operate around the clock. As head bookkeeper, Darwin looked on with growing concern as his ponderous ledger books filled up in as little as four months. Darwin persuaded John Larkin to order a custom-made index volume with space for 96,000 customer names, which Darwin filled in by working entirely after hours during a two-month period in 1883. His weekly salary was raised from $9 in 1882 to $12 in 1884.[45]

| fig. 16
Larkin Company, 1878

| fig. 17
Larkin Company, 1885

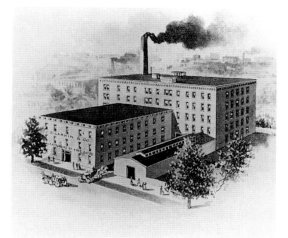

| fig. 16

| fig. 17

Shortly after the Larkin ledger index was completed, Darwin agreed to spend his evenings selling his brother William's stove polish to Buffalo shopkeepers.[46] He threw himself into the work with such abandon that he soon became ill and depressed, causing Hubbard to advise him to "quit the evening work."[47] But Darwin's industriousness was not a characteristic he could change. In 1883, in addition to his obligations to the Larkin Company, he wrote 116 letters and twelve postcards, attended seventeen plays, and read at least nine books. In September of that year he purchased a lot near the Larkin factory for $200, and the following May, with the sponsorship of John Larkin, he contracted to build a small, $800 house for the rental income it would generate.[48] In November 1883 he enrolled in a bookkeeping class at the YMCA, where his books became a model for the rest of the class, and by January 1884 he was instructing the class himself.[49]

While work was a place of refuge for Darwin, a realm where he could gain recognition, acceptance, and praise from his peers and superiors, his work habits cost him dearly. In addition to severe bouts of depression in the fall of 1883, he noted thirteen separate illnesses in the first eight months of the year, a pattern that would recur throughout his rise to success with even more serious consequences in the future.

Darwin had begun to write letters exhorting his father to join him in Buffalo shortly after his arrival there in 1879; and he continued to do so until early in 1884, when Hiram finally relented, moved to Buffalo, and rented a shop for his shoe-repair business at 373 Seneca Street, behind which he and Darwin set up their living quarters.[50] Life with his father proved troublesome for Darwin, however.[51] Hiram complained, threatened to leave Buffalo for lack of customers, deceived Darwin about money (which he sent to his wife in Nebraska), and, after many years of preaching abstinence, turned to drink. Once he arrived in Buffalo, Hiram Martin is rarely mentioned in his son's diaries.

Around the same time Hiram Martin moved to Buffalo, John Larkin and Elbert Hubbard began to show appreciation for Darwin's service and dedication. Larkin invited Darwin to Idlewood, his family camp on Lake Erie, on four summer weekends in 1884. Beginning in April 1884, Hubbard invited Darwin to his home in East Aurora almost every weekend over a seven-month period, and in the following summer these visits were extended to several weeks at a time.[52] Hubbard's large Queen Anne house was a welcome refuge from industrial Seneca Street. Hubbard reintroduced Darwin to horseback riding, encouraged him to make use of his substantial personal library, and engaged him in discussions of farming and literature over dinner.[53] Darwin's health improved noticeably throughout 1884 and 1885, despite his being so busy at work as to have written in his diary, "My time so fully occupied I have to hurry to do everything."[54]

In August 1885 Hubbard suggested that Darwin catalogue his personal library in East Aurora. While visiting the Buffalo Public Library, Darwin realized that a card file would be superior to the cumbersome index volume he had created for the Larkin Company two years earlier, because it could be accessed by several people simultaneously. Darwin ordered 35,000 index cards from a local printer and, working day and night for over two months, transferred all of the customer names onto them.[55] Characteristically, he worked himself sick, but the finished product proved to be a landmark invention in the history of business.[56] The card index was also timely, as it enabled the Larkin bookkeeping department to keep abreast of the influx of orders that had resulted from the sales innovations of the early 1880s. Hubbard rewarded Darwin with a fine horse and carriage and raised his salary to $20 per week.[57]

In October 1885 Hubbard created the "Combination Box," a sales device of such compelling public appeal that it eventually propelled the Larkin Company to the top ranks of American business. The original Combination Box of Sweet Home soaps offered one hundred bars of hand soap for $6, along with an assortment of toilet soaps and related articles.[58] Its success depended on the direct-mail solicitation of customers, the inclusion of a "premium," or bonus gift item, in each box, and the bulk purchase of such items at a low cost. Initially, Darwin recognized in the Combination Box a potential bookkeeping nightmare, but within a matter of weeks he struck upon a historic solution: the customer accounts would be posted directly onto cards rather than in the big ledger volumes, and the "card index" would become a "card ledger."[59] From 1886 on new sales ideas drove factory production upward at a sometimes astonishing rate, but never beyond the capacity of Darwin Martin's card ledger.

Early in 1885 Darwin began to call regularly at the home of Mr. and Mrs. Alexander Reidpath, storekeepers on Seneca Street who were the parents of three daughters. Darwin was drawn to the happy familial atmosphere and especially to Isabelle, a quiet, attractive girl of fifteen | see *fig. 4* [60] who suffered from recurring ulcers of the eye. His attachment to her and to the family intensified during the spring as Mr. Reidpath's health deteriorated, culminating in his death on June 8.[61] Darwin, caught up in the family's emotional distress, wrote in his diary, "Begin to think I am in love,"[62] but because of Isabelle's age their courtship was protracted over three years.

Darwin proposed to Isabelle in July 1887, and in September he purchased a lot on Summit Avenue in Buffalo's Parkside neighborhood, a half block north of the site on which he would eventually commission a complex of residential buildings from Frank Lloyd Wright. Darwin threw himself into the house-building project with his customary zeal, consulting others, sketching and drawing plans with Isabelle in the evenings, and working closely with his architect, C. R. Percival.[63] On December 9 he wrote in his diary, "At architect Percival's office 10–4 P.M. without dinner; after talking house six hours with Percival, more than an hour with Father, and all evening with Belle, my head ached so I could not sleep."[64]

The house was completed, except for minor details, in the following June at a cost of $3,580.92, more than $1,000 above Darwin's budgeted amount | *fig. 18*.[65] It was small and rather simply massed as Queen Anne houses go, and Darwin was disappointed. "[Nine] to 11:20 at new house. Everything very nice except the tower which is squatty. Don't like it at all. Spoils whole appearance in my eyes."[66]

Darwin and Isabelle moved into their new house shortly after their wedding on June 26, 1889. The adjustment was difficult for Darwin, who was accustomed to being completely self-sufficient and who tended to be as demanding of others as he was of himself.[67] His work habits became a source of friction, as he often carried both lunch and dinner to the office in case he had after-hours work to do, and he sometimes arrived home on the 11:15 P.M. Belt Line Railroad. At home he constantly occupied himself with house-related activities. In his diary he wrote, "Belle had a hard summer trying to adjust to living with an exacting husband."[68]

Once they settled into their home the Martins entertained small groups of family members, friends, and occasionally Darwin's business associates. They joined the nearby Episcopal church; their children, Dorothy and Darwin R. Martin, were born in 1896 and 1900, respectively. Thus Darwin Martin surrounded himself with home and family, but he continued to cling to the ideal of reassembling his siblings in Buffalo—an ideal that proved difficult to realize.

| *fig. 18*
C. R. Percival, Darwin
D. Martin House,
Buffalo, New York,
1888. Elevation

Hiram Martin joined Darwin and Isabelle in their new home in July 1889, but feeling uncomfortable there, he returned to boardinghouse living in September 1890.[69] The following year he moved to Chicago to live with Delta and George Barton, and then with William and Winifred Martin. He passed away in Chicago on January 29, 1893.

Frank Martin continued to work as a traveling salesman with some success following his departure from the Larkin sales force in 1881, but he squandered much of his earnings on women and alcohol. Darwin tried to help Frank in a succession of ill-conceived soap-related ventures.[70] In 1890 Darwin set Frank up in a perfume and sachet-powder business based in Buffalo, in the hope of drawing Frank closer to him; but there is no evidence that Frank ever resided in the city, and on the rare occasions that he visited he proved to be a difficult guest, especially for Isabelle.[71]

Alta Martin was even more dissolute than Frank, but despite his indifference during Darwin's early, lonely years in Buffalo, he allowed Darwin to persuade him to move his family from Newark, New Jersey, to Buffalo in 1895, when Darwin offered him a night watchman's position at the Larkin factories.[72] Alta lasted less than a year, however, and with his departure another filament of Darwin's familial dream slipped from his grasp.[73]

Ultimately, Delta Barton, upon whom Darwin had so depended for her frequent "sisterly letters" during his early years in Buffalo, became the principal recipient of his considerable generosity. Delta and George Barton moved from Auburn, New York, to Chicago in 1888, when William Martin made George a partner in his stove-polish business. Problems arose, and in 1895 Darwin brought George and Delta to Buffalo and gave George a position in the Larkin Company.[74] Thus for a few brief months in 1895, with the Bartons arrived, Alta signed-on as a watchman at the Larkin Company, and Frank's perfume business well established in Buffalo, Darwin nearly achieved his cherished dream. But then there was William | *fig.* 19, who proved to be problematic in an altogether different way.

After two years as a soap slinger in the early 1880s, William joined Frank Gano, a manufacturer of stove polish in Chicago, as a partner.[75] By 1888, with help from Darwin, William was able to buy out Gano.[76] In 1890 he married Winifred Kirby of Mount Ayr, Iowa.[77] The stove-polish business prospered with the help of some guaranteed business from the Larkin Company.

| *fig.* 19
William E. Martin, circa 1915

Throughout the 1880s and 1890s William made frequent overtures to Darwin to join him—first as a soap slinger[78] and later as a partner in the stove-polish business.[79] Darwin declined because of his own success at the Larkin Company and his involvement with Isabelle Reidpath, but in 1887 he offered to mortgage his Maurice Street rental house and buy out Gano if William would agree to move his business to Buffalo.[80] This time William demurred, establishing an impasse that would never be resolved. William, too, was motivated to reassemble the Martin family. In addition to his overtures to Darwin, he succeeded in attracting Delta and George, he got Hiram briefly, and Frank bought into his stove-polish business.

Despite this impasse, Darwin and William Martin were drawn together by a series of extraordinary circumstances during the 1890s. In April 1894, while trying to repair a jammed metal-stamping machine at his factory, William severed three fingers from each hand.[81] Darwin immediately dispatched Isabelle to Chicago to help out. (Darwin visited only briefly.) During her stay Darwin wrote to his wife:

> My Darling:
> I am home safe and sound. Poor Will. Have wired him and George [Barton]. Asked the latter to wire reply. Bless you darling for your note saying "I'm willing to do my share, if I have to go without things." Think, dear, if my hands were maimed. How helpless I would feel for many long months. I have sent Will $50 and to solace him assured him he should have a home while I did. God grant I need never have to make you regret it. I could spare them $500 a year to live quietly in a little cottage you know dear, it don't mean I will ask you to yield up your ideal of a home.
> Your loving husband.[82]

Significantly, at this tragic moment in the life of the relative closest to him, Darwin Martin expressed no direct concern for William's personal feelings and no consideration for Winifred, for their new baby, or for William's business. The entire letter is constructed around the idea, and the ideal, of a home.

The penultimate surge in the fortune of the Larkin Company began with Elbert Hubbard's $6 Combination Box. In 1888 the Larkin Company made its initial attempt to induce its customers to seek out additional new customers, an idea that eventually became a mainstay of the enterprise.[83] Customers were given the option of paying off a $6, thirty-day account by sending in six new $6 Combination Box customer orders.[84] Hubbard did not anticipate that many of these new customers would also seek out six new customers, thus creating an exponential increase in orders. Nevertheless, Hubbard forged ahead in 1892 with a new $10 Combination Box, for which there was a single premium offered, the attractive Chautauqua Piano Lamp, valued at $10 retail but purchased by the Larkin Company from its manufacturer in great quantities at a low wholesale price. Thus for $10 the customer received a $20 value—the lamp and a year's supply of soaps. The public responded enthusiastically and the volume of business increased at an even faster pace.

As a result of these developments, Darwin Martin's staff increased from six assistants in the beginning of 1888 to twenty-four by the end of the year.[85] That he was able to attend to Isabelle, maintain his horse, speculate in real estate, build a house, and operate his brother's perfume business in the face of the accelerated growth of the Larkin business is a testament to his energy, his dedication, and his mastery of the organization; but again, a toll was taken. In 1890 and 1891 diary entries such as "Too busy to think"[86] and "Busy all the time, not a minute to spare, J.D.L. & Co., garden, poultry, L.F.M. & Co., etc., etc., can't read or sit and rest. Blood all out of order"[87] appear, and in 1892 he abandoned the diary altogether.

The tumultuous events of the early 1890s within the Larkin Company and Darwin's ascendant role in them are a reflection of the increasingly unorthodox behavior of Elbert Hubbard. Sometime between 1886 and 1888, Hubbard, then secretary of the Larkin Company and a married father of three children, fell in love with Alice Moore, an East Aurora school teacher.[88] Hubbard's wife, Bertha, became aware of the affair after she had unwittingly allowed Alice to move into their home. Alice relocated to Hull, Massachusetts. During the ensuing few years Hubbard managed to carry on an affair with Alice and grew increasingly restless with both his business career and his family life.

On September 20, 1892, John Larkin informed Darwin that Hubbard planned to withdraw from the business with the intention of entering Harvard College to study law.[89] Darwin seized the opportunity to negotiate for Hubbard's stock[90] and to assume his position as secretary of the Larkin Company. Hubbard resigned on January 5, 1893, after twenty years in the business. Darwin wrote, "[Mr. Hubbard] spoke some v[ery] kind words to me, I was much moved. Tears stood in his eyes. After I reached home I could not restrain my feelings; I wept."[91] The loss of his long-time mentor, a man of singular charisma, must have been devastating to Darwin, and that sense of loss was compounded a few weeks later with the death of Darwin's father, Hiram, in Chicago.

Despite a contentious departure, wherein Hubbard demanded his considerable share of the Larkin Company in cash, in the face of the national depression of 1893, the former secretary continued to wield influence over the business through his marketing ideas and his continuing friendship with Darwin.[92] His principal legacy, the $10 Combination Box, became the cornerstone of Larkin sales for the following twenty years. As secretary, Darwin's approach to marketing was fundamentally different from Hubbard's, however. Whereas Hubbard constantly experimented and took risks, Darwin preferred to stick with a proven success. His strength lay not in imagination but in figures and in attention to detail.[93] He simply expanded the premium offerings and added soap-related products in increasing quantities each year. Following the single-premium offerings of 1892 and 1893 (the Chautauqua lamp, followed by the Chautauqua desk), enough premiums were added by 1894 to warrant a sixteen-page catalogue; and by the early 1900s hundreds of premium items were being offered by the company. The bookkeeping became increasingly complex, but with Darwin's card-ledger system it was only necessary to increase personnel in order to keep abreast of the work.[94]

As a result of these developments, the Larkin Company underwent a transformation during the 1890s from a soap manufactory to a mail-order business based on the sale of soap. This change is a reflection of Darwin's systematic mind. The brunt of the premium buying, advertising, bookkeeping, and the supervision of office personnel fell to him, while John Larkin occupied himself with soap production, land acquisition, finances, new building construction, and the overall supervision of the business.

The mounting concerns of the business began to oppress Darwin in the mid-1890s. Letters to Isabelle in Chicago in 1894 reveal signs of depression and convey a sense that his painful childhood was never entirely out of his consciousness.[95] Late in January 1897 Darwin was completely overwhelmed by the demands of the business and suffered a severe nervous collapse, causing his physician to recommend an extended leave of absence from the company. John Larkin convened the board of directors around Darwin's bed to assure him that his plans for the business would be carried out in his absence. Darwin and Isabelle spent eight weeks at Old Point Comfort, Virginia, after which he was able to return to work in May.

As a result of Darwin's illness and after long deliberation, John Larkin invited William R. Heath, a Chicago attorney who was married to Mary Heath, a sister of Elbert Hubbard and of Mrs. John D. Larkin (née Frances Hubbard), to join the company. Heath began on April 1, 1899, as personnel manager and soon began to share the burden of the day-to-day operation of the Larkin Company with Darwin Martin.[96]

Due to the frantic pace of his life and work during the second half of the 1890s, Darwin was unable to maintain a detailed autobiographical record, as he had in the 1880s,[97] yet these years hold special interest because they immediately precede, and to a certain extent condition, Darwin's and William's initial reaction to Frank Lloyd Wright. Fundamental to what would transpire with Wright was Darwin's annual salary, which rose from $1,500 in 1893 to $5,000 in 1896,[98] to $10,000 in 1898 following his nervous breakdown, to $25,000 in 1899[99]; by 1906 it is said that Darwin Martin was the highest paid executive in the United States. By 1907 his personal assets had reached $1 million, and by 1912 they exceeded $2 million.[100]

The Larkin Company plant on Seneca Street grew apace with the growth of the business, with the construction of the C, D, and E buildings in 1895 and 1898 | fig. 20, steadily expanding alphabetically through to the mammoth R, S, and T Building (also known as the Larkin warehouse) in 1912—altogether to a total of 3 million square feet. By late 1902, when negotiations with Wright for the Martin complex began, Darwin, as secretary of the Larkin Company, would have been very familiar with the processes and problems of building construction, albeit of the large-scale, industrial kind. Equally significant was the meteoric rise of his personal wealth in the years before income tax. He had almost unlimited funds for

| *fig.* 20
Larkin Company, 1898

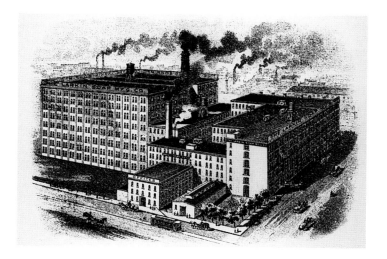

the project and was only restrained by his innate frugality. Indeed, it was in the juncture between Darwin's unlimited wealth and his tendency toward frugality that Wright would have to operate.

Toward the end of the 1890s, Darwin and William Martin began to correspond more frequently, drawn together by additional family tragedies in the wake of William's loss of his fingers and Darwin's nervous collapse. In 1898 Isabelle contracted typhoid fever, and only after she recovered was she informed that her sister, Nettie Reidpath, had died of the disease. Two years later Darwin and Isabelle's son, Darwin R. Martin, nearly died as well. Darwin again invited William to move his family and his business to Buffalo; failing in that, he used his wealth and his extraordinary knowledge of business to draw William closer to him.[101] Among the twenty-four letters exchanged by the brothers from 1898 to 1902, Darwin wrote many long, cogent essays on indebtedness, lawsuits, and life insurance. Many of William's responses reveal him as sometimes blunt and tactless.[102] One letter concludes, however, with a simple postscript, "NB Ever investigate Christian Science any?" which drew a sarcastic response from Darwin, although all of the Martins would eventually convert.[103]

In early August 1902 William wrote the letter to Darwin expressing a desire to move out of the city of Chicago that began the chain of events that would lead the Martin brothers to Frank Lloyd Wright. Darwin's return letter offered William a loan at five percent interest and is rich in advice based on Darwin's experience with building.[104] William responded on August 18, 1902, with a lengthy discussion of the neighborhoods that interested him and an invitation to Darwin to "visit Chi[cago] & look over the ground with me, for I would like to have your approval in what ever I do in this matter."[105]

Darwin responded on August 22 with a discussion of location, cost, and commuting time, and again on August 25 with a long and carefully considered discussion of the issues, based in part on converstions he had had with William R. Heath, who had lived in Chicago for ten years.[106] In this letter Darwin agreed to go to Chicago on September 11 in order to conduct some Larkin business and to help William in his quest for a home. It was on Saturday, September 13, 1902, that the two Martin brothers drove out to Oak Park and "discovered" Frank Lloyd Wright.

May 26, 1907

Dorothy Martin and
other family members in
the Martins' automobile
in 1907

Chapter Two

THE BARTON HOUSE: TESTING THE WATERS

THE NOVEMBER 1902 meeting between Frank Lloyd Wright and Darwin Martin was momentous for both men. Wright's practice was flourishing in the aftermath of the publication of the first prairie-house design in the *Ladies' Home Journal*, a widely read popular magazine, in February 1901 | see *fig. 7*, and his reputation was growing as prairie houses began to proliferate in Oak Park, River Forest, and elsewhere in the Greater Chicago area.[1] In 1901 and 1902, Wright designed approximately forty-five buildings, of which about thirty were built—a lifetime of work for many architects.[2] As Wright began negotiations with his Buffalo clients, he and his office staff (some seven to twelve assistants, depending on circumstances) were working on an average of twenty, mostly domestic, commissions at a time. Wright's readiness to assume additional work, including a substantial office building, is an indication that he was eager to explore the full range of possibilities of the new prairie form.

The Buffalo commissions held two major attractions for Wright: whereas most of his work up to November 1902 was concentrated in the vicinity of Chicago and in southern Wisconsin, the city of Buffalo, five hundred miles to the east, represented a penetration into a potentially vast new market. Moreover, the commission for the Larkin Administration Building, which would be realized as a five-story, steel-framed, brick-clad headquarters for the Larkin soap and housewares mail-order operation, offered Wright an opportunity to break out of the realm of domestic design into the more visible and lucrative realm of commercial architecture—a realm with which he had nearly five years' experience in the offices of Adler & Sullivan.[3] Wright may have also inferred from conversations with William Martin and in the early stages of becoming acquainted with Darwin Martin that he had found a client of substantial wealth and generosity.

Wright and Martin had much in common: their ancestors hailed from Great Britain; they were both close in age (Martin was two years older), below average in stature (Martin was shorter than Wright), highly intelligent, well read, and passionate about their work. Both had endured the loss of a parent; both had distant, older fathers; and both had spent a portion of their youth living in parts of Iowa and in the Boston area. Both had a connection to the arts and crafts movement and began work in booming Great Lake cities under the direction of prominent men to whom writing was important (Louis Sullivan and Elbert Hubbard, respectively).

On the other hand, as artist and client, Wright and Martin were not on an equal footing in the relationship. Neither were they similar in manner or appearance: Wright had an aura of authority and a charisma born of his supreme self-confidence, personal charm, and extraordinary design ability.[4] Martin, in contrast, was bowlegged, red haired, freckled, pock-marked, deaf in one ear, and given to stammering. In 1886 the famous phrenologist Orson Squire Fowler concluded that Darwin was "deficient in continuity, self-esteem, secretiveness and language," and later that year, Darwin described himself as "nervously constituted."[5] As Wright would soon discover, outside of the realm of business, where he was comfortably in command, Darwin was a perpetual student, intellectually curious, driven to learn, open to new ideas, and an enthusiastic admirer of creative individuals although not creative himself. Wright had many kinds of clients, but he especially enjoyed those like Darwin Martin, who were willing to learn from him.[6] In short, the Buffalo venture looked promising to Wright.

But what accounts for Darwin Martin's extraordinary receptivity to Wright's architecture and for the enthusiasm and loyalty that would endure over thirty-two sometimes difficult years?

The majority of Wright's early clients were friends, neighbors, relatives, or friends of friends, clustered in Oak Park and River Forest. As Leonard K. Eaton has demonstrated, Wright's clients (Eaton defines the husband as the client) were generally upper-middle-class professional people, usually industrialists, who were self-made, inventive, progressive, politically conservative, and often musically inclined. Eaton characterizes their wives as "individuals."[7] Most clients were Protestants, and a relatively large number were Christian Scientists.[8] The Martin brothers fit Eaton's client profile reasonably well, but unlike the clients in suburban Chicago who knew Wright as a neighbor and saw his work evolve from the early 1890s, the Martins encountered his work in measured increments that were destined to amplify the significance of the work and the impact of Wright's personality. Initially, they responded directly to the houses as they saw them during their September 13, 1902 visit to Oak Park; then they learned about Wright's ideals and principles through their conversation with Walter Burley Griffin at Wright's studio that same day; and finally, following a period of gestation, William met Wright himself. Darwin was further prepared for his initial encounter with Wright through the mediating effect of his brother's effusive letter ("one of Nature's noblemen") of October 22, 1902.[9] Thus for Darwin, a considerable mystique formed about Wright in advance of their first meeting in November 1902, a mystique that would never entirely dissipate, one that Wright recognized and exploited, and one in which Wright probably exceeded Darwin's expectations. The conditions of receptivity couldn't have been better.

Darwin Martin's predisposition toward liking Wright was further conditioned by a cluster of circumstances. The letters written by Darwin to Elbert Hubbard and by William Martin to Darwin in September and October of 1902 express as much excitement about Wright himself ("highly educated...a splendid type of manhood...with *high ideals*") as about the work. William was excited about the quality of the work ("he will build you the finest, most sensible house in Buffalo") and the status it would bring ("you will be the envy of every rich man in Buffalo"), while Darwin's letter to Hubbard focused upon the style ("simplicity itself") and its monetary value ("he makes $8,000 look like $15,000 in a house"). The letter is also significant because it represents a conscious acknowledgment on Darwin's part of the similarity between Hubbard and Wright and perhaps a subconscious acknowledgment that in Wright he had found someone to fill the role that Hubbard had occupied in his life for so many years—as a creative and unconventional counterpart to Darwin's methodical, uncreative self.

William Martin's enthusiastic letter powerfully reinforced Darwin's predisposition toward Wright and was, in turn, further reinforced by Hubbard's response to Darwin ("he [Wright] is certainly a genius in his line") and by William Heath's readiness to commission a house by Wright in Buffalo for himself and to lend support to Darwin's campaign to have Wright design the Larkin Administration Building.[10] In fact, despite the Martin brothers' reservations about John Larkin's willingness to employ Wright, Larkin's initial interest in Louis Sullivan as a candidate constituted a major step toward the acceptance of the progressive ideas that were fomenting in the Chicago and prairie schools of the Midwest.

Darwin Martin's enthusiasm for Wright was conditioned as well by the course of life and work that he had chosen. Both Darwin and William Martin rejected their agrarian experiences on the Nebraska frontier for the commercial-industrial world of urban America in the late nineteenth century, an era that witnessed the greatest concentration of inventions and innovations in history. One of Darwin's primary functions as secretary of the Larkin Company was to keep abreast of the products of American industry and to evaluate and select a wide variety of household goods for the Larkin premium catalogue.[11] Thus Wright's prairie architecture appealed to Darwin as "the latest thing" in houses, as a product, and as a good investment. Darwin wrote to John Larkin, "A Wright house is like an oriental rug, it increases in value, is better understood and admired ten years after its erection than when new and will be worth more yet in twenty years."[12]

In the final analysis, the power of Wright's personal appeal was anchored in his work. Whatever positive inclinations Darwin Martin may have experienced toward Wright, the ultimate attraction was the work itself: the prairie houses, whose sleek vessel-like lines, natural materials, and fine crafting so defied convention and held the promise of a house that would transcend all other houses, the "Home Sweet Home" of Darwin Martin's long-cherished dream.[13]

THE BARTON HOUSE

From Frank Lloyd Wright's initial visit to Buffalo in November 1902, a full year passed before he was given a contract for the Larkin Administration Building. The delay was partly attributable to Darwin Martin, who apparently discussed his own house commission with Wright but made its realization, along with that of the Larkin Building, contingent upon the successful design and completion of a small house for his sister and brother-in-law, Delta and George Barton.

Darwin selected a design for the Bartons—that of the J. J. Walser House in Austin, a Chicago neighborhood adjacent to Oak Park | *figs.* 22, 23—while on a fact-finding visit to Chicago with Isabelle in March 1903. He reported the results to John Larkin:

> I selected a plan of Wright's for a simple, inexpensive house which he can furnish blueprints of with no work on his part...and which I will proceed at once to build....In a few months, therefore, we will all be able to better judge the consistency and practicability of Wright's ideas in so far as a little house can exemplify them.[14]

| *fig.* 22
Frank Lloyd Wright,
J. J. Walser House,
Austin, Illinois, 1901.
First floor plan

| *fig.* 23
J. J. Walser House.
Principal elevation

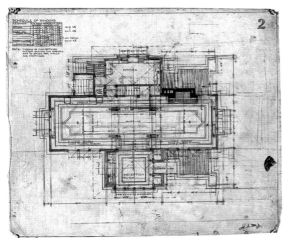

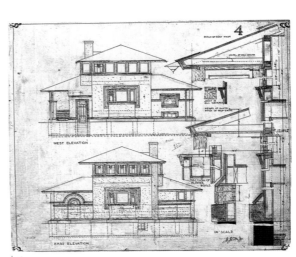

| *fig.* 22

| *fig.* 23

Darwin asked Wright for a house that would cost around $4,000. He did not propose the six-building complex that eventually materialized but wrote somewhat vaguely in terms of "two houses, a greenhouse and a barn."[15]

Given the derivation of the Barton House from the preexisting Walser design, Wright's commitment to portraying his clients in their buildings had little bearing on this commission. The Bartons were, in fact, only nominally clients. Darwin Martin commissioned, oversaw construction of, and paid for the Barton House with the understanding that the Bartons would rent the house from him when it was completed.[16]

Darwin was powerfully motivated to be generous toward his sister, Delta. Following the death of their mother, she was consigned to a foster family—the Weavers, in Auburn, New York—with the result that Darwin did not see her again for seven years. The Weavers raised Delta as their own and objected when George Barton, a man of rather dim prospects, began to court her. They eventually reconciled themselves to the relationship, and Delta married George in 1884. Despite the siblings' long separation, Delta was Darwin's closest living female relation and sustained him with frequent, affectionate letters throughout his lonely early years in Buffalo.[17] Even then, Darwin was protective of Delta. He wrote to his father in late 1881, "Please write to [Delta] soon Father it makes her feel bad to be neglected."[18] In another letter, Darwin proposed that the whole family—Hiram, Frank, Alta, Delta, William, and himself—live together in Buffalo, with Delta keeping house for them.[19] By the mid-1890s, Darwin was able to provide George Barton with a position as a clerk in the Larkin Company, a position he held for the rest of his career. The Bartons settled a few blocks from Darwin's 1888 Summit Avenue home and remained there until the summer of 1904, when their new Frank Lloyd Wright–designed house was completed.

Just what the Bartons thought about their Wright-designed home remains a mystery. No family photographs of the interior have come to light, nor is there mention of the Bartons' feelings about the house anywhere in the extensive Martin Family Papers. George and Delta and their adopted daughter, Laura, lived at 118 Summit Avenue from 1904 until George's death in 1928, after which Delta moved to Laura's home in Bryn Mawr, Pennsylvania.

While the Barton House has little to do with portraiture, the circumstances of its realization are rich in insights into Wright's and Martin's personalities, their relationship, and their methods of work. Moreover, the Barton House does play a significant role in the conception of the Martin complex as a portrait of Darwin Martin. For Wright the commission presented an opportunity to rethink and transform an earlier design while simultaneously envisioning its implications for a proposed complex of buildings. The commission was also an opportunity to elevate Darwin Martin's thinking toward more ambitious aesthetic, and more costly, goals. Insofar as the Martin complex is a coherent whole—and the Wasmuth portfolio plan certainly suggests that it is—its story begins with the Barton commission.

Darwin Martin's overzealous involvement in the commission was a function of his personality and his considerable experience in building construction, both on his own behalf (he commissioned four houses) and as a leading executive in the Larkin Company (which built fifteen large-scale industrial buildings during his tenure there). Because he lived less than fifty yards away from the site of the Barton House, he was able to monitor its progress very closely and frequently intervened in disagreements between Wright and Oscar S. Lang, the contractor—a practice that was to continue throughout the construction of the rest of the Martin complex. Darwin's notion of ideal client behavior is outlined in a letter to his brother William, who was then building his own Wright-designed house in Oak Park: "It is very important that you should yourself personally see your home about twice a week, part of the time three times a week. Be thoroughly familiar with all the specifications. Be able to see in your mind what each item is and then see in the house that it is there. Do not depend on Wright, much less on McLeod [William's contractor]. Don't depend on anybody. Don't think you cannot spare the time. Don't turn this down because you are wiser than I. You will have a much better house if you take my advice."[20]

The Walser House is a modest wood-frame and stucco prairie house. Its principal living spaces—the living and dining rooms on the first floor and the bedrooms on the second—occupy the two-story portion of the house, while the single-story crossing axis, parallel to the street, is comprised of an entry and reception room to the south of the principal mass and a kitchen protruding to the north. The principal elevation is symmetrical. The Walser

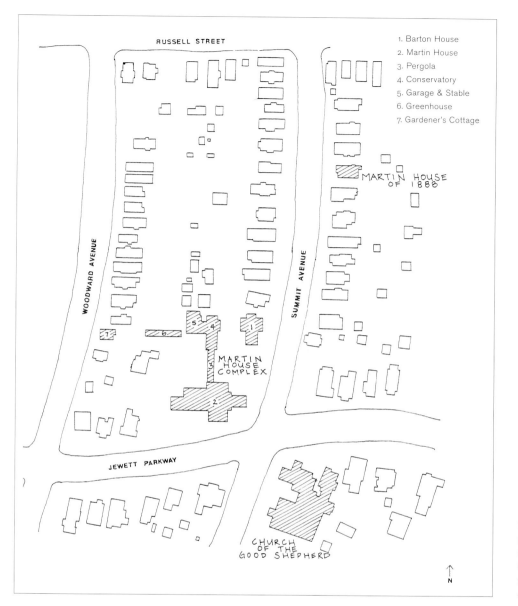

RUSSELL STREET

1. Barton House
2. Martin House
3. Pergola
4. Conservatory
5. Garage & Stable
6. Greenhouse
7. Gardener's Cottage

MARTIN HOUSE
OF 1888

WOODWARD AVENUE

SUMMIT AVENUE

5 4
7 6
1
3 MARTIN
HOUSE
COMPLEX

2

JEWETT PARKWAY

CHURCH
OF THE
GOOD SHEPHERD

N

| *fig.* 24
Map of the Parkside
neighborhood, showing
the 1888 Martin House
by C. R. Percival and
the Frank Lloyd Wright-
designed Martin Complex

walls are solid at the first floor level with tripartite Chicago-type windows cut into the fabric of the east, south, and west walls. On the second floor generous eaves protect casement windows that extend in a series across the entire front and rear elevations and wrap their corners with a single additional window. Shortly after selecting the Walser plan, Darwin wrote to Wright:

> With this letter I return the sketch of the J. J. Walser, Jr. house, the plan of which has been approved by the Bartons. We wish you to prepare blue prints and complete specifications as early as possible, for a house with brick and plaster exterior on this plan reversed so that all the doors and windows now facing North will face South and vice versa.[21]

Late in March 1903, shortly after Darwin received blueprints | *figs. 25, 26* and specifications for the Barton House from Wright, he fired off a volley of criticisms. He and Isabelle were particularly concerned about the footprint of the building, as it threatened to encroach upon the neighboring lot to the north. Darwin voiced his wife's reservations about the design along with his own:

> Just like a woman! Mrs. Martin wishes now that we had seen the interior of the little (Davenport?) house at River Forest—the one that was locked. She feels as though a snugger design might better coincide with her views. However, it is still my humble opinion that the Walser is a pretty good plan. My only objection is the amount it encroaches on the lot. The more Mrs. Martin turns the matter over in her mind, the more unhappy she becomes about your exteriors. I think that awful Fricke approach | *fig. 27* and entrance is what distresses her, and possibly the (Hertley?) has something to do with it. I think she fully agrees with me that the interior of our own home will be safe in your hands, and that only the exterior causes anxiety.[22]

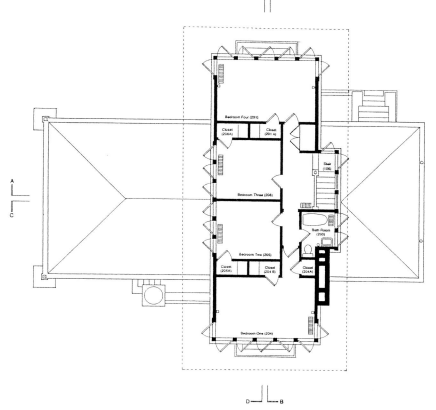

|fig. 25

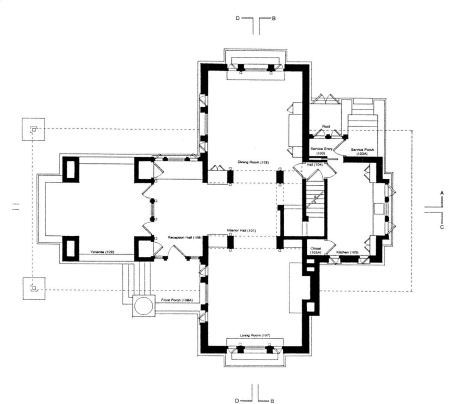

|fig. 25
George and Delta
Barton House. Second
floor plan

|fig. 26
Frank Lloyd Wright,
George and Delta
Barton House, Buffalo,
New York, 1903–04.
First floor plan

|fig. 26

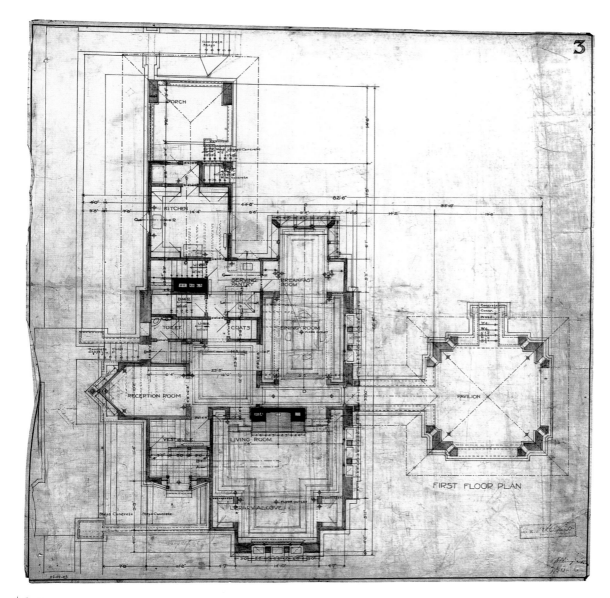

| *fig.* 27

William G. Fricke House,
Oak Park, Illinois, 1901.
First floor plan

The Martins were troubled by the porch Wright added to the south wing of the Barton House, which increased the width of the house to fifty feet (the width of two typical house lots on the street) and, owing to the placement of the house on the extreme northern edge of the site, brought the kitchen eaves to within five feet of the neighboring lot. In questioning both the dimensions and the proportions of the house, the Martins threatened to undermine the integrity of Wright's design, causing him to rise to its defense with this carefully argued letter:

> Dear Sir: Concerning the width of the Barton House—It seems to me that a house which is rather free in outline will do better what ought to be done in the proposed position, considering its association with your own house, than would a more tightly compacted one. The fact that the porch extends beyond an imaginary 50 ft. lot line should not figure, as the projecting veranda will form a sightly feature which will add rather than detract from the effect of the association of the two buildings. We can hold this projection down close if you wish it. It would not be advisable to trim the eaves, I think, as the proportion of the house would easily suffer....
>
> The Walser plan could hardly be improved upon for the site, exterior or interior. It is certainly snug without being "dinky." The Davenport House is also 50 feet wide and is not nearly so adaptable to your conditions. [23]

Wright then shifts his discussion from proportion to the nature of his clients in an effort to win over Isabelle Martin:

> I am sorry Mrs. Martin is still unhappy over our exteriors. If she has not seen enough to assure her of a certain capacity and versatility in creating beautiful homes I can say nothing to comfort her unless she might be pointed to the fact that each client is finally satisfied and

our enthusiastic advocate. They are people of more than ordinary cultivation too. Many of these people had misgivings and no one of them saw just the building which pleased them, indeed how could they, or why should they when each treatment is peculiar to the individual for whom was it designed? Many saw things which were as distasteful to them as the things you mention are distasteful to her.[24]

Wright's concluding remarks are permeated with the idea of the house as a portrait:

> The buildings you saw were in no sense samples submitted, from which you were to determine your own house, but merely evidence of a capacity on the part of your architect to understand and appreciate your feelings and wants and his strength to characterize them in truly beautiful fashion for you—as he had done for others. It is impossible for one to realize the extent to which this has been done for another—I know that perfectly well. But if Mrs. Martin could not feel in the atmosphere of the work, something as true and simple as it was broad and capable, she would be a very foolish woman to entrust me with the designing of her home. She would be wasting the opportunity of her life for no opportunity seems to me quite so much THE opportunity of one's life as the building of the home unless it is the choosing of one's wife or husband, as the case may be.[25]

Wright's letter is bifurcated: his message to Darwin—that the projected porch is a "sightly feature which will add rather than detract from the effect of the association of the two buildings"—is addressed to the aesthetics of the Barton House, while his remarks to Isabelle are socially framed and employ language calculated to challenge her judgment.

Wright was persuasive. The correspondence between him and Martin diminished significantly in the spring of 1903, an indication that the "sparring" period was over and that Wright's office staff was preparing the working drawings for the Barton House.[26]

FROM FRANK LLOYD WRIGHT ARCHITECT
FOREST AND CHICAGO AVENUES OAK PARK
ILLINOIS TELEPHONE OAK PARK FIFTY THREE
IN CHICAGO BY APPOINTMENT ONLY ▼ ▼ ▼ ▼

My dear Mr.Martin:-
    I have begun work on the Jewett Avenue
property, and find a difficulty at the outset
which should be determined and I write to ask
if you find an objection to squaring your
building with the Barton's, disregarding the
Jewett Avenue frontage as far as a parallel
is concerned, thus;

No two of the lot lines are parallel and the
front of the house might break away gently in
several offsets to coincide approximately with
the slope of the street.
    I think it important that the Barton house
and your own stand square with regard to each
other, leaving square angles in the court between, barn and all.

    I know the buildings along that street
(except the church?) are set parallel with it
but it is in a corner anyway which makes a
positive lining up impossible. What do you say?
    I shall come to Buffalo as soon as I have
your sketches in shape.
    The delay in getting positive information
as to lot lines has kept us back somewhat on
office building plans and perhaps I would better come down once more to get the width of
the annex determined.
    You have not yet written me the memorandum
Mr.Larkin suggested. Perhaps it is unnecessary?
It shall be as you think best.
    With regards to Mrs.Martin.

                    Yours sincerely
                    Frank Lloyd Wright

Mr.D.D.Martin,
Buffalo, N.Y.

May 11, 1903.

| fig. 28
Frank Lloyd Wright,
letter to Darwin D.
Martin, May 3, 1903,
containing initial sketch
of the Martin Complex

As soon as the Barton House was underway, however, Wright turned his attention—somewhat precipitously—to the design of the entire Martin complex. His letter to the Martins of May 11, 1903 includes a crude sketch of the complex as it was then understood | *fig. 28*:

> My Dear Mr. Martin:
>
> I have begun work on the Jewett Avenue property, and find a difficulty at the outset which should be determined and I write to ask if you find an objection to squaring your building with the Barton's, disregarding the Jewett Avenue frontage as far as parallel is concerned, thus [sketch of Martin complex]. No two of the lot lines are parallel and the front of the house might break away gently in several offsets to coincide approximately with the slope of the street.
>
> I think it important that the Barton house and your own stand square with regard to each other, leaving square angles in the court between, barn and all.
>
> I know the buildings along that street (except the church?) are set parallel with it but it is in a corner anyway which makes a positive lining up impossible. What do you say?
>
> I shall come to Buffalo as soon as I have your sketches in shape....
>
> With regards to Mrs. Martin.
>
> Yours sincerely,[27]

Darwin wrote immediately to correct Wright's misunderstanding regarding the alignment of the Jewett Avenue houses.[28]

Nothing was heard from Wright until July 1903, when he unexpectedly wrote to the Larkin Company asking to be paid $2,000 for his as-yet-unfinished work on the administration building.[29] Wright's premature request threw Darwin into a frenzy of concern about the escalating costs of the Barton House. On July 24 he asked Wright for a copy of the contract costs of the Walser House, which proved to be $8,000, nearly twice what Darwin had originally requested for the Barton House. On August 4 he reminded Wright that the Barton House, with its south porch and brick veneer, was more elaborate and hence would be even more expensive than the Walser House, adding, "What can we do to cheapen the house?"[30] Then, upon receiving a revised estimate from the contractor for the Barton House, Darwin wrote to Isabelle, who was vacationing, "My dear: Mr. Lang made his report last night on the Barton House. The bids aggregate at first sight, including architect's fees, $10,500. Isn't it awful? Instead of a little house, every man who figured on it referred to it as a big house, Lang constantly reminding them that it was a little house."[31] Darwin suggested a variety of ways to trim costs, but he concluded the letter with a decisive shift in the direction of enlightened patronage:

> Wright's houses do cost astonishingly. The big roofs cost; the heavy
> masonry costs; the long room 50' x only 18' costs; putting the kitchen
> on the opposite side of the house instead of behind the reception
> room, adds a lot of outside wall and cost. We simply must recognize
> that if we are going into art in architecture that money is too gross
> a subject to take into account.[32]

Despite this hint of enlightenment, Darwin continued to try to diminish costs and even went so far as to suggest that they scrap the Walser plan altogether in favor of something entirely different and fifty percent lower in cost. Wright wrote asking, "Why worry about the cost?"[33] to which Darwin replied, "Really Mr. Wright, it isn't so much the cost, as it is the consciousness of disproportion that worries us."[34]

Faced with these additional criticisms, Wright fired off a somewhat belligerent letter on August 22, 1903. This and a second letter written six days later constitute a rare record of Wright's persuasiveness:

> My dear Mr. Martin:
> History has a knack of repeating itself *ad libitum, ad nauseum*. I will
> have to come down and wipe up the ground with the whole Buffalo
> contingent.

The figures on your house are for something in the imagination of the several contractors not for the substance of the shadow traced by our plans.

If you really would like to know what the work is worth in quantity and what would be a fair price for the work scan the following schedule.

Masonry — solid brick	2300.00
Mill work (complete)	650.00
Carpentry	1100.00
Lumber	425.00
Heavy Hardware	50.00
Painting	300.00
Plumbing	600.00
Heating	526.00
Electric work	80.00
Tile	600.00
Trimming Hardware & Electroliers	275.00
Glass	250.00
Total	$7156.00
Plastering	460.00
	$7616.00

You remember we have added a tile roof, a porch, and brick in place of plaster to the original Walser House together with a few other desirable details.

This is not so bad?

We are going to build the house at that figure if you will just sit tight and hold fast.

We want a tile roof most certainly, a delicate shingle tile of the right color, not like anything in the vicinity I can assure you.

The porch is a necessary luxury, we must cling to that too with the strength of despair.

[The William R.] Heath [House in Buffalo] is coming out about $2,000 better than thought when I last wrote you. Perhaps there is a glimmer of hope, "afar off" and dim, but still a glimmer.

Your masons are robbers. I will prove it to them when I come down with my surveys of quantities. We will ask them for prices on these quantities in the wall and for nothing else, or in place, or according to schedule and for nothing else.

The way of the "art architect" is as hard as that of any other "transgressor."

Lend us a hand when I come down and let us see if combined effort can't make something desirable happen. We will pull the Barton House out of the shadows.

Yours as ever,

N.B. [handwritten] A brick veneered house here is somewhat more expensive than a solid brick one. The solid brick *turned* is good enough for any body—and has an integrity denied the average veneered article. I do not see how Mr. Lang saves the money

—FLW[35]

Darwin responded with a little sarcasm:

Dear Sir: I have been endeavoring to extract comfort from your letter of Aug. 22nd, wherein I am assured that if I will but sit tight and hold fast my little $6,000 house *may* be completed, including architect's fees and Buffalo superintendence, for $7,842.70. I suppose I should be happy and am inconsiderate in refusing to be so. Assuring you that I am perfectly willing to lend a hand as requested if you can show me the propriety of my spending $1,842.70 more than I intended, I am, Yours very truly[36]

Undaunted, Wright wrote again on August 28:

My dear Mr. Martin:

Regarding the items in yours of the 8/19/03.

1st. "The figures are awful." I think in this connection we have all of us to shift our conception of a fair price. We have formed our conceptions on an earlier state of the market—outgrown and not likely to occur again. The old standard is obsolete. Compare the prices of such staples as lumber, brick, labor, and the technical appliances entering into the construction of an ordinary house today with the prices you paid when building your own house or your flat building. We are learning this lesson here by degrees and sweating blood in the process....

3rd. Concerning the disproportionate cost, it is disproportionate only in comparison with make-shifts.

The plan you have is economical to a degree in arrangement it is a perfect thing of a simple kind calling for good workmanship and good material. The only sort of building a far-sighted man with means could afford to build.

It is distinguished only because it is genuinely the thing mentioned above. You are paying no premium for the "peculiarities" of an architect after you are square with his brains. This is, at the moment, a matter for your intuitive judgment to grasp rather than a matter to be mathematically demonstrated. Nevertheless it is true....

5th. I must disagree with Mrs. Martin about the veranda, waiving its advantage to the Barton house itself which is greater proportionately than any saving to be effected by cutting it off, it is essential to the balance of the whole as a finished work, that is, of the group of buildings. The Barton House itself would lose an important feature which it needs.

6th. There will be sun to shade in the Living Room windows with the porch roof where it is.

7th. The $8,000.00 house has come to take the place of the $5,000.00 of earlier days.

I think the Barton House plan will carry itself with 4/5 of the better class of modern home makers. You can afford to take your chances on the remaining 1/5. Besides there is sufficient private exit from the kitchen to the Second Story to satisfy the requirements of common decency and a servant's room if specially desired as such could be partitioned off the rear bedroom as it has been done in the Walser House.

Referring now, to your letter of the 8/25/03. We will guarantee our estimates of quantities and will forward them immediately.

Our estimate on lumber was given us by [Elmer E.] Andrews who built the Walser House and our millwork we can send you from here at the price quoted.

I am beginning to see the force of Woodruff's position at least in relation to work of an "unusual" character. If I had the necessary financial backing I should be tempted.

"There's millions in it," apparently.

I am perfectly willing to redraw the chimney and in any case to omit the Second Story fire place. I am loath to reduce the size of the chimney, however, and hope you will not make shift by shingling the roof nor deprive the Bartons of the modest luxury of their veranda by mutilating the balance of a well nigh perfect composition to save say—$350.00.

Yours sincerely,37

Although Wright's letter reveals a certain willingness to compromise on an interior feature, when it came to the overall impact of the design of the house and of the projected complex, he remained resolute and adamant. Darwin finally acquiesced early in September 1903: "Sometime ago I asked you for instructions for staking out the house. I have not rec'd them. Will you send them at once? Mr. Lang was to see me last evening, and as Mrs. Barton is partial to the veranda I told Mr. Lang that we would go ahead with the house blind and see how it came out."[38]

As construction got underway in October, the correspondence between Wright and Martin diminished again, but Wright wrote on October 27, 1903, in response to a demand made by the Building Department of the City of Buffalo, that the ten-foot, flat-arched span between the reception area of the Barton House and the unit room should be reinforced so as to safely carry a portion of the second story above it. Wright's tone is noticeably jaunty:

> My dear Mr. Martin:
> About those beams. Put them in if the department wants them with my compliments to the dept. It—the dept.—is evidently a good one.
>
> They probably thought the wall was carried across the openings solid, as a matter of fact the weight of brick to be carried is really insignificant as it is only a pressed brick veneer above the roof line, laid over the roof sheathing against the sheathed studs, and the opportunity for wooden construction, in accordance with specification, more than ample, and as safe but as expensive, too, probably as the beams. So let us have the beams.
> Yours truly,[39]

A little more than a week later, Wright wrote this somewhat lighthearted letter to Darwin:

> Dear Sir:
> All right my dear Mr. Martin. You now have the plans and specifications with details. When the building is finished I hope to be permitted to see it and in the meanwhile let us both pray.
> Yours most sincerely,[40]

| fig. 29

George and Delta
Barton House. Elevation

The Barton House was framed up by the end of January 1904; on May 27, 1904, Darwin wrote to Wright that he was anxious to see the building completed; and by August 5, 1904, the Bartons were able to move into the building | *fig. 29*. The installation of the gutters, some furnishings, the decorative light fixtures, and other details dragged on over a period of two years, however.

Every alteration that Wright made to the original Walser drawings on behalf of the Bartons had an important impact on the design of the full Martin House complex. The placement of the Barton House close to the north edge of the site left Wright the maximum amount of space with which to site the additional buildings. His insistence on adding the porch to the south side of the Barton House shifted the axis of symmetry from east-west at Walser to north-south at Barton and changed the character of the Walser model from a self-contained, symmetrical, and rather uninteresting plan to one that decisively gestured toward the (future) main Martin House. It established a Latin-cross plan that would be repeated in the main house and in the conservatory and echoed in the garage/stable. Moreover, the juxtaposition of the Barton plan with its north-south axis and the Martin House with its east-west axis suggests the rotational relationship of four versions of the "Home in a Prairie Town" depicted on a single block in the *Ladies' Home Journal* of February 1901 | *fig. 30*. The juxtaposition of the Barton porch and the Martin east porch also constituted a touching reminder of Darwin's relationship with his sister.

By using Roman brick and a brick tile roof instead of the wood frame, stucco, and wooden shingles of the Walser House, Wright established a higher level of expense for the Martin complex and an elegance that could not be matched in lesser materials. He liked to say that the Roman bricks, deeply raked on the horizontal, were as fine as "corded silk"; but because the Barton House was wood framed with a brick veneer that reached only to the sill level of the second-floor windows, the brick also enabled him to dramatize the rift between the walls and the great shelf of eaves that protected the windows.

No mention is made in the correspondence between Wright and Martin of the fact that the Barton House is larger than the Walser House by two feet. Did Wright sneak that by Martin? Was it even possible to sneak such a thing past this wily client? Probably not, but the result had an impact on the scale of the entire complex. The Barton House ultimately

| *fig. 30*
"Home in a Prairie Town," *Ladies' Home Journal*, February 1901. Rotated block plan

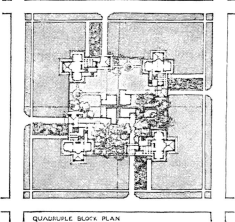

QUADRUPLE BLOCK PLAN

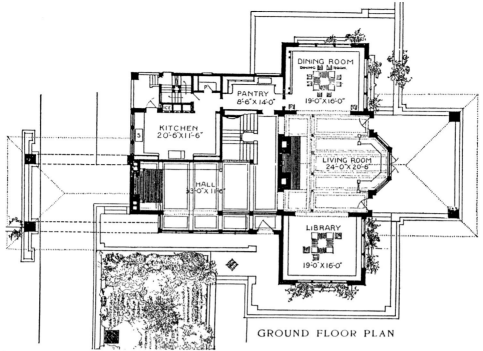

DINING ROOM
19'-0"X16'-0"

PANTRY
8'-6"X14'-0"

KITCHEN
20'-6"X11'-6"

LIVING ROOM
24'-0"X20'-6"

HALL
33'-0"X11'-6"

LIBRARY
19'-0"X16'-0"

GROUND FLOOR PLAN

| fig. 31

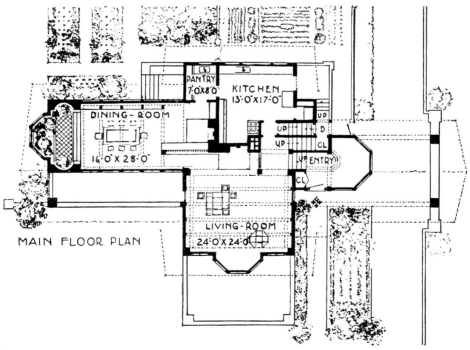

PANTRY
7'-0"X8'-0"

KITCHEN
13'-0"X17'-0"

DINING-ROOM
16'-0"X28'-0"

UP
UP
D
CL
UP ENTRY
CL

LIVING-ROOM
24'-0"X24'-0"

MAIN FLOOR PLAN

| fig. 32

| fig. 31
"Home in a Prairie
Town," *Ladies' Home
Journal*, February 1901.
Plan

| fig. 32
"A Small House with
'Lots of Room in It,'"
Ladies' Home Journal,
July 1901. Plan

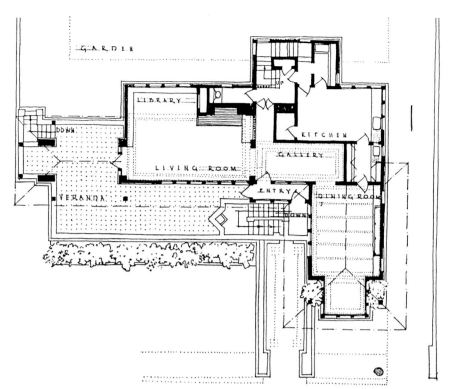

|fig. 33

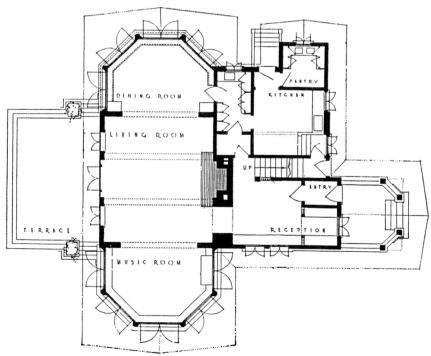

|fig. 34

cost $12,000, three times the amount Martin originally specified. Thus Darwin Martin and John Larkin found out what it was like to work with Wright: it was very expensive. They went ahead anyway.

THE RELATIONSHIP OF THE BARTON HOUSE TO THE MARTIN HOUSE COMPLEX

Wright's first prairie-house designs, the "Home in a Prairie Town," |*fig. 31*; cf. *fig. 7* and "Small House with 'Lots of Room in It,'" |*fig. 32*; cf. *fig. 8* published in the *Ladies' Home Journal* of February and July, 1901, respectively, established two plan prototypes: the first is T-shaped (or slightly cross-axial) and features the triple spatial unit (dining room, living room, library) along the shorter axis; the second is L-shaped and takes on a pinwheel character, with the dining room and living room juxtaposed at right angles to one another. Wright's Frank Thomas House of 1901 is one of the first realized versions of the L-shaped plan of the "Small House with 'Lots of Room in It'" |*fig. 33*.[41] The "Home in a Prairie Town" plan was first materialized as the Warren Hickox House, in Kankakee, Illinois |*fig. 34*; cf. *fig. 9*, and in the Henderson House, in Elmhurst, Illinois (both of 1901), but was most grandly realized as the plan of the principal Darwin D. Martin residence |see *figs. 46, 47*, as well as in the Barton plan.[42] The Barton plan is closest to the "Home in a Prairie Town" in its cross-axiality and its three-rooms-in-line sequence, though the space between the living and dining rooms is occupied by a hall, and there is no separate library.[43] At roughly 990 square feet, the main floor of the Barton House is smaller than either "A Home in a Prairie Town" (1,600 square feet) or "A Small House with 'Lots of Room in It'" (1,300 square feet); but the Latin cruciform plan made possible by the addition of the Barton south porch to the Walser plan and the triple spatial sequence within represent the principal themes that Wright would elaborate in forming the full Martin House complex, themes that would prove crucial to the special coherence that distinguishes the Martin plan from the plans of Wright's other large-scale, multiple-building domestic complexes.

Insofar as the Barton House was a test to see what Wright was like, the test worked both ways. Darwin Martin found Wright to be expensive but also persuasive, brilliantly in command of his work, and fascinating as a personality. Wright found Darwin Martin to be amicable, susceptible, and apparently somewhat in awe of Wright's talent—altogether a promising prospect.

Chapter Three

THE MARTIN HOUSE: DESIGNING A DOMESTIC SYMPHONY

IN THE CLOSING decades of the nineteenth century, domestic architecture in the United States drew inspiration from two venerable historical traditions—the classical and the picturesque. The latter—irregular, romantic, calculated to appeal to the imagination—grew out of ideas developed in English landscape design in the eighteenth century and was reinforced in the nineteenth century by Gothic revivalism and the writings of John Ruskin (1819–1900), Augustus Welby Pugin (1812–1852), A. J. Downing (1815–1852), and others. The S. Bayard Dod House in East Orange, New Jersey | see *fig.* 11, designed by Arthur B. Jennings in 1885, with its complex massing, irregular profile, rich surface detail, and aggregation of living spaces around a spacious central hall, is a conspicuous example of picturesque ideals adapted to American domestic taste in the 1880s.

Classical alternatives to the picturesque derived their inspiration from the houses of eighteenth-century colonial governors, wealthy merchants, and plantation owners and were descended from ideals developed during the Italian Renaissance transmitted to England in the seventeenth and eighteenth centuries. Inaugurated around the time of the American centennial, the colonial revival in the United States was reinforced by the classically based teachings at the École des Beaux-Arts in Paris, where many American architects were trained in the second half of the nineteenth century. Colonial revival houses such as the circa 1890 Edward Hayes House in Buffalo, New York | *fig.* 35, designed by the local firm of E. B. Green and William Wicks, employ the formal vocabulary of classicism (columns, moldings, pediments, balustrades, etc.), bilateral symmetry, and harmonic proportions. They were typically rectangular in plan with a central stair hall dividing the house, front to back, into two equal halves.

Frank Lloyd Wright explored both of these approaches briefly during his formative years. The first Hillside Home School in Spring Green, Wisconsin, designed by Wright in 1887, is a picturesque, shingle-style design; the George Blossom House, built in Chicago around 1892, is colonial revival. But Wright apparently found the colonial style too staid and constraining, the picturesque style too arbitrary, and both "sentimental."[1] He absorbed their lessons but moved swiftly beyond them in search of something less derivative of historical precedent, more modern, and more authentically American.

Wright often characterized his intentions in architecture as "breaking the box," by which he meant freeing his spaces from the confining corners of traditional architecture in

| *fig.* 35
Green and Wicks,
Edward Hayes House,
Buffalo, New York, ca.
1890

78

pursuit of a greater unity between the interior of the building and the external world of nature.² This impulse, which reflects his youthful exposure to Unitarian-Transcendentalist thought, was first manifested in the pinwheel configuration of his own house in Oak Park of 1889 | *fig. 36*. Wright's ability to pursue this ideal was curtailed, however, during his years in the office of Adler & Sullivan (1887–93), when he was obliged to shroud his after-hours commissions in a cloak of convention.

After parting ways with Adler & Sullivan, Wright abandoned compact plans based on Queen Anne and classical precedents in favor of linear plans consisting of elongated rectangles joined in various ways to octagons, as in his A. C. McAfee (1895) | *fig. 37*, Chauncey Williams (1892), George Furbeck (1899), and Joseph Husser (1899) houses. Wright's preoccupation with the octagon during the mid-1890s is consistent with a growing ambition on his part to break the box of conventional architecture; but despite the apparent spatial freedom of the octagon (each of the corners represents a 135-degree angle), octagons are hermetic and inward-turning and they resist a fluid integration with other geometric forms and with nature. The Joseph Husser House plan | *fig. 38*, the last of Wright's linear plans of the 1890s, is awkwardly conceived but rich in potential. Its incipient cross-axiality anticipates the plan of "A Home in a Prairie Town" of the following year; the double prows leading onto its east porch foreshadow the prow tucked under the great cantilever of the Robie House porch; and the radial buttresses of the breakfast room prefigure the directional piers that will eventually terminate the unit room of the Martin House.

In his "Home in a Prairie Town" of 1901 | see *fig. 31*, Wright struck upon a radical solution for integrating the space of the house with the space beyond, which took the form of a cross-axial plan with a substantial chimney and fireplace at the intersection of the axes. By locating the hearth at the crossing of axes that lead outward in the four cardinal directions, Wright achieved a powerfully symbolic plan grounded in the experience of the American landscape and an organic scheme in which the chimney mass stands as the nexus of a structural-spatial system opening progressively outward along the axes. Wright's desire to "break the box" and transcend the conventional distinctions between indoors and outdoors was accomplished by the extension of the axes and the use of terminals that provided a more fluid transition into nature than a simple window wall could ever achieve. In the fifteen-odd prairie houses

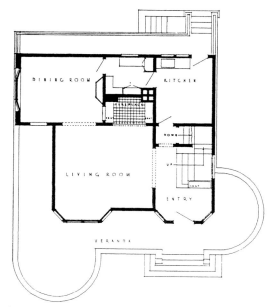

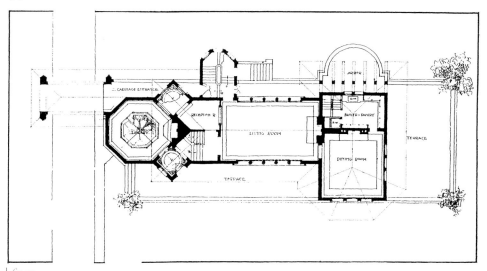

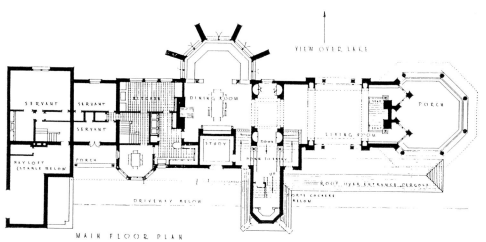

|fig. 36

|fig. 37

|fig. 38
Frank Lloyd Wright
Home, Oak Park, Illinois,
1889. First floor plan

|fig. 37
Frank Lloyd Wright,
A. C. McAfee House,
1895 (project). First
floor plan

|fig. 38
Frank Lloyd Wright,
Joseph Husser House,
Chicago, 1899. First
floor plan

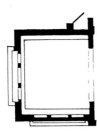

"A Home in a Prairie Town," 1901

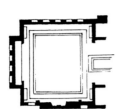

Isidore Heller House, 1897

F. B. Henderson House, 1901

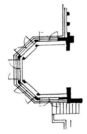

"A Small House with 'Lots of Room in It,'" 1901

| fig. 39
Room terminals in various
Wright homes

Ward Willits House, 1901

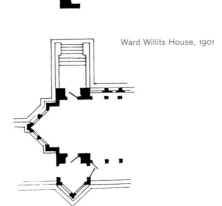

designed in 1901 and 1902, Wright employed cruciform, L-shaped, T-shaped, and in-line plans with five types of terminals: the simple squared end; the extruded square bay; the extruded half octagon; the half octagon; and the prow | *fig. 39*. Among these, the squared end was the least dynamic.3 The others, which created pockets of space that were variously cupped onto the buildings, hardly represent integral solutions. Wright achieved the most effective synthesis of structure and space in the Darwin D. Martin House, but the solution required nearly fifteen months of work on his part.

As crude as Wright's May 1903 sketch of the Martin complex is | see *fig. 28*, it represents the formation of an idea in the mind of the architect. The drawings and letters pertaining to the building of the Martin complex indicate that the programme that materialized between May 1903 and the summer of 1904 included a house for Darwin and Isabelle Martin, their two children, and several live-in servants; a house for the Bartons; a greenhouse; a pergola connecting the Martin House to the greenhouse; and a garage with a chauffeur's apartment above and a stable to the rear. Plans for a gardener's cottage were first discussed in 1905, but the building was not constructed until 1908.4 As the greenhouse took shape, Darwin complained to Wright that it was more a conservatory than a "growing house," so he purchased a 60-foot-long, commercially designed greenhouse and had it installed west of the garage/stable structure.5 Wary of the intrusion, Wright offered to "put a little architecture on it."6

Wright's May 1903 sketch contains only the Martin and Barton houses, the garage/stable, and a pergola that leads northward from the main house to no specific structure. An additional appendage to the main house, the only structure drawn without cross-hatching, may represent a greenhouse. The cross-axial plan of the Martin House is recognizable in this sketch, but the house is rotated 90 degrees from its eventual alignment with Jewett Parkway, and the entire building complex is rotated 90 degrees to align the principal facade of the main house with the driveway Wright used to delineate the west boundary of the site. Darwin was quick to correct Wright's misunderstanding of the relationship of the houses on Jewett Parkway to the street but otherwise gave short shrift to Wright's sketch, owing to his preoccupation with progress on the Barton House and the Larkin Building.7

Wright completed a more fully developed preliminary plan of the Martin complex some-time late in the fall of 1903, when the Barton House construction was well in hand | *fig.* 40. On December 26, 1903, Darwin wrote to Wright, "Mrs. Martin says if we are to build we may as well have done with it. It don't seem as though our little house will hold us come another Christmas."[8]

In the preliminary plan, the main house is repositioned as it would eventually be built, with its long, east-west axis parallel to Jewett Parkway and its cruciform plan, interior spaces, porch, porte cochere, and pergola all in place. However, the pergola in the plan has twenty bays rather than the eleven that were finally constructed, and it leads to a small, shedlike appendage on the east side of the garage. The garage is nearly square and the stable is drawn as an exedra-like addition to its north elevation. The garden west of the pergola is treated with a classical formality that is noticeably at odds with the freer rendering of landscape features on the pergola's opposite (east) side.[9] It too has a small, exedra-shaped bay in the wall at its northern terminus, screening the entrance to the garage.

The first-floor plan of the main house in this drawing follows the general spatial organization of Wright's "Home in a Prairie Town" of 1901 | see *fig.* 31, but the spaces here are tightly compartmentalized. The exterior walls of the library and dining room meet at reentrant corners; clusters of four piers forming 7-foot squares appear rudimentarily in the living room, but in this drawing they have not yet been developed as the principal structural motif and organizing feature of the entire house. (They do not appear in the kitchen, for example.) The axis running northward through the entrance hall and pergola cleaves the house into two distinct halves. The west walls of the library and dining room emphatically close those spaces off from the entrance hall; the staircase is compacted into a tight square space on the west side of that hall, and the dining room–living room–library spatial sequence (or "unit room") features the living room as a large, slightly rectangular space oriented east-west, flanked by matching rooms with Greek-cross plans that are oriented north-south. On the whole, the main house in this version has narrow, attenuated spaces that appear to have been conceived separately.

Darwin Martin, whose principal concern was the size, and hence the cost, of the house, sent this response to Wright's preliminary plan on December 29, 1903:

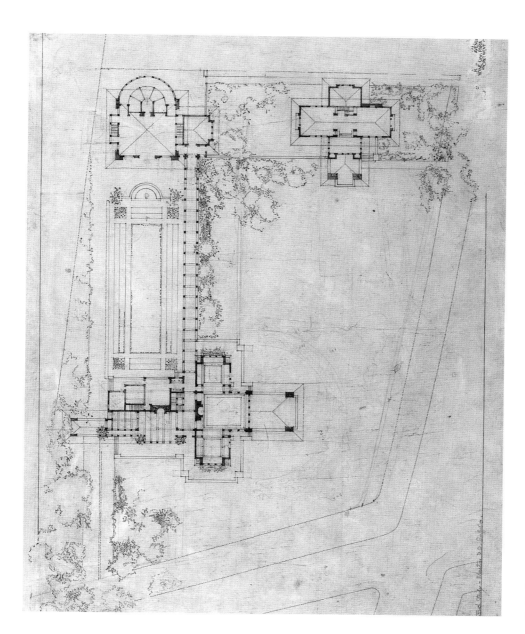

|fig. 40
Darwin D. Martin
Complex, late fall 1903.
Preliminary first floor
plan

The sketch made by you, exclusive of the porte cochere & veranda, covers 5400 sq. ft. The house we live in covers 1100 sq. ft. You remember the Swede who missed the ferry boat by 20 ft. He said he could have made it in "two yumps." From 1100 to 5400 ft. is too much for one yump. You will have to build us an intermediate house of say 3000 sq. ft....I have bet an apple with Mr. Heath that I will get a reply to this letter. He bets I won't because he has written 3 without an answer.

Wright's response began in a similarly jovial tone. Regarding the Barton House, he wrote: "The raked joint with the Roman brick should be very fine and dandy,—as close in grain as a corded silk—what's the matter? 'You might as well kill a fellow as scare him to death.'" But it turned persuasive with regard to the Martin House:

You lose the apple!

I wish I could get together with you and your good wife for a few minutes so that we might have a heart to heart talk about the present plan. We will try to carry out all the requirements you mention, somehow, but if we are going to realize the home you are entitled to and ought to have you will have to "ring off" on the square foot business and comparisons with anything in previous existence. You could put the whole first floor of your present home in W[illiam] E. M[artin]'s living room and his room is small compared with every other in a dozen houses we have planned this year. You will say when you see it that it is not a large room. In fact it is not large enough.

I sympathize with your desire for a larger garden,—we will get it, together with all of Mrs. Martin's practical requirements, but don't freeze your architect down to certain areas for various parts of the plan, "proportion" must determine these things within reasonable limits, and give him a free hand within that limit; stretch the limit until your discretion deflects to the breaking point, let her break, even, for once and you will be pleasantly shocked by the result.

We will make another sketch for you, embodying your suggestions in some way to preserve the harmony and proportion of a consistent arrangement and will bring it down with me, for I expect to see you soon.[10]

Martin and Wright exchanged additional letters regarding the size of the Martin living room during January 1904, but from the end of January until May, a four-month period during which Wright twice visited Buffalo, no correspondence exists. Wright had other important projects, including the Larkin Building, on the drafting boards and may have set aside the Martin House for a time.

A revised first-floor plan of the main Martin House | *fig. 41*, drawn sometime in the late winter of 1904, contains important improvements to the preliminary plan. Most notably, the new plan is more compact and the individual spaces, less attenuated; the pier clusters have emerged fully as the internal structural system of the house; and the principal stairway has been reconfigured from its position to the west of the entrance hallway so as to wrap around a vertical shaft of space within the hallway, thereby bridging the east and west sides of the plan. This vertical space, an important counterpoint to the horizontal expansiveness of the house, was to culminate with a skylight, which was never realized.[11] The exterior corners of the library and the dining room are now detached from walls and consist of two large piers juxtaposed at right angles with an extruded block at their conjunction and a reentrant angle on their interior side, forming an M-shape in plan. These heavy corners are not consistent with the looser, freer character of the rest of the building's pier-based structure, but they mark an important step in the direction of the final resolution of the corner condition.

Wright's office completed construction drawings of the plans for the garage/stable and conservatory | *fig. 42*, the next buildings to be constructed on the site after the Barton House, on May 7, 1904. Shortly thereafter Darwin made a note that read, "Visit from Mr. Wright. Plan of our new house practically settled."[12] On May 16, ground was broken for the garage/stable.[13] Nevertheless, Darwin was troubled by Wright's lack of communication and

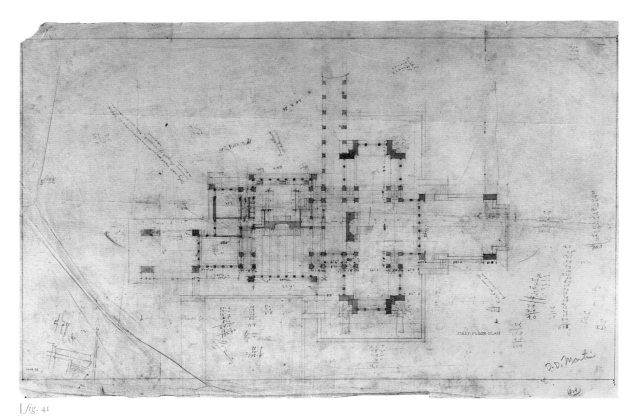

| *fig.* 41

Darwin D. Martin
House, late winter 1904.
Revised first floor plan,

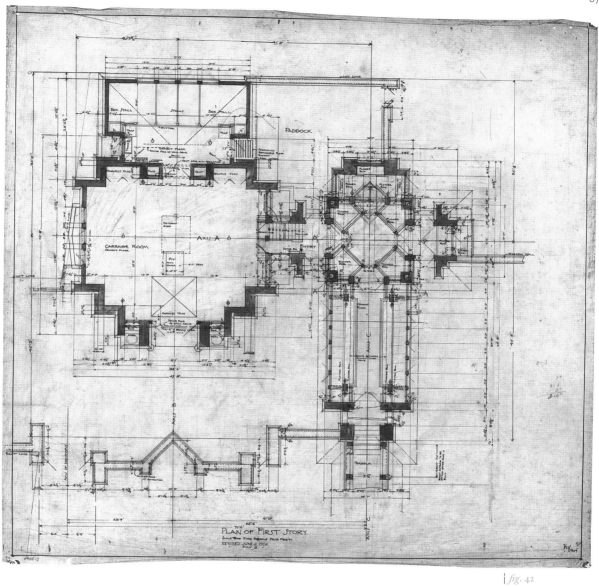

i *fig.* 42

Darwin D. Martin
Complex, garage/stable
and conservatory. July
27, 1904. Revised first
floor plan

turned to his brother William to find out what was going on in Wright's Oak Park studio. William wrote:

Dear Brother:

Your telegram requesting [garage/stable] plans was received, and I called up Wright that evening, when I found that he had gone to Hillside for three or four days; this, notwithstanding that he came in town [Chicago] with me that morning and did not say that he was going out of town, but led me to think that he would give some of my matters his attention that day and inform me of proceedings,—so I was much surprised to find that he had gone away that evening.

If you discover any way in your dealings with him, whereby you are able to keep tab on him, I would like to know how you do it.

I called at his office yesterday morning, and one of the *draftsmen* said that he had been working on the plans, and mailed them to you Thursday, but knew nothing regarding the brick. He said that when Mr. Wright returned from Buffalo, he threw the plans into one corner of the office,—which, by the way, has been torn up from stem to stern for the last two weeks,—and said nothing about any alterations until Wednesday or Thursday morning when he inquired if the plans had been altered, and, much to his surprise, he was told that nothing had been done, as nothing had been said about it, by him. They then got busy, and by working all day and part of the night were able to return the plans, as stated.

Certainly if Wright's *plans* appear to be "queer," his business methods are more so. Probably his loose methods are a mere indication of his great genius,—because if a man is a genius, he must be a little off in other respects (?) I have fully concluded that while I thoroughly appreciate his plans and ideas, I would not give two

cents for his superintendence of a job. As a matter of fact, the superintendence ought to be on *his* part of the work,—to get him to do
the right thing at the right time,—and when I take him to task
about his dilatory practices, he lays it all on the "boys" and says they
are to blame for the whole "show."[14]

Darwin also wrote to Wright asking for the garage/stable blueprints,[15] to which Wright
replied, "Please don't push—just shove gently: 'Don't shoot the performer, he's doing his
best.' P.S. This operation at least has a robust 'physique.' I wish you would quit Larkin and
come and manage for me.'"[16]

Darwin continued to hound Wright with regard to information about the garage/stable:

Am anxious to see the specifications, if only in the rough, that I
may have an inclination of what I am getting into. I have not yet had
a chance to study the plans.—Have been out of town, but will tonight.
Lang says they are full of angles and that the cost of the building will
be surprising, away beyond Mr. Wright's est.[imate] of course.[17]

On May 25, 1904, Darwin issued Wright an ultimatum regarding the completion of the
entire complex. "By-the-way, the whole plan has got to be fixed P. D. Q. because the house
absolutely must be all finished March 1/05 so it will be ready for the June 26th blow out.
Heath says we had better plan to finish by Christmas."[18]

Two days later Darwin wrote to remind Wright that the cost of the Barton House had
risen to $10,500. "We [Darwin and Oscar Lang, the contractor] figured that if we have
stamina enough to make the changes in the stable and greenhouse plan in accordance with
my letters to you of this week, that we may be able to put up the buildings for $14,000, but I
do not know how to get out of it now."[19] The conservatory and garage/stable have undergone
an extraordinary transformation in the construction drawings of May 7, 1904. The conservatory, which had begun as an insignificant appendage to the garage, emerges as the cynosure
of the entire Martin complex. Within this cruciform crystalline structure, a full-scale replica

of the Nike of Samothrace, elevated on a square plinth, commands the site. The facade of the adjacent garage, initially little more than a box, now advances in three diminishing planes framed by a stepped succession of brick corners and piers, the whole subsumed under a roof of elegant simplicity. The stable is suppressed to the rear. In developing these two structures, Wright, who always regarded his designs as part of something greater than the functions they served, appears to be playing the garage—the massive, masculine container of the machine—against the lighter, more feminine conservatory, bearer of Nike in her bower of flowers.

Another hiatus in correspondence began on May 27 and lasted until July 12, 1904, evidently indicating a period of intense work in the Wright studio. The plans of the garage/stable and conservatory were revised on June 1, and foundations were begun on June 13. A week later ground was broken for the main house.[20] Darwin continued to agitate for faster results, causing Wright to write on July 14 (having just visited Buffalo) to explain the nature of the work in his Oak Park studio:

> My dear Mr. Martin:
>
> Your [garage/stable] plans you have by this time, no doubt. I think you understand me to say that the plans had to be figured before they could be printed and that it would be done right away, as soon as I got home. As but one man could work on each plan at a time and as they have been working so continuously since the plans returned, from 8 in the morning until 7 at night, and then a special messenger took them in to the blue printer's and waited for them to send them to you with the least possible delay, I have that modest assurance of conscious worth that makes W.E.M.'s onslaughts and your own harmless.
>
> If the making of plans were as simple and as quickly to be performed as you think I for one should be glad.
>
> The steel schedule the boys are now working at, and they will stick at it until done.

We hope to have it off today,—but don't declare a broken promise if you don't get it tomorrow. Do try and have faith that we will serve you as best we can, for we will so serve you, but drawings are not going to leave this office for your buildings until they are right and fit to use as nearly so as we can make them at least, even if you wander homeless for the rest of your mortal days. Write us your needs and rest assured that we will hasten to give you whatever you require but if you don't receive it next day don't assume neglect, default or unnecessary delay. It takes some time to arrive at correct information.

You fellows down there put a Chicagoan to shame in your get-there-gait, but be persuaded that the best results in buildings don't come with that gait.[21]

The tardiness of Wright's production on Darwin's behalf continued to trouble the client. In a letter to William on August 1, Darwin wrote:

Half the specifications and details are also lacking for stable and green-house, tho' they are half built. Certainly with the start of a month—after every point was settled—the intellectual dep't ought to keep pace with the physical dep't, especially when the latter isn't—can't be—vigorously pursued. Wright is a fine fellow and a genius as an architect, but how can I recommend him to anybody.[22]

Darwin's letter moved William to defend Wright. In so doing William provides additional insight into the workings of Wright's studio:

Dear Brother:
I found the trestle boards in the drafting room covered with drawings and sketches for [the Larkin Administration Building]. Whether

this had been specially arranged for my benefit or not I am unable to say, as I telephoned Mr. Wright on my return home last eve that I would be down after dinner. However, the lay-out did not look as though it had been specially arranged, but did have the ear marks of having been earnestly worked upon.

It is my conviction from the nature of your complaint, that you do not fully comprehend the scheme in all its details. I coaxed Mr. Wright to let me have a pencil sketch that I am sending you under separate cover | *fig.* 43. He has been using it to enable him to fully comprehend the scheme and to enable the draughtsmen to know what the blue prints were to fit. He did not want this sketch to go out of the office as they need it to refer to constantly, and you will therefore return it as quickly as possible.

The little sketch that he showed you in the first place does not convey as good an idea as you will have after viewing this one; and as blue prints are very uninteresting to laymen, and in fact convey little or no meaning to half the mechanics who use them, I think you will get considerable satisfaction from this sketch.

It is my opinion—and you will realize it later on—that you are trying to rush this job too fast. What your object is in doing so, I do not know. But if I were building a house of this character, especially of brick, I would not attempt to complete it within two years. If it were my house, I would not try to do more this year than to enclose it and possibly give it one coat of plaster, and then the house would stand until spring. If you continue to push and crowd Mr. Wright, not only will it cost you more, but you will prevent him from giving you his best, which he has been honestly endeavoring to do.

It will, however, be harder work for you to spoil this job with Mr. Wright at the helm than it would if you were dealing with ordinary men. Most architects get tired of being urged to give something

| *fig.* 43
Darwin D. Martin
House. Perspective
sketch

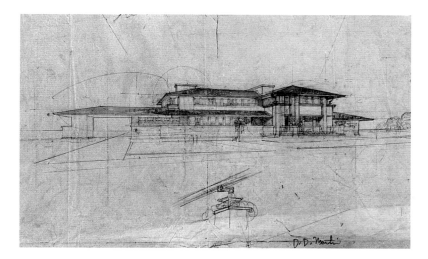

that they had not yet produced themselves and would give you any old thing to pacify you. However, Mr. Wright thinks too much of his work to allow you to excite him, although you have galled him under the collar many times.

You have been so accustomed to seeing your plain, massive factory buildings erected in a jiffy that you think your house ought to move along with the same sort of speed,—and this is where you are making a great mistake. The plans for your house are not made and sold by the yard, and the only wonder is, that Mr. Wright is able to perform his part of the labor as rapidly as he does. Some day, when the house is completed and you have forgotten your troubles, you will reflect how you pushed the work and you will wonder how you escaped having it spoiled.

The labor required from Mr. Wright is simply immense. You ought to come to Chicago and spend two or three days in his office and you would then better understand how they are better able to arrive at, and create such homes. Mr. Wright showed me several sheets of paper on which he had been drawing designs for the [art] glass for your barn, and had only just arrived at what he wanted. Any one of the designs that he had discarded would have satisfied an ordinary man, and only he knows when the thing is right or wrong, and unless he gets it right he keeps on trying.

It is the same throughout the house. His tracing cloth shows the results of his labors, as it is ragged in many places where changes have been made repeatedly.

I am really surprised that you are so ungenerous and unsympathetic with Mr. Wright, and you are doing him and yourself a great injustice by your present methods....

One would think to read your letters that all Mr. Wright has to do is to turn the crank and plans are produced. There is not the slightest detail in connection with your plans that Mr. Wright has not given his personal attention and authority, and so far as I know, he has never allowed any makeshift or "that's good enough" to stand in his way of making it a perfect job. He can only move so fast. If you must move faster, my advice to you would be to find some other architect.[23]

William's letter indicates that Wright showed Darwin Martin a small, apparently rough elevation sketch of the Martin House sometime early in the development of the full plan, but that otherwise discussions between architect and client had been confined to the plans of the complex until William borrowed the perspective sketch cited above.[24] The sketch is held in the Archives of the Frank Lloyd Wright Foundation. A comparison of this sketch with Clarence Fuermann's photograph from a similar point of view indicates that certain details, such as the large pier at the west end of the second floor, the placement of the secondary chimney, and the inclusion of additional urns at the west end of the facade, had not yet been resolved; but this drawing—which attenuates and dramatizes the elevation somewhat—probably represents Darwin Martin's first opportunity to share Wright's vision of the house that he was building.

Early in August 1904, Wright completed a revised preliminary plan of the full Martin complex | *fig. 44* that closely resembles the house as it was built. [25] There is not much concern with landscape in this drawing, but the 100-degree angle formed by the conjunction of Jewett Parkway and Summit Avenue is accurately depicted, the formal garden to the west of the pergola is slightly revised, and there is a faint trace of the "floricycle"—the semicircular garden that would eventually surround the east porch. The most important changes represented in this plan are the opening of the corners of the main house by the juxtaposition of two large piers at right angles and the introduction of the two-sided living room fireplace. The pergola has fourteen bays here, as opposed to the eleven that were ultimately built, and Wright retained this fourteen-bay configuration in the plan of the Martin House as he redrew it for the *Architectural Record* of March 1908 | *fig. 45* and for the Wasmuth portfolio of 1910 | *fig. 46*. The bursar's office at the west end of the main floor of the Martin House is depicted as fully glazed on its south and west elevations.

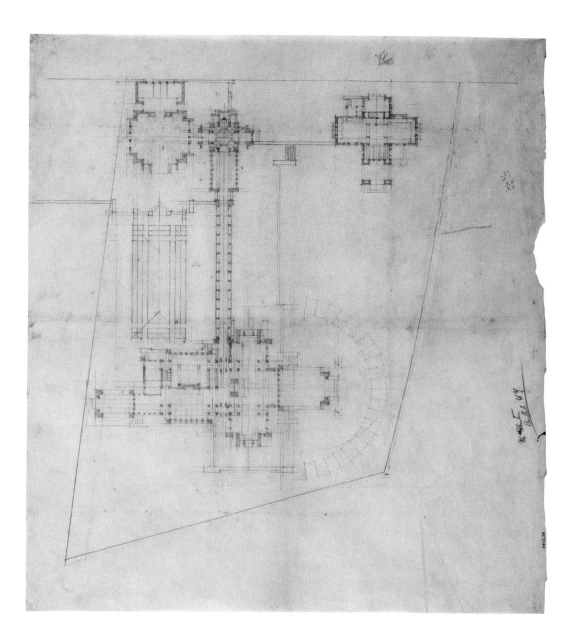

| fig. 44
Darwin D. Martin
Complex, circa August
1904. Second revised
preliminary first floor plan

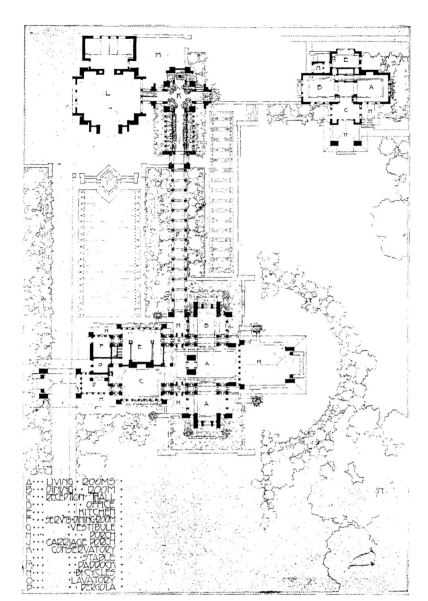

| fig. 45

| fig. 45
Darwin D. Martin
Complex, as published
in Frank Lloyd Wright,
"In the Cause of
Architecture,"
Architectural Record,
March 1908. First floor
plan

| fig. 46
Darwin D. Martin
House. First floor plan

A · · · LIVING · ROOMS ·
B · · · DINING · ROOM ·
C · · · RECEPTION · HALL ·
D · · · · · OFFICE ·
E · · · · KITCHEN ·
F · · · SERVTS · DINING·ROOM ·
G · · · · VESTIBULE ·
H · · · · · PORCH ·
J · · · CARRIAGE PORCH ·
K · · · CONSERVATORY ·
L · · · · · · STABLE ·
M · · · · PADDOCK ·
N · · · · BICYCLES ·
O · · · · LAVATORY ·
P · · · · PERGOLA ·

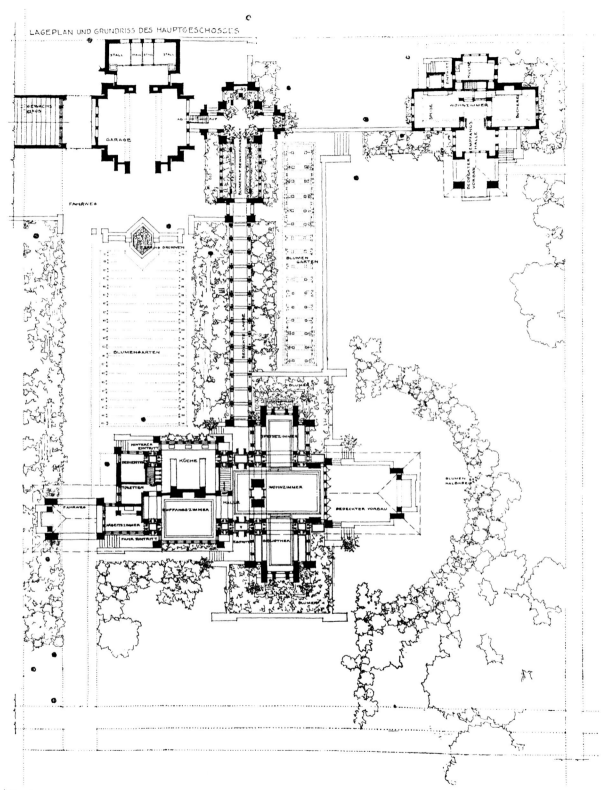

LAGEPLAN UND GRUNDRISS DES HAUPTGESCHOSSES

fig. 46

As soon as Darwin had a chance to examine the new plan he wrote to Wright, "No back in Living Room fireplace. Mr. Lang thinks this intended, but I cannot believe it. Please send us a correction."[26] Wright responded, "The Living Room fireplace has no back,—it is the latest in fireplaces. Will send you the full development of the idea later on."[27] Darwin shot back a reply two days later:

> The Wig Wam style of fire-place may be, as you say, the latest in fire-places. It won't, however, be the last, for every time my boy sees this smoky arch, *he* will be the latest thing in fire-places. He won't be a healthy boy if he uses the door when he can just as well use the fire-place. Visitors finding two fire-places in the reception hall cannot complain of the coldness of their reception.[28]

Wright responded, firmly, "Wig Wam fireplace stands pat."[29]

This site plan of early August may well be Wright's final rendition of the entire Martin complex prior to construction. It is highly unlikely that Wright would have had any reason to produce a construction drawing of the full complex, as the scale of the individual buildings would have been too small for a contractor to read; or, conversely, at a readable scale the drawing would have been too large and unwieldy. He had already produced a construction drawing of the conservatory and garage/stable, and another for the main house would soon follow. No such drawing exists for the pergola, though three pergola bays appear on the construction drawing for the main house.

Close in time to this second preliminary plan, Wright produced a landscape scheme for the entire site | *fig. 47* that contains the footprint of each building, a few key exterior piers and walls, and most of the plantings positioned as they would appear in the plan as it was redrawn for the 1908 *Architectural Record*.[30] The formal west garden is softened in this drawing, and pencil overdrawing indicates the first iteration of the prow-shaped end wall that would screen the garage from the garden in the final plan. Moreover, a newly conceived formal garden of longer, narrower dimensions has been added to "bank" the east side of the pergola, to balance the composition, and to intensify the connection between the main house and

| *fig. 47*
Darwin D. Martin
Complex, summer 1904.
Site plan with axes

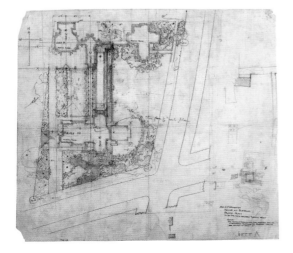

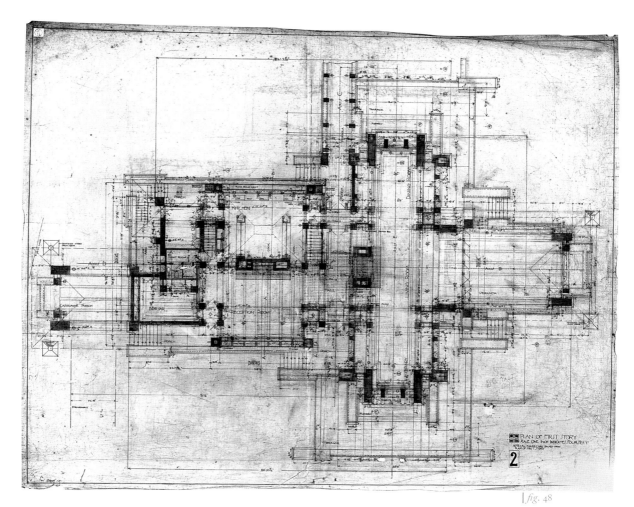

fig. 48

Darwin D. Martin House,
August 1904.
Construction drawing of
first floor plan

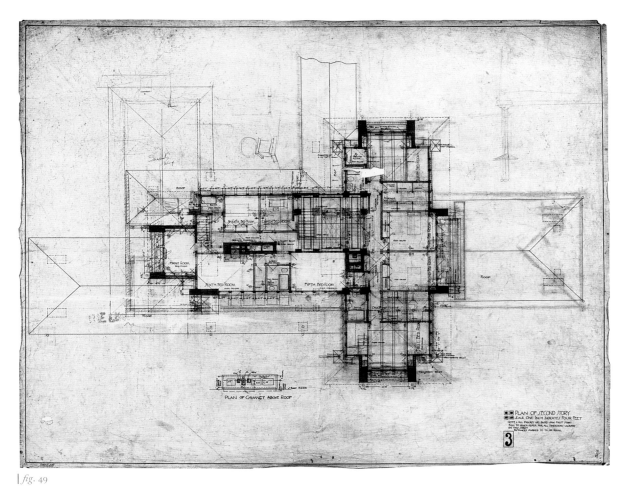

| fig. 49

Darwin D. Martin House.
Second floor plan

the conservatory. This drawing is accurate as to the number of bays in the pergola (eleven) and the nonrectilinear siting of the complex vis-à-vis Jewett Parkway and Summit Avenues. The ends of the library and dining room are, however, delineated with paired deep piers but without the lesser flanking piers that would eventually comprise the corner treatment, which would so effectively "break the box" of the final building.

Wright's office produced fully detailed construction drawings of the first and second floors of the Martin House sometime around June 20, 1904, when ground was broken for the house [*figs. 48, 49*]. The first floor plan matches the revised preliminary plan very closely, except that the walls of the bursar's office now appear as solid masonry. The windows that appeared in the earlier drawing have been elevated above the level at which the plan was cut, so that Darwin would not be distracted by the view of the exterior while working in his home office. A comparison between this plan and the preliminary plan from the fall of 1903 [*fig. 48*; cf. *fig. 28*] reveals that, generally speaking, walls have disappeared and spaces have coalesced toward the ideal that Wright expressed when he told Darwin Martin, "Whole first floor is living room with subdivisions."[31]

TOWARD A GREATER UNITY

During the fifteen months that Wright refined the preliminary design of the Martin House, none of the eight rooms on the first floor changed location or function, and yet the plan underwent a complete transformation. In his quest to achieve the maximum possible continuity between the interior and the exterior of the building, Wright created a unique structural system comprised of four pairs of internal pier clusters, complemented by additional groups of piers at the four extremities of the building. The internal pier clusters [*fig. 50*] are primarily structural in nature, but unlike traditional load-bearing walls they work together with the terminal piers to carry the second floor and thus allow for a perimeter glass membrane—much of it art glass—around the entire building. The internal pier clusters also contain radiators; carry book shelves, sconces, and internal lay lights (a form of art-glass skylight that employs an incandescent bulb); serve as the springing points for the system of detached oak beams that define individual rooms within the larger unit space [*fig. 51*]; establish the A–B–A rhythms of the building's tartan grid; and, by their presence inside the perimeter of the building, help to define the larger spaces without fully enclosing them. Where necessary—

at the entrance to the bursar's office through a pier cluster, for example—the pier-cluster function is altered. All of the piers, whether internal or on perimeter walls, are constructed of a core of common red brick faced with Roman brick, hence there is no significant change in the fabric of the building from exterior to interior.

While the internal pier clusters have stability by virtue of their square plans, the piers at the extremities are strongly orthogonal and are positioned so as to enhance the sense of outward movement. This is especially evident on the east porch | *fig. 52*, where the structural system is free of windows. The hipped roof of the east porch is carried on two large piers, which are positioned at the point where the width of the porch suddenly narrows, as though to accommodate them, and then extends beyond them in the form of an extruded bay | *fig. 53*. Whereas Wright consistently relies on principles of compression followed by expansion in his interior spaces, at the perimeter of the building the order is reversed: spaces are suddenly narrowed and, propelled by the energy of their axes, they jet outward much as a river accelerates as it enters a narrow canyon.[32]

The north (dining room) and south (library) ends of the Martin House unit space are nearly identical and each terminates with three pairs of piers of differing dimensions that are separated from one another by glazing | *fig. 55*.[33] The largest piers are two stories tall and 9 feet by 2 feet in plan and carry the upper roof. A second set of piers, similarly colossal in scale and measuring 5 feet by 3 feet in plan, is juxtaposed at right angles to the principal piers. These lesser piers do not reach the roof but are cut off at the sill level of the second story, carry part of the load of the second floor, and double as drains for the roof run-off. A third set of smaller piers stands between the principal piers as if to help to carry the second floor or possibly the spandrel between the first and second floors. In the resulting arrangement | *fig. 54*, the A-B-A rhythm of the Chicago window, which Wright had simply cut into the solid walls of the Barton House, has been made an integral expression of the building's structure.

This elaborate arrangement of major and minor piers and windows at either end of the unit space effectively dissolves any sense of traditional corners in the library or the dining room in favor of piers leading out of the house in the cardinal directions. The largest piers are aligned north-south, begin 5 feet within the building, pass through the glass membrane, and extend 4 feet into the surrounding landscape, their deeply raked horizontal joints forming

| *fig.* 50

| *fig.* 50
Darwin D. Martin
House, living room. Pier
cluster

| *fig.* 51
Darwin D. Martin
House, living room. Pier
cluster with beams

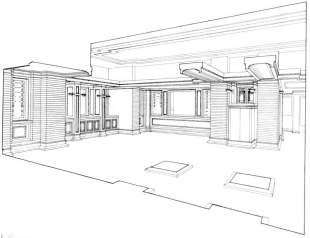

| *fig.* 51

| *fig.* 52

Darwin D. Martin
House, east porch

| *fig.* 53
Darwin D. Martin
House, east porch.
Plan detail

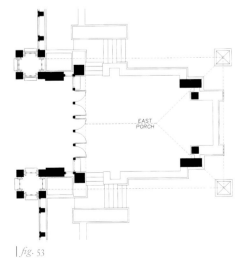

EAST
PORCH

| *fig.* 53

scores of orthogonals that accelerate the outward thrust of the space and thus the continuity between the interior and the exterior of the house.

The opening of the back side of the living room fireplace into the entrance hall, which Darwin initially found so troubling, is particularly important to the interpenetration of space and mass, and space and space, within the Martin House. By giving the fireplace two sides, Wright made it more effectively the centerpiece of the house, brought together the east and west halves of the house, and injected new authority to the east-west axis. This axis passed through the open center as a counterforce to the powerful parallel north-south axes that passed through the entrance hall and pergola and through the unit room.

Wright worked for fifteen months to achieve the unique synthesis of structure and space that characterizes the Darwin D. Martin House, and yet, even though he continued to use piers, cantilevers, art glass, central chimneys, Roman brick, articulative wooden moldings, and cross-axial plans in most of his subsequent prairie houses, he did not repeat this system again. In fact, he returned to less dynamic room terminals—especially the square bay—in the majority of his prairie houses. Why would he do this? The answer lies in Wright's determination to idealize his client in the building. The genesis of the design of the Martin House lay in the personality of Darwin Martin.

| fig. 54

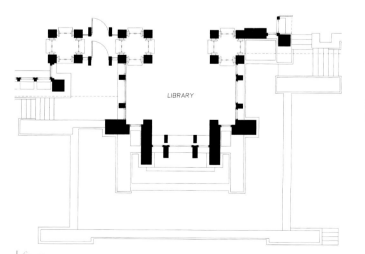

LIBRARY

| fig. 55

| fig. 54
Darwin D. Martin House.
Elevation from Jewett
Parkway

| fig. 55
Darwin D. Martin House,
library. Plan detail

Chapter Four
CONSTRUCTING THE MARTIN HOUSE

THE PROCESS OF constructing the Darwin D. Martin House differed from the design phase in that—at least hypothetically—this phase was more a matter between Wright and Oscar S. Lang, the contractor, than between Wright and his client. Darwin Martin continued his vigilance, however, because change orders and errors would cost him dearly, because he had an imagined (if unrealistic) deadline for completion, and because it was in his nature to do so. He recorded the progress of construction in a series of seventy-nine photographs taken between July 23, 1904, when the foundations of the garage/stable and conservatory were laid | *fig. 56*, and May 9, 1905, when the Martin complex was almost completed.[1] Photographs taken on the site illustrate the buildings' progress from July to the end of November 1904 | *figs. 57–60*. The roofs were completed and interior plastering began in mid-December 1904, just into the winter season. A reporter for the *Illustrated Buffalo Express* visited the Martin site and published an article entitled "A House of Many Oddities" on October 9, 1904, about halfway into the construction phase. The article benefited from the author's firsthand experience of the house and included interviews with some of the personnel on the site.[2] The writer highlighted the more sensational aspects of the design and the technological innovations associated with them:

> Jules Verne might well be the designer of a house that is being built at the northwestern corner of Jewett and Summit avenues in this city. It may be destined to be termed the freak house of Buffalo when it is finished. But it will be a very convenient house for its occupants. Moreover, it will be a very attractive dwelling, with its great simplicity of architecture and its beautiful setting of flower-covered terraces and shrub-dotted lawn.
>
> The freak feature of the house is that it will be built entirely of angles. Except for two arched fireplaces, there will not be a curve anywhere, from the walls that form the shell of the house to the spindles that help form the banisters of the stairways. Even the rungs in the chairs in the house will have four sides. The brass bedsteads will be made of square posts and square rods. Curved or round objects

| *fig. 56*
Darwin D. Martin
Complex, garage/stable
foundation, July 23, 1904

will be almost as rare as ice on Lake Erie in August. Bowling and croquet balls and eggs will be about the only exceptions.

But in this house of successively multiplying series of sharp angles will be about as comfortable as a home can be made on earth. It will be lighted by its own electric plant. It will be heated by its own hot water plant. All the water supply will be filtered. The hot water supply will always run hot immediately because it will be "on circulation." The house will be supplied with flowers from its own conservatory, a passage 100 feet long underneath a pergola will connect the house with the stable. The passage will also be utilized as a bowling alley.[3] The flowers in sixteen huge vases on piers outside the house will be watered simultaneously by the turning of a single faucet inside the house.

It may prove to be a house of puzzles to the undiscerning visitor. No steps will be seen by the coming guest although there will be two sets in the front portion of the house, to say nothing of two more sets leading to a broad veranda. And when the guest gets inside the house, he'll have a hard time finding a way to the second story. There will be one stairway for the family and its guests. But it will start unobtrusively from a spot that has 33 reproductions.[4] So there will be only one chance in 34 of finding the stairway. As the architect expresses it "we mortify our staircases"—they are a means to an end and never a feature. The owner of the house is Darwin D. Martin. The architect is Frank Lloyd Wright of Chicago whose specialty is building beautiful homes without curves. He is trying to found a simple style of American architecture. Two finished houses show his work in Buffalo. O. S. Lang of the Parkside district built Mr. Wright's first two productions in this city [the Heath and Barton houses] and he is now engaged in putting up the Martin. The peculiar construction of the building demands his constant

| *fig.* 57
Darwin D. Martin House, foundations of main house, August 26, 1904

| *fig.* 58
Darwin D. Martin House garage/stable and conservatory under construction, November 6, 1904

| *fig.* 57

| *fig.* 58

attendance on the scene. Every few minutes a puzzled workman comes up to him with some problem arising out of the departure from beaten paths of architecture. It is an expensive house to build, not only on account of the cost of the high quality of material being put into it, but because the most intelligent skilled mechanics in their respective classes have to be employed, who must proceed slowly and carefully.

The house is being built on a lot having 200 feet on Jewett avenue and 300 feet on Summit avenue. It faces on Jewett. The stone foundation walls are up, the concrete base is finished and the walls of the superstructure are now three feet high. The house will be 155 feet wide, while its deepest dimension will be 88 feet. It will be only 33 feet high. It will have a deep basement and two stories. Above the base of white concrete the walls are of brick faced with slender Roman vitreous brick running in this from tan to orange. The face brick is laid with half-inch sunken joints, thus serving to bring the beauty of the coloring into greater relief "like corded silk." These walls will run up to a low hover hip roof of red tile with cornices 5 1/2 feet beyond the face of the building. The outline of the building will be broken up by many angles always perfectly balanced by angles on the other side. Every point in the building will be balanced by some other point. Errors in construction can not be tolerated, to correct one the work must be undone and a new start made. Fractions of inches are being dealt in abundantly by the builder. A broad veranda on the east side of the house is balanced by a large porte-cochere on the west side. The projection from the front wall of the building made by the extension of the library is balanced by a similar projection of the dining-room from the rear wall.

A pergola 80 feet long and ten feet wide will connect the house with a conservatory in the rear lot. The walls of the conservatory are

fig. 59
Darwin D. Martin House, walls up to second-story windowsills, November 6, 1904

fig. 60
Darwin D. Martin House, with I beams in position, November 27, 1904

fig. 59

fig. 60

already in position. The building is eighteen feet wide by 60 feet long and fifteen feet high. To the left or west of the conservatory is the stable, which is practically finished. Both conservatory and stable are faced with the Roman brick and contain series of balanced angles of their own. All the buildings will be fireproof.

Most of the rest of the article deals with the house as it will be when it is completed. While much of the text is merely descriptive, the author's informant(s) provides insight into Wright's judicious use of terraces to modulate access to the buildings:

> The outside steps of the house will be concealed by piers of the face brick topped by concrete coping on which will be placed stone vases four feet across. Although the top of the basement windows will be three feet above the level of the ground, they too will be hidden. A series of terraces will effectively bar them from outside observation. Yet they will shed a profusion of light into that section of the building.
>
> The house and its connected buildings will have an artistic setting. In nooks and niches on the outside of the building, made by the angle construction, will be placed concrete boxes of flowers. Dropping away from the level of the first floor of the house will be terraces of earth devoted to perennial flowers. Along the east side of the pergola will be a terrace thirty feet wide planted in flowers. This terrace will connect with the narrower terraces about the east side of the building. On the west side, will be a formal garden ending at the north with a foundation and exhedra [sic] to screen the stable doorway. On the east and south of the house will stretch a wide expanse of lawn to Summit avenue and Jewett avenue.
>
> The interior of the house will have a simple elegance more costly than ornate embellishments. The hidden steps in front lead

to a porch eleven feet square. From the porch a wide doorway opens into a vestibule. Once inside the vestibule one has an unobstructed view down a hallway and through the pergola to a fountain playing in the end of the conservatory before a niched piece of statuary 180 feet away. The vestibule spreads to the left into a reception-room twenty feet wide and twenty-four feet long. To the left of that room is a study and a coatroom. The remainder of the left wing of the house downstairs is given up to a large kitchen and servants' dining room. To the right of the hall, beginning at the front, is the library. Then in order named come the living-room and dining-room. All three are under one ceiling, divided only by airy partitions coming within a foot or two of the ceilings. The library, projecting half its length beyond the front wall of the house, has light on three sides. Opening off the right of the middle of the living room is a family veranda 22 by 32 feet. It is also reached from the lawn by two sets of concealed steps. On the left or west side of the living-room is a new kind of fire-place that is open also on the hall side. The dining room, projecting beyond the regular rear line of the building, also has light from three sides. Its rear windows overlook the terrace of flowers along the pergola.

In the western end of the basement are a laundry, drying-room and storeroom. The main section of the basement is given up to a children's playroom, with a great fireplace and wide brick hearth, where nuts galore can be cracked with impunity.

The playroom and all the interior of the first and second stories, including the pergola, will be cabinet finished, fumed quartered oak now being prepared in a factory in Milwaukee. All the interior walls and ceilings will be trimmed in panels of this beautiful wood. Within the panels will be a common plaster of rough finish, tinted in rich colors. Throughout the house will be supporting piers of faced brick of the same hue as that in the outside walls, only the sunken joints will be gilded. All the floors except the sleeping-rooms will be of dull red tile.

Guests in winter time will wonder how the heat is furnished. They will see neither register, radiator nor stoves. Yet there will be pleasant gentle even warmth, like that given by a summer sun. Hot-water radiators will supply the heat in every room, but they will be concealed in quartered-oak boxes, which will be part of the finish of the room. The heat will come out of openings, which will look like part of the decoration of the room. The house will be lighted by electricity, but there will be gas jets in all the rooms in case of emergency. The windows will be of metallic sash, an advance on leaded panes, done in designs of crystal plate and iridescent glass embracing straight lines and angles only. All but the stationary windows will be hinged on the side. The shade rollers will be concealed and the ends of shade sticks will slide in grooves like those in a Pullman car.

The furniture of the house will be designed and placed by the architect. He will see to it that not a curve is slipped in on any of the furniture. It will be the simple, solid, substantial so-called mission type of furniture. All the wooden furniture will be of the same quartered oak as the inside finish of the house.

The stable in the northwest corner of the lot will be a model. It is 40 feet wide and 60 feet long. In the basement will be the heating plant, hot-water supply and the electrical lighting plant. On the ground floor in front will be the carriage-room. There will be no crawling beneath an automobile when Mr. Martin's motor car gets out of order. A trapdoor in the floor of the carriage-room can be opened, disclosing a sunken floor four feet beneath the other floor, and about three feet square. A stubborn automobile can be straddled over this place and then the chauffeur can get at its engine-room while standing up in the pit. There is also an entrance to this little pocket from the basement. In the rear of the first floor of the barn will be the stalls of the horses. Upstairs the coachman's quarters and a loft for hay.

Work was started on the house and other buildings on June 1st. It is figured that Mr. Martin will be able to move into his new home in June of next year.

Construction of the Martin House ran fifteen months beyond the completion date cited in this article. The delay can be attributed to Wright's working methods, to the complexity of the design, and to the logistics of a project that involved scores of craftsmen, artists, and manufacturers scattered all over the eastern and midwestern United States. The art-glass windows were manufactured by the Linden Glass Company, the fireplace mosaic was created by Giannini and Hilgart, and the window fastening devices were made by Spencer Adjusters, all of Chicago; interior trim was made by the Matthews Brothers in Milwaukee; tiles were produced in Zanesville, Ohio; electrical fixtures were manufactured by the Wilfred Lumley Company of Pittsburgh; window screens came from Portland, Maine; and furniture door hinges and locks were supplied by Soss Invisible Hinges and the Corbin Lock Company, respectively, both of New York City. Many Buffalo firms were involved in production as well.

Chicago-based architectural photographer Clarence Fuermann's 1907 Jewett Avenue elevation of the Martin House | *fig. 61* conveys a deceptive simplicity of materials, little more than horizontally coursed Roman bricks, cement copings, and crisp roof edges interlayered with deep shadows broken only by the shimmer and glint of art glass. In fact, the Martin House was composed of nearly every construction material then known to man. Foundations were made of mortared rubble stone; the floors, of concrete reinforced with metal mesh and steel I beams, surfaced with 3/4-inch tile on the main floor, magnesite in the basement and on the second floor, and linoleum in the kitchen. The walls and piers were built with cores of common red brick, faced with slender, yellow-brown Roman brick. The roofs were framed in wood but were extensively reinforced with steel beams, some measuring 28 feet in length and 18 inches in height, manufactured in Pittsburgh by the Carnegie Steel Corporation.[5] Eaves, cantilevered as much as 5 1/2 feet beyond the building's outer walls, carry soffits surfaced in sand-floated plaster made with sand from Rockaway Beach, Long Island, and a system of double copper gutters, one within the other, that conceal the sloping line necessary to the proper functioning of a gutter.[6] The exterior trim is of cypress, while most of the interior is articulated with a fine grade of fumed quartersawn oak, much of it veneered over an oaken core.[7] In addition to the 394 pieces of art glass employed throughout the complex as windows, lay-lights, skylights, and cabinet doors, numerous large-scale clear plate windows were installed. Heavy-gauge glass formed the balcony floor above the east porch and the sun traps outside the reception room. Three-quarter-inch-thick, white Novus sanitary glass, a pigmented heavy-gauge glass, was used to line most of the kitchen | *fig.* 62 and bathrooms. The fireplace mosaic | *fig.* 63 was made of glass tesserae, cut in the form of purple blossoms and green wisteria leaves veined with gold, which cascade over a grid of golden-brown tiles 3 inches square. Roof tiles were of terra-cotta; copings of concrete were cast in place; and the finials, or "birdhouses," atop the conservatory were carved from Indiana limestone.

At face value, the division of responsibility for realizing the Martin House was as deceptively simple as the house itself: Frank Lloyd Wright provided the artistic vision and the drawings for the project, Oscar Lang interpreted the drawings and oversaw the construction process, and Darwin Martin paid for the professional services. In reality, however, the process proved highly complex. Wright's creative process was ongoing and developmental in nature, giving rise to frequent, costly delays and change orders. His office produced hundreds of drawings and blueprints, ranging from conceptual sketches | see *figs.* 28, 44 to construction drawings | *figs.* 64, 65 to small clarification drawings | *figs.* 66, 67.[8]

The logistics of organizing and constructing the Martin House were formidable. Lang supervised a regular crew of around sixty-five men | *fig.* 68. In addition, he had to coordinate the delivery of supplies and, in some cases, the installation teams of more than sixty subcontractors and manufacturers | see APPENDIX. The assembly of individual parts of the buildings,

|*fig.* 61

|*fig.* 62

|*fig.* 61
Darwin D. Martin House,
Jewett Avenue elevation

|*fig.* 62
Darwin D. Martin House,
kitchen

| fig. 63

Darwin D. Martin
House, living room fire-
place, with mosaic by
Orlando Giannini

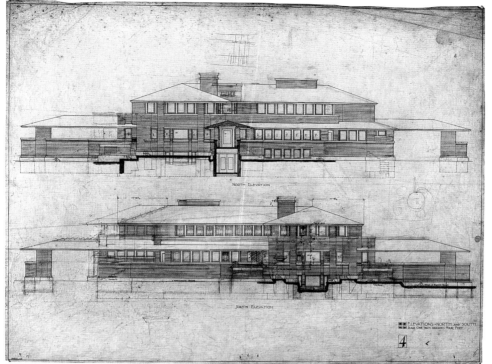

fig. 64

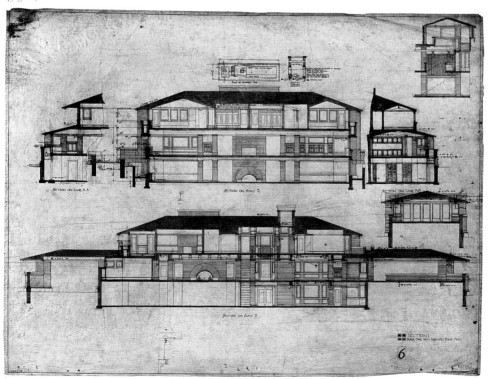

fig. 65

fig. 64
Darwin D. Martin House.
Construction drawing of
longitudinal section
through north-south axis

fig. 65
Darwin D. Martin House.
Construction drawing of
longitudinal section
through east-west axis

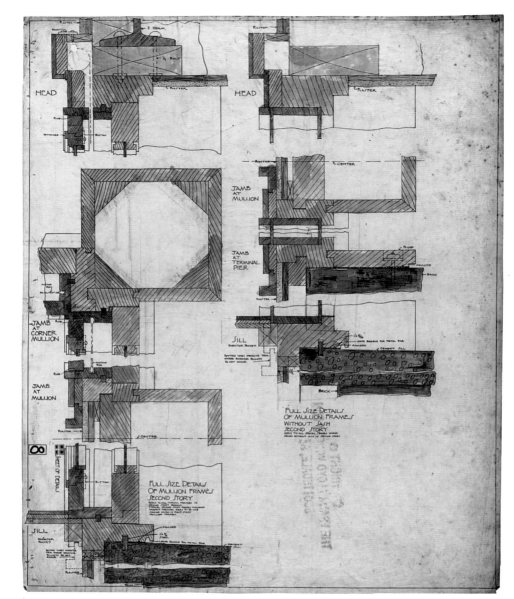

| fig. 66
Darwin D. Martin House.
Detailed construction
drawing

| fig. 67
Darwin D. Martin House.
Wall section

overleaf
| fig. 68
Darwin D. Martin House.
Construction crew

| fig. 66

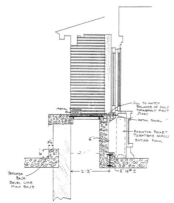

MARTIN HOUSE
SECTION THROUGH RECEPTION ROOM
OUTSIDE WALL
SCALE THREE QUARTER INCH

| fig. 67

like the Novus glass surfacing of the kitchen and bathrooms, was frequently contingent upon the timely receipt of goods from other manufacturers, such as plumbing and fixture suppliers, as well as Wright's timely production of construction drawings. Wright's frequent failure to produce interpretive details on time was compounded when, on more than one occasion, he or his staff made errors. An additional layer of difficulty lay in the interpretation of Wright's designs produced in Oak Park, Illinois, by Lang and his crew working nearly five hundred miles away in Buffalo.

Lang's letterpress book covering June 1905 to October 1906 contains 291 letters to manufacturers, subcontractors, and suppliers, but given the absence of a comparable volume (or volumes) covering the first nineteen months of the Martin project, it is likely that Lang may have written more than five hundred letters altogether.[9] An additional 421 letters, mostly from contractors and suppliers, written to Lang between 1904 and 1906, provide additional evidence of the scope of the work and bear witness to the problems that occurred with individual products and their manufacturers.[10] There are, for example, fifty-six letters to Lang from the Penn-American Plate Glass Company, supplier of the Novus glass, and another twenty-three letters from the Linden Glass Company regarding the Martin House art glass. The lining of the ceiling of one of the Martin House bathrooms with Novus glass presented particular problems, as this letter from the president of the Penn-American Plate Glass Company to Oscar Lang indicates:

> Dear Sir; –
>
> We have been considerably concerned about the installing of the ceiling in Bath Room No. 3, to comply with the request of Mr. Martin and Mr. Wright, the architect, in having it in one piece. For from the cramped position in which we would have to work in getting this plate into position, and the very slight bearing we would have on the side panel, and our inability to work from the top in order to get the proper fastenings into the glass to support it, and we think it best in order to make a safe and satisfactory job, to divide the ceiling for this room into 4 pieces; by doing this we can fasten it

| *fig.* 68

on to the ceiling without showing any fastenings on the face of it, and we will divide it into four equal parts....

W. L. Krause, President
Penn-American Plate Glass Company[11]

Darwin Martin was always quick to intervene in the construction process. A letter to the Linden Glass Company of September 14, 1904, which begins with a complete list of the glass required for the stable and greenhouse and quotes $1.25 per square foot for the work, provides a case in point. The letter continues:

> Be careful to thoroughly wrap the glass in paper before packing [it] in sawdust. The Barton glass furnished last spring continues to shed sawdust every time it is washed.
>
> Do you test the windows under air pressure? This should be done. Windows which contain apertures to admit cold air in the winter will be very unsatisfactory.
>
> Please acknowledge receipt of the letter and advise me when glass will be shipped. [12]

Lang deserves considerable credit for his role in the construction of the Martin complex. In addition to managing the complexities inherent in Wright's design, Lang had to contend with an extremely demanding client in Darwin Martin, who was himself a master of logistics.[13] Martin constantly inserted himself into the building process and used his vast knowledge of American industry to assist in the acquisition of products, but his help may have been a mixed blessing for Lang.[14] The following exchange reveals just how demanding Darwin could be and how his demands could affect others. During a heavy downpour on the evening of June 5, 1905, Martin visited the house and observed the results. Before Lang arrived at the site the following morning, he had left a sheaf of notes, which read in part:

Have you ten carpenters fit to put on trim? I understand we were to use cabinets makers. There must be no hammer marks. I expect you will give this work your close personal inspection as it progresses.... .

I hoped last evenings extraordinary downpour might bring you over to see the effect of it on your undertakings. I was there two hours. The water in stable basement was three courses of brick high, our side of pit. In pit to knee. The siphon didn't work voluntarily but finally worked a little and I hope (now 6:30 a.m.) continued all night. The pergola basement was dry. The playroom had in most places 1/2 to 1 inch of water which came up through the floor. The finished basement had an inch of water which evidently came in through area doors, the drain in area receiving <u>no</u> water. John spent part of the night mopping basement. The drain at foot of steps in pergola basement is not trapped. Every drain requires investigation to see if it receives water and if trapped. The siphon must be made to work & ball soldered on. Please indicate by a drawing to me the location of drain tiles on the ... three sides of east projection of conservatory and I will pass it to Foster to add to the chart. To stop inflow through those walls must we dig all around down to the floor level and cement and asphalt outside? Were not walls cemented outside? Wasn't that part of Frank's contract? See unfinished lintel over door in ... house basement area although frame is painted and called finished. Height of conservatory doorway must not be decreased. Can metal lath and cement?

Though storm threatened last eve house was left with many windows opened including several in reception hall where trim is stored. Wonder if monolith will be safe in playroom? What will effect of moisture from beneath be? Are verandah rain basins at Barton grade? If so ground in hemicycle is mostly six inches too low and rain last eve formed a moat there. All the soil coming off from front lawn can be used there. Wheelbarrows, not wagon will be required.

M[15]

Lang's response, which reveals a wound to his pride, refers to a conversation that followed Darwin's early morning memo, in which Darwin resorted to sarcasm with Lang, as he sometimes did with Wright:

> The foreman from Matthews Bros. Mr. Wernike hires and discharges all men for inside trim. The men I furnished are Carpenters. I shall inspect the work as it progresses. . . .
>
> As to my worrying about my <u>undertakings</u> last night. I have too much confidence in the work to worry or come over to see if it was right. I <u>knew</u> it was as near right as I could make it and follow out the plans; I have pride enough in my work Mr. Martin to feel it very keenly when you insinuate that I am not sufficiently interested in any point concerning your house. After the talk we had this morning over the points mentioned in your memo, I am of the impression that with the strain I am under in keeping all ends up, that you should assure me the I have the hearty cooperation, sympathy and support of the <u>owner</u> or that I do not for I have worked for no one else's interests . . . .
>
> Lang[16]

The essential nature of Lang's role in the construction of the Martin House notwithstanding, the driving force behind the conception and realization of the project derived from the dynamic interaction between Wright and Martin. In his comment to Wright of May 24, 1904, regarding the garage/stable and conservatory—"We may be able to put up the buildings for $14,000, but I do not know how to get out of it now"[17]—Martin set the tone of reckless abandon that would characterize his financial dealings with Wright throughout the project and for many years thereafter. Just as construction was about to begin in August 1904, Darwin sent Wright a lengthy letter filled with questions concerning a myriad of details. Wright answered item by item and then seized the opportunity to try to expand Darwin's vision for the project:

> I think I told you that you couldn't hope to get out on residence proper for less than $35,000.00 and we have inched some since,— fireproof floors, and tile floor covering, more meat in piers and breast works. Say up to $40,000.00 which is a modest sum to expend for the house of a representative Buffalonian?
>
> You ought to spend $75,000.00 on it instead of $40,000.00 just to leave Buffalo something worth having, something to live up to, you know.[18]

In responding Martin ignored Wright's bid to double the budget for the house and expressed his growing frustration with Wright's failure to provide details on time:

> Have you any idea by this time how exceedingly aggravating it is to a client to have to tease and coax and wheedle for past due details? For details that obviously require only concentrated industry, not courting of the Muse, to produce. You do not have to court a Muse to produce detail for our stable door. We want to hang the doors soon and we don't want to wait much longer for brains. We will make them without 'em.[19]

In mid-October 1904 Darwin wrote to Wright to report the first of many errors in design: the basement of the Martin House was built according to one plan and the superstructure after another, making it necessary "to start at the bottom and build the piers farther apart."[20] Darwin seems to have taken the error in stride and concluded the letter with a light but pointed postscript, calculated to remind Wright, however gently, of the escalating costs of the project:

> P.S. [William E. Martin] says his trip here will save me. I accused him of having a conversation like this when he met Wright.
> W. E. M. (to Wright)—"Have you thrown the hooks into DDM?"
> Wright—"Yes"
> W. E. M.—"Well, throw them in again."
> Now, W. E. M. is penitent and says you have thrown them in at plenty, and he will tell you to let up....
> DDM[21]

Wright responded to Darwin's letter on October 13 with an epistolary gem calculated to draw Darwin into the all-consuming swirl of his own creative fury (or so he wished Darwin to believe):

> W. E. M. will be rather late at this end to stop the carnage now. He would better organize himself into a red-cross society and help save the pieces at the Buffalo end.
> No quarter, no! not until D. D. M. has the most perfect thing of its kind in the world,—a domestic symphony, true, vital, comfortable. A real something to show for his years of hard work, and a translation of those hard, faithful years into a permanent record that will proclaim him to subsequent generations as a lover of the good! the true! the beautiful! For did he not consider the lilies of the field? = "For I say unto thee that Solomon in all his glory was not arrayed like one of these."

Was his home not as a lily of the field: the field?—the human soul.

There now,—will you be good?

WRIGHT[22]

Darwin must have been disarmed by Wright's passion and answered, somewhat meekly,

> DOMESTIC SYMPHONY Will I be good? Well, I will. I hear a rumor that you will be here next week. We will be glad to see you, but take warning, do not come unless prepared to deliver McNulty's plaster bid, complete interior trim, specifications and details for Buffalo bids and Milwaukee bid. Meanwhile we must receive sun trap details.[23]

Another expensive error in construction was discovered in November, which Darwin accepted with equanimity:

> Redrawings of conservatory have been received. The ripping out of the error in the copper skylight cost us $50.00 (we do not lay it up against you, but you could have warned us). Now we will proceed valiantly to rip out the false work already completed in the rectangular part of the conservatory and conform to the redrawing. We will dicker with Farmer, who, having the contract for the cement, has the advantage of us, for the cost of this work and of the changes in the square section. We cannot introduce the mullions in the doors because they are made and Linden is making the glass.
>
> How we do earnestly wish that you would get in your finest thinks in time.[24]

Early in December 1904 Wright fell ill for a six-week period, during which Darwin Martin and Oscar Lang corresponded with Wright's office superintendent, Walter Burley Griffin regarding the art glass, plastering, and other details. Wright recovered and returned to the Martin House project with a letter on December 28 expressing sympathy for the family of William Martin, whose seven-year-old daughter Eunice had just died.

The letters between Martin and Wright of January 1905 address interior trim, skylights, and other finish work, and are mostly routine in nature.[25] On January 26 Wright wrote to announce closure on the general construction phase of the Martin complex. He concluded with the following:

> I think our service is about all in now—except the special furniture and planting plans. The planting plan is underway but the furniture can await my return. When I see you next week, I shall have delivered the goods in the way of plans and details for the D. D. Martin domicile. We leave the 15th ult. [next] for the West. With regards to yourself and family. I am Yours truly[26]

Wright refers to his trip to Japan, about which he must have informed Darwin verbally during a recent visit. Wright, along with Paul Mueller, the Chicago-based supervising contractor for the Larkin Administration Building, dined at the Martins' home on the evening of February 11.[27] When, on February 15, 1905, the Wrights and the Willitses set off for Japan, the architect apparently felt that the Martin complex, the Larkin building, and his commissions elsewhere were well enough along to allow for his absence.

February of 1905 was not an opportune time for Wright to leave the country, however. His work on the Martin House and the Larkin Administration Building was hardly complete, and a number of other commissions were in progress as well. Nevertheless, Darwin's reaction was curiously benign: "I note you say that 'we leave the 15th of February for the west.' I take it that Mrs. Wright will accompany you. I am glad for both of your sakes." [28] Perhaps Wright had confided in his client about his extramarital relationship with Mamah Borthwick Cheney, the wife of Edwin Cheney for whom Wright had designed a small house in Oak Park during the previous year. If this was indeed the case, then Darwin Martin would have sanctioned Wright's trip as an effort to repair his marriage. Regardless, the personal nature of the exchange indicates a growing closeness on the part of Wright and Martin—one that would be tested during the architect's three-month absence, as finish work got underway and Martin found himself dealing with the architect's representatives in Oak Park.

Chapter Five

THE *TOUT ENSEMBLE*

OSCAR LANG AND his men worked throughout 1905 and began to withdraw from the Martin House late in the year, when they were supplanted by teams of highly skilled artisans and craftsmen who would execute the building's landscaping and interior finish. Some two hundred letters exchanged between Darwin Martin and Frank Lloyd Wright from December 1905 until November 1906 provide a detailed narrative of many aspects of the completion of the Martin House. Lively and revealing discussions of some of the more contentious issues, such as those pertaining to the art glass, the fireplace mosaic, the dining room furniture, and the fees for Wright's services, provide an indication of the ambitiousness of the undertaking. The results of all the craftsmen's toil, and the resolution of these issues, can be seen in a series of approximately thirty-five photographs, taken by Clarence Fuermann in 1907.

When Wright went to Japan in early 1905, leaving Walter Burley Griffin in charge of the Oak Park studio during his absence, problems arose almost immediately regarding the art-glass windows in the Martin House. Wright had already redefined both the nature and the role of decorative colored-glass windows by replacing the opaque pictorial imagery of Louis Comfort Tiffany (1848–1933) and John La Farge (1835–1910) with transparent compositions, in which combinations of clear plate- and colored-glass elements were suspended in architectonically conceived frames made of rigid zinc and copper caming, rather than the traditional, softer lead. Wright made varied caming widths a vital part of the design of his windows,[1] and he made the windows themselves an integral element of the larger composition and experience of the building. Although they were often abstracted from natural forms, the designs of these windows are best understood as delicate exfoliations of the building's pervasive post-and-beam system, analogous to the leaves and buds of a tree. Called "light screens" by Wright, the windows organize the viewer's visual experience of the natural world beyond the confines of the building's interior. Conversely, since the glass pieces do not constitute a single plane, they tend to inhibit views into the building and thus provide its inhabitant with additional privacy.

Wright designed unique art-glass patterns for each of the structures in the Martin complex and four distinct patterns for the Martin House itself: the tree-of-life window | *fig. 69* for the second story of the house; the wisteria pattern | *fig. 70* for most of the main floor rooms;

a lightly gridded variant of the wisteria window pattern for the bursar's office | *fig. 71*[2]; and a high-density scheme with cascading chevrons for the small paired casement windows for each pier cluster | *fig. 72*. There are numerous variations on the principal designs. There are tree-of-life and wisteria patterns expanded to door size, and there are tree-of-life patterns with single-tree designs and four-tree patterns in addition to the standard three-tree pattern. Wright also designed art-glass skylight, lay-light, and cabinet-front patterns for both the Martin and Barton houses.

Problems arose when Griffin pointed out to Darwin, shortly after Wright's departure, that

> It is Mr. Wright's will that the windows of the reception room, 1st story, be of the general design of the 2nd story [the tree-of-life pattern]. The Linden Glass Co. will be glad, no doubt, for you to withhold your consent because these lights are costing them so much and have written you, as you request, before proceeding.[3]

Darwin not only opposed Wright's choice of windows for the reception room, he also objected to the wisteria pattern on the grounds that it did not provide a sufficiently clear view to the outside. To this Griffin responded, somewhat testily, with comments that offer insight into the way that Wright's windows were understood within his office:

> Dear Sir:
>
> You certainly are making us trouble with this last suggestion as to the glass, for the idea of the pattern [of the wisteria window] is a uniform texture given by the bands, enlivened by the sprinkling of falling golden flakes, as it were. At any rate, to give the open center would render necessary starting on a new tack altogether, for any violation of the old idea would be so obvious as to make it forever unrestful. Moreover, the Linden Glass Company have twenty-three of these lights cut. All but two of the type excepting the reception room, undecided.

| *fig. 69*
Darwin D. Martin House. Tree-of-life window, second floor

| *fig. 70*
Darwin D. Martin House. Wisteria window, first floor

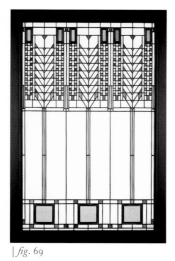

| *fig. 69*

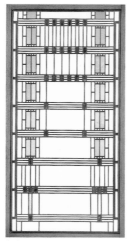

| *fig. 70*

They explain this fact as a matter of self-preservation for themselves in that cutting a single light for pattern would be a four fold expense per square foot and that they had assumed a light to be settled finally when approved by Mr. Wright.

However, considering the matter as far as concerns these lights already made, I do not believe that you intend your suggestions as to shut-off outlook to apply, for they are in each case subordinate to clear center windows of plain plate except where opening on to veranda, where they improve the outlook.

The reception room, which doubtless you are thinking of primarily, had been planned for the second story design as you know, which preserves a clear outlook to one seated.

If you can finally come to decide in favor of the original intention, you will be doing the best thing, but if you cannot, had you better not advise the Glass Company to continue with all other first story lights and us to try to please you when it comes to this room.4

The window pattern in question is divided by eight horizontal bands of four closely aligned metal cames, somewhat like the staffs of musical notation.5 In Darwin's windows two abstract patterns—apparently based on wisteria blossoms—cascade downward over the outer quadrants of these horizontal bars, diminishing as they descend. The upper center of the composition contains thin rectangles arranged vertically and accented with gilded squares, leaving the central two-thirds of the window relatively open.

Wright's art-glass patterns generally either grow upward from a base or downward from the top with a suspended quality, like a stalactite. They are positioned according to how Wright wanted the building to be experienced. At the Martin House, the suspended wisteria pattern occurred alongside clear plate windows so that viewing out was less an issue than it might be elsewhere in the house. Nevertheless, the wisteria pattern was considerably less dense than the tree-of-life pattern. The tree-of-life window was conceived for the second floor where it provided more privacy and where its chevrons gave a vigorous upward thrust

| *fig.* 71
Darwin D. Martin House.
Bursar's office window

| *fig.* 72
Darwin D. Martin House.
Pier-cluster casement window

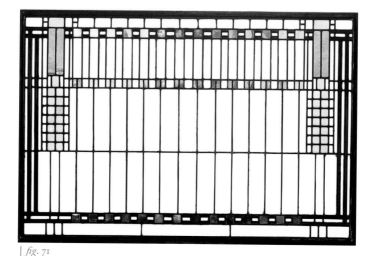

| *fig.* 71

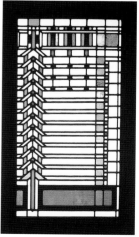

| *fig.* 72

to the roof.[6] In his concern for practicality, Darwin Martin appears oblivious to the degree to which these window patterns are integral to the design and the experience of the building. He replied to Griffin:

Dear Sir:

The fact that the Linden Glass Co., have two lights for first story cut, does not, it seems to me, have a material bearing on the case. There would be very little of it wasted even if my suggestion for a modified design is adopted. The modification I suggested may produce an unrestful result; certainly the design as submitted, is unrestful and would always be a thorn in the side.

Of course, your arguments that we could forego the pleasure of using those windows and instead use the clear center windows, is some inducement but not a recommendation to the design under discussion. We positively cannot entertain the idea of putting into the Reception Room [the] second story design, for when one stands up it is utterly impossible to look out of the room. It seems to us this design is quite impossible for the place suggested.

You say "when it comes to this room." We have already come to this room, and it is suffering for lack of glass.

We cannot possibly entertain the idea of waiting Mr. Wright's return before this room is glazed. Perhaps the most practical thing will be to glaze with clear plate.

I am in hopes that this letter will reach you so that the matter can be pretty thoroughly discussed with Mr. Lang when he is there on Saturday.

The effect of the first story glass is very similar to that in W.E.M.'s house, so we have had a pretty good opportunity to judge it and we did not admire it when we saw it there, neither Mrs. Martin nor the writer, though of course we would not have them

know this. . . . I will discuss with Mrs. Martin the feasibility of accepting the first story design for the rooms other than the Reception
Room, and leaving it open whether we shall glaze that with clear
plate or with some modification of the first story design. The point
we insist upon is, that those windows shall be available for viewing
the street, whether one is standing or sitting, and this seems to us
not an unreasonable demand.[7]

Wright's view prevailed, the full tree-of-life pattern was installed in the reception room, but
the Martins were not satisfied with the result. On May 28, 1906, Darwin wrote to Wright:

Contrary to all expectations and predictions the reception room has
not proven enticing or even inviting though the whole south side is
windows. We conclude that it is because of the long harsh line of the
register enclosure which together with the abnormally broad ledge
outside of the windows makes the distance from the real interior of
the room to the skyline too great. Mrs. Martin has made the excellent suggestion that the radiator box in front of the three middle
windows be removed, lower radiators be put there and a low, broad
seat constructed. What do you think of this and will you furnish the
detail to work by?[8]

In 1909 the seven south-facing tree-of-life windows (but not the single east- and west-facing
windows) in the reception room were sent back to the Linden Glass Company in Chicago,
where the 4-inch iridescent base squares were removed and replaced by thin vertical rectan-
gles that allowed for a clearer view toward Jewett Parkway | *fig. 73*. Wright wrote to Darwin,
"If Mrs. Martin would be happier I should remove the iridescent glass entirely from the
squares you mention and substitute clear glass."[9]

    Also noteworthy during Wright's absence is Darwin's decision to include a skylight in
the east wing of the living room, just inside the porch | *fig. 74*. The living room, surrounded

| *fig. 73*
Darwin D. Martin House.
Tree-of-life window,
as modified for the
reception room in 1910

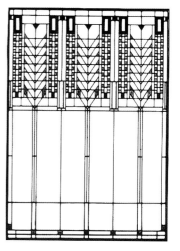

on four sides by the east porch, the library, the dining room, and the entrance hall, did not receive any direct sunlight and was consequently darker than the rest of the interior. The new skylight measured 3 feet 5 inches by 10 feet 5 inches and admitted a shaft of colored light into the east alcove during the morning hours:

> I have finally decided to put the skylight into the living room. The French windows are now glazed and we have confirmation of all our fears of the darkness of this room and it can only be relieved by a skylight. It comes to me at last that instead of the skylight seeming to be a makeshift and a too-apparent effort to escape a difficulty, that it will be a very desirable, attractive feature. [10]

Griffin replied, "Glad you have 'seen the light' as to the ceiling window in living room. Your decision has sent 'gallery west' about a week's work here on the trim and transom details." [11]

Wright returned from Japan late in May 1905, in a singularly exuberant mood, and immediately wrote to his faithful Buffalo client:

> My dear Mr. Martin:—We, Mrs. Wright and I, have come back much improved in health and spirits—can lick my weight in wild-cats. How would you like to be a wild cat?
>
> A three month's absence and entire change of scene meanwhile has given me my clients and friends in perspective and the spirit of one D.D. Martin shines out clear and white. I shall be glad to see him in the flesh once more. I hope that he and his are well and will be glad to see me too.
>
> Expect to arrive at Buffalo Sunday morning. [12]

Martin and Wright immediately resumed their avid correspondence. Approximately 140 letters were exchanged over the eighteen-month period from May 1905 until the Martins'

fig. 74

Darwin D. Martin House,
living room. East alcove

open house in November 1906—a frequency attributable to the detailed nature of the finish work and to Darwin's increasing impatience as his cherished wedding anniversary passed unmarked by celebration on June 25, 1905, and as he and his family prepared to move into the still unfinished house on November 20, 1905. Wright visited Buffalo monthly throughout the remainder of 1905 and continued to write approximately one letter for every three written by Martin. Much of the correspondence dealt with routine matters (insofar as anything about the Martin House could be considered routine), but the final, "symphonic" nature of the design depended on the close monitoring of the skilled craftsmen who would complete the work.

Martin and Wright began to discuss furniture for the house shortly after the architect's return from Japan. Its design and manufacture would require six additional months. Interior wood trim, art-glass windows, and Novus Sanitary Structural Glass—manufactured in Milwaukee, Chicago, and Pittsburgh, respectively—began to arrive by the traincar load in June 1905. The installation of the trim and Novus glass required five additional months and the art glass, considerably longer.

On May 19, 1905, Darwin sent Wright a list of twenty-six furniture items including a variety of tables, bookcases, cabinets, wardrobes, dressers, and side chairs, to which Wright added four easy chairs, a baby grand piano case, six library chairs, four tabourettes, and six side chairs, with no consideration for the time and effort that would be involved in their production. An undetermined number of additional pieces, such as the beds and blanket boxes for the master bedroom, were also designed and produced.[13] Wright's response concluded with the provocative comment, "not yet designed on paper—will be soon FLW."[14]

On June 3, 1905, Darwin reminded Wright of the need for the design and fabrication of the 150 square feet of glass mosaic that had been planned for all four sides of the living room fireplace | see *fig. 63*. Darwin expressed a concern that the chimney would settle, causing the mosaic to crack,[15] but Wright breezily assured him, "Our chimneys never settled,—try one,—Mosaic is O.K. and I have the man to make the stuff, right here in Chicago. Will send you a bid soon. Gianini [sic] is his name and he is a cracker jack."[16] Wright's concluding comment, "Furniture and fixtures already designed only necessary to put them on paper,"[17] suggests again that he was able to envision his work quite fully in his mind before committing it to

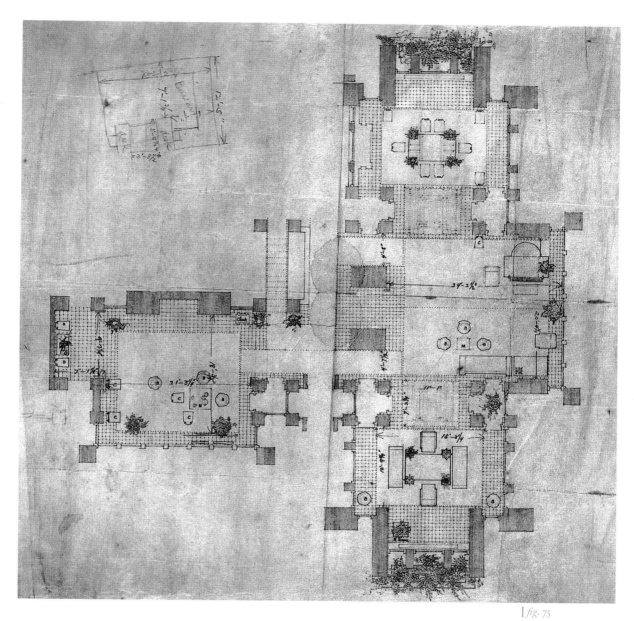

| fig. 75

Darwin D. Martin House.
Wright's furniture place-
ment plan, first floor

paper. Mr. and Mrs. Frank Lloyd Wright visited the Martins in Buffalo on June 11, 1905.[18] But despite this personal attention, Darwin's frustration mounted during June and July 1905.[19] "The house can be finished in 5 to 6 weeks if we could have now all the plans and the architect, viz., glass, mosaic, light fixtures, adjusters and hook fasts, the tables, the chairs. We are prepared to make a cyclone finish but for the architectural delays."[20] Wright allowed Darwin's frustration to rise to the bursting point before sending off this gem of self-absorption:

> My dear D.D.M.:
> The cartoon for windows over sideboard is finished—very pretty!—
>
> The cartoon for the fireplace complete is also finished—Superb!
>
> Gianini [sic] has a considerable section of the design worked out in gold for your approval—ship it to-morrow—great piece of work!
>
> Furniture drawings and gas fixture details are my daily trouble —dream of them at night!
>
> Linden has all the drawings that he had a right to expect from us—jump on him!
>
> Spencer [a manufacturer of window fastening devices and a former officemate of Wright's] I have tried to get some reliable information from and failed, but have O.K.d drawing for hook-fast and told him to go ahead with adjusters—think he lied about the condition of same in letter to you—blow him out of the water!
>
> Have detail finished for lily pond in circular hollow,—the proper scheme at last!
>
> Going to New York Sunday night,—returning to Buffalo Wednesday—will see you then, a complete walking Compendium with a panacea for interrogation points.—Gaily,
> Wright[21]

Darwin continued to press Wright in July and August 1905, pausing on August 26 to express satisfaction with a first-floor furniture placement plan | *fig. 75*, which Wright had just sent. "Your *tout ensemble* sketch is *magnifique*," he wrote. "We are much impressed not only with the unsparing labor bestowed, but with its taste and beauty. We will never move a chair or footstool from the indicated positions."[22] The Martins were critical of specific pieces of furniture, however:

Samples of all but dining chairs should be made immediately. The library couches and the living room davenport, and living room and reception room tables can be made at once.

We must ask you to modify the library and dining tables in these particulars. You promised Mrs. Martin that the dining table would be made so that when desired the entire table could be covered with one cloth, i.e., that the sides would be straight. The corner features are acceptable to Mrs. Martin if made removable, but when removed must be made an orthodox table. With the sides cut in the extending corners eliminate 5 1/3′ around the entire table that cannot be utilized for plates. Can you have the projections made removable so that the table could be used as a plain rectangle when desired?

When the Martin family of five dine with the Barton family of 3, no somersaults have to be turned. The everyday table seats 8; but when the Barton family of 3 dine with the Martin family of 5, in the new house, the table as sketched will have to be extended, because only 6 can be seated without extension. Could not this be readjusted?

Now as to dining chairs—they are to be leather-seat?—Mrs. Martin objects to the boardy back; does not like it at all; wants chairs as light as possible she likes the Barton and W. E. M. (Unless it is Waller) dining chairs best of any Wright dining Chairs she has seen (p.s. so do I). You need not make ours just like them, but make them light. Will you send new sketch for them?

The library table has cupboard doors only 5″ back of edge of top. The cupboard is sufficiently raised from the floor to not interfere with the feet of one sitting at table, but the cupboard door would have to be opened to make room for one's knees. So we rebel here. Please remedy this.

In the library couch sketch there appears a piece of furniture not shown in the tout ensemble or anywhere else. It looks like the stalking ghost of a bookcase. Don't do it.

The reception room book-stand and jardinière stand are no doubt O.K., but when you come again show us.[23]

Darwin concluded with a request for plans for a gardener's cottage, the final building of the Martin complex:

The gardener's cottage is very pretty and plan more practical than Lang's. The lot is 37.9′ wide. Where would the house be located? When can you furnish complete, unamendable plans and specifications, and can you send us a man to build the house according to said plans and specifications complete, key in owner's pocket, for $2750? We will get him a Wabash [railroad] half-rate ticket.[24]

Despite Darwin Martin's apparent enthusiasm for this project, several years would pass before the gardener's cottage | fig. 76 was actually built.[25]

Progress on the main house was not always smooth. In late August 1905 Darwin found it necessary to chastise Wright when it became apparent that his furniture placement plan did not coincide with the placement of electrical outlets on the original first floor plan, necessitating the costly ripping up of some of the newly laid floor tiles. Darwin wrote, "And I suppose if you keep on drawing changes I will be chump enough to keep on paying workmen to wreak these changes in cement, tiles and steel." He concludes the letter, "P.S. and N.B. I felt it all the while we were laying these conduits and outlets that you didn't know where they ought to be at."[26]

| fig. 76
Frank Lloyd Wright,
Darwin D. Martin
complex, gardener's
cottage, designed 1905,
constructed 1908.

Darwin's sense of urgency intensified as the November 20, 1905, move-in deadline approached.[27] He wrote eight letters in three weeks, to which Wright only responded once. In late October, Darwin wrote to Wright that he had learned Adam and Westlake, the manufacturer of his lighting fixtures, had never received any drawings from Wright's office.[28] In his reply Wright blamed Griffin but deflected attention onto Orlando Giannini, who, he said, was making good progress on the fireplace surround. Wright added that he would arrive "late this week when I shall daub your walls for you good and plenty,"[29] a comment that suggests that Wright mixed paint colors for the house intuitively on-site.[30] On October 30, Darwin wrote to tell Wright that he had learned that it was unlikely that Giannini would complete the mosaic by December 15. He added, "As we intend to occupy the house as soon as the wall decorations are completed, we shall cover the chimney with burlap and glaze the windows with plain glass."[31]

Wright reported on Giannini's progress on the mosaic on November 2:

> My dear D.D.M:
>
> I stopped to verify your pessimistic view of the fire place mosaic— Gianini [sic] pleads lack of foreknowledge of what he had still to do when he reported to me 3 weeks ago that he would be on time—I saw, then, on the benches over 2/3s of the facing cut and fired—It is now all cut and fired but one small portion of one section—but he is handling it gingerly in a one-horse way, finding trouble with the mitered edges, working two men only on it because it is difficult work etc., etc., etc. He is working over time on it from now on—he swears a horrid Italian oath that he will have it in place within three weeks, but he is a natural born liar like all his race—we can do nothing—we are simply held up. The window is however as I told you all cut and pieces partly glazed. It will come along surely within days....I will come Monday night—bringing planting plan of "Floricycle" with me, schedule for light fixtures and bids on same.[32]

Wright traveled to Buffalo on November 8 and stayed two days.[33] As the move-in date drew closer, Darwin's letters to Wright became increasingly repetitive, even nagging. On November 14 he wrote, "This is to remind you that you did not mail last Saturday the sample of colors for curtains....This is to remind you that I bet you didn't go to Milwaukee today, as agreed, but I hope you will go without delay, because we get no furniture until you do."[34] And on November 16, Darwin wrote:

> This is to remind you that it is Thursday and I have not rec'd color sample which you were to mail last Sat. or Mon. This is to remind you that the Adams and Westlake Co. wrote me under the date of the 16th that they are still without sufficient info. from you to enable them to name a figure on my lighting fixtures, When will you enable them to bid? Pardon me for mentioning that you wrote last Feb. that your services for the Martin house were all in. We begin to live in the house next Monday, but up to this date we are without architect details for the important lighting fixtures.[35]

At this point Wright informed Darwin that the lighting manufacturer, Adams and Westlake, had dropped the Martin commission without notifying anyone involved, and he added, "I am getting discouraged but will make some desperate efforts this coming year to build up a coterie of capable, honest workmen, or manufacturers, who don't want to get rich quick and who love fine work for its own sake. Perhaps you have an idea of the difficulties attending that ambition?"[36] He concludes, "I went to Milwaukee last Thurs. and settled all furniture with Crosby; modified the chairs making them all lighter and somewhat more comfortable."[37]

Despite Wright's efforts, the Martins had become increasingly concerned about his design for an oversized morris chair and for their dining chairs | *fig. 77*, which had only three legs. Darwin complained in a letter of November 11, 1905:

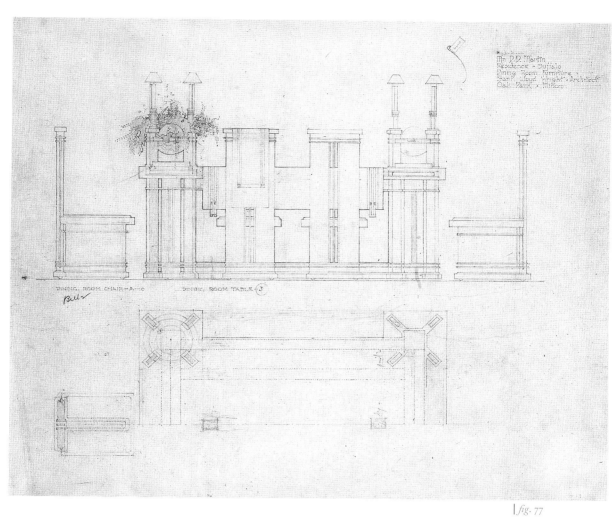

DINING ROOM CHAIR-A-10   DINING ROOM TABLE-3

fig. 77

Darwin D. Martin House.
Drawing of dining table
with three-legged side
chair

Mrs. Martin quite insists that the dining chairs be made with ortho-dox legs. She insists that the design submitted is a stunt, and she doesn't want to be responsible for a stunt. The Morris chair will be too heavy to move when made full size. We must insist that our chairs be portable, as you have made the back one solid board. Every one who has seen it agrees that spindles would be much preferable. Please lighten the chair up considerably. Make it so a woman or at least two women can move it about.[38]

The Martins moved into their house as scheduled on November 20, 1905. Aware of the inconvenience to the Martins and of Darwin's immediate presence on-site, Wright pressed ahead with completion, but problems persisted. Darwin reported to Wright on November 23, "Gianini [sic] says 'mosaic shipped'....Crosby [of Matthews Brothers, Milwaukee] says dining chairs still without [four] legs. Have instructed him not to make them yet but to rush tables. Please give the chairs legs so that when one sits on a chair-corner it will not tip over, and so it will look more orthodox."[39]

At this point Wright expressed apprehension over the scope of the furniture project—a total of over fifty individual pieces—and the amount of time it would require to design them: "I could wish you no worse luck than to have to furnish designs for *everything* in a modern, up to date, residence. I am beginning to realize the magnitude of the task, if, indeed, it is not beyond the pale of reasonable effort."[40] Wright also took the opportunity to vent his feelings concerning some of the craftsmen: "Foster [the plumbing contractor] has wriggled about here for an hour with the usual slimy nothingness as a net result...Soak the Penn American for me; they are trimmers, crawfishers, and bellyachers."[41]

Progress continued nevertheless. The gardener's cottage drawings were completed on December 5, 1905, and a few days later Giannini's assistant came and mounted the fireplace mosaic. On December 7 Wright wrote to say that drawings for clothes poles were done, that lamps for the newel posts were ready, that he was anxious to get the life-size cast of the Nike of Samothrace in place in the conservatory, and that William Martin and Paul Mueller had found a rug at Marshall Field's for Darwin's house.[42]

On the day before Christmas, 1905, Lang wrote to Wright to announce "the completion (save a few minor details)" of his work on the Martin House:

> I appreciate the accuracy and completeness of the plans and details, as worked out in your office. Mr. Martin's residence is generally conceded to be the most complete and artistic house creation in the city of Buffalo. No one can appreciate more than I, the great amount of careful thought which you have devoted to it.[43]

Approximately a day later, Wright forwarded Lang's note to Darwin Martin, appending it with the following: "My dear D. D. Martin:—This is a copy of an unsolicited 'testimonial' from your building superintendent. Wright."[44] Darwin wrote to Wright twice on December 26. The first letter concerned the design for the dining chairs:

> Dear Sir:
>
> DINING CHAIR. We rec'd yesterday afternoon the 2nd model for dining chair. After carefully considering it we still protest against any design even approx'g this. Yest.[erday] p.m. a lady of more than ordinary intelligence, sat down in the chair to try it and nearly tipped over. We do not want chairs that will cause even one per cent of our guests to wildly clutch the air and ejaculate, as this design would surely do.
>
> Please do not hug this child you have invented so close to you that you cannot see with others its impracticality.
>
> We would like to have our dining chairs at once. We think that we have been very patient. We think that you should respect our wishes. You have shown your capacity of making good dining chairs. Make us some. You could not get your friend Mr. Waller to accept this design.[45] Do not make a chair that makes housekeeping cares burdensome.

We do not want a cabinet-maker's product. We do not want a sectional bench. We want chairs, made up without any boards, of legs and spindles. Long ago you knew Mrs. Martin's objections to boardy chairs. It is merely a waste of time and money to continue hoping that we accept anything like the design now before us.

Yours.[46]

The Martins eventually received the four-legged, spindle-backed dining chairs | *fig. 78*.[47]

Darwin's assessment of some of the major furniture pieces—a rare example of such testimony—appears in a letter written to Wright's office on February 1, 1906:

The library table is here and is beautiful, excepting the corner superstructure. The living room table is a joy forever. The dining table is here but awaits Mr. Wright's next visit before its return to Milwaukee for reconstruction.

The round chairs [barrel chairs], barring their weight, are pronounced by Mrs. Martin (I have not seen them. They are still at the upholsterer's) highly satisfactory. The two small tables please us.[48]

With the exception of some discussion of repairs to the Giannini mosaic, the principal issue between Martin and Wright during the first five months of 1906 concerned Wright's fee for services. Darwin's second letter of December 26, 1905, indicated that he had recently perused a copy of his debits to Wright's account. "I had never footed them up before and am greatly astonished that they amount to almost $6,000.00, which is doubtless a thousand dollars more than I shall owe you."[49] Still, Darwin's letter included sincere praise for the house:

Our hearts are filled with gratitude for the new house these Christmas days. Both guest rooms were full and there was quite a sizeable party around the Christmas tree yesterday morning. The

fig. 78

Darwin D. Martin House.
Dining room

gifts from your family will I trust be duly acknowledged by Mrs. Martin and Dorothy, and they give us all pleasure. We thank you for your expressed good wishes and earnestly wish you a happy and prosperous New Year.[50]

This letter may have encouraged Wright to make a plea for additional funds, the need for which he explained in terms of his considerable debts ("an increase in my home mortgage to care for three thousand dollars floating indebtedness"[51]) and dim prospects ("Unity Church is the only thing immediate"[52]). As justification, he claimed, "I have devoted more time on the ground in Buffalo to the Martin Residence than to the Larkin Office Building,"[53] and noted further that by paying Mueller to supervise the Larkin Building he had assumed an expense that the Larkin Company should have shared.

In response, Darwin disputed Wright's exaggerated claim of superintendence but agreed to pay fifteen percent for the furniture designs. After questioning the wisdom of Wright's recent purchase of a property adjacent to his home, which followed the Wrights' expensive trip to Japan—where the architect had spent lavishly to acquire a collection of woodblock prints—Darwin expressed some dismay over the state of Wright's finances. He then offered six principles whereby Wright might improve his relationship with future clients:

1st. Follow the precedent you have already established for yourself in the Unity Church, of building within the appropriation, or approximately, not as in Mr. Heath's case, way beyond, nor in my case, way, way, way beyond.

2nd. FIX you [sic] plans.

3rd. Make adequate drawings and specifications. I am aware that you never have agreed with me that you ever have failed on this point, and I am aware that when you deliver you give full measure and running over, but the stubborn fact remains that in our case at least a very great deal of planning was verbal.

4th. Be punctual. Though the heavens fall, be punctual. Delays of months running into years are killing. Only an unlimited supply of enthusiasm will live down such adverse conditions.

5th. Be mejum. As Samantha said to Josiah, "if you cannot be mejum, be as mejum as you can." You get nothing but rebuffs and bumps from all sides when you are extreme. Take your wise and good wife into your plans. When she tells you you have overdone it 100%, believe her 10% at least and modify your plans in the direction of conservatism. Eschew your over-elaborate simplicity. It is the extremes that are expensive to you and to your clients and profit the least in the end. It is the extreme things only in our house that we would change. Take as an example the elaborate light units. Believe me, they are a dream, i.e., the realization is not all you saw in your imagination. And again, No. 1 Bedroom. It is the extremes only that scare people.

6th. Keep alive every day your perfectly evident capacity for letter-writing. You can encompass your wonderful ability with all the commonsense practice necessary to fill your office with business to over-flowing. Do not sacrifice so much to your exaggerated idea of the province of an architect to be the arbiter of the esthetic, for your only return will be reproach, whether candidly expressed or not, for a selfish gratification of riotous invention.

In conclusion Darwin wrote, "Mrs. Martin finds the protraction of the completion of the house beyond endurance."[54]

Darwin's letter gives expression to nearly three years of his own frustration over the difficulty and expense of bringing Wright's artistic vision into a built reality. As a practically minded businessman, Darwin Martin must have found Wright's somewhat cavalier attitude toward time and money painful to bear; but one wonders if Wright had been more punctual and "mejum," cost-conscious and communicative, how the Martin House would have turned out. It is not clear what Martin meant by the "extremes" represented by Wright's light units and master bedroom. The lights—opaque glass globes held in filigreed brass brackets | *fig. 79*—were handsome, shed little light, and may have projected danger-ously into the living spaces. As for the master bedroom, we only know that Isabelle Martin moved into a nearby bedroom—exactly when is not known—perhaps to gain more privacy than was possible in a room that projected toward Jewett Parkway and contained fifteen art-glass windows on three sides.

Wright responded to Darwin's guidelines with a spirited self-defense on January 2, 1906:

My dear Mr. Martin:

Your six articles are well stated and in no mean spirit, I am satisfied. I shall gratefully acknowledge them "my profit in the job."

Evidence in rebuttal of several points might be effective though probably not useful. I sense, I think, your temper and spirit in the mat-ter. There may be a few kicks lurking beneath the temper,—of the spir-it there is no doubt. But I should like to say that my purchase of prop-erty five months ago, was, like the light units, a dream; but based upon my supposed prosperity and resulting only in the forfeiture of a small sum of earnest money when "I found out." I still owe for the other things.

And in passing I should like to enquire as to what can be expected of "light units" without light? I am still infatuated by them,—likewise Bedroom No. 1.

You do not seem to realize that to the Architecturally initiated Wright is a "conservative" and every critical review of his work so far accords him the "safe and sane" position in the progressive move-ment. I am not especially proud of it either. I don't know that I want my capabilities, (if I have any) hedged about with the practice of so-called "common sense" people. I find that the class arrogating to themselves especially this property are usually poetry crushers of the expedient type, without imagination, rather hard, with their eye on the side of the dollar that says "In God we trust" but with the men-tal reservation that all others shall pay cash.

| *fig. 79*
Darwin D. Martin House.
Light sconce

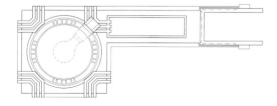

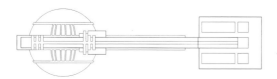

No, I don't want them. I am not cut out for a "successful architect." I don't like the kind I have seen who enjoy that distinction. I am used to rebuffs and bumps,—they don't count so very much except to make a fellow look kind of battered up, but as long as his wife loves him what's the difference?

I have been rebuffed and bumped in a good cause anyhow, the extremes of today are the substantial commonplaces of tomorrow. Your "common sense" variety is only trafficking today in the cast-off extremes of yesterday! Let it go at that.

I still insist that a reasonable interpretation of plans whether by letter or in person constitutes superintendence, and I dislike to profit in pence by Lang's mistakes only,—but I shall have to get off where you will,—you have "an agreement."

I don't blame you for your view of the matter, you have had little or no occasion to investigate the custom relating to professional practice of this nature, and though your native shrewdness and good sense tells you where you might have had more, still you don't know by comparison what your surplus is over and above the average service that has fixed the rates.

You have stood up pretty well,—the contractors, workmen, all say Martin is a pretty white proposition, and the architect shall not be behind. When Martin knows, he *is* a white proposition. But there are some things, I think Martin will admit it, that Martin don't know, although he is extraordinarily capable.

You see I am in accord with Article six keeping alive my capacity for letter writing.

I want to say finally that your only real trouble has been what "fixed plans of an adequate nature," (see prelude to Martin's of Dec. 30.) Wright rendered you and your salvation, always, the "verbal explanations" referred to.

In conclusion I have to confess that I have never yet made an investment of any nature, from the food I put into my children's mouths to the multitude of Japanese prints I give away, that I have not miscalculated my means and my obligations to my creditors and I don't suppose (though I still hope) that the day will ever come when it will be otherwise,—for I sell something I have no right to sell, I ought to give it. There is no unearned increment in my business, not even the advantage of "repetition" nothing but the unceasing effort of emptying myself of my best and highest qualities for hire, from day to day, whenever someone wants a little beauty and nobility "mixed in" with the theatre of his animal habits.

Yours as ever[55]

Wright visited Buffalo on May 10, 1906 and attempted to negotiate an additional payment of twelve hundred dollars from Martin,[56] who wrote twelve days later,

My conscience does not…smite me a mite in saying that if One Thousand Dollars ($1,000.00) spot cash will bring from you a receipt in full of all demands including the future things that may be considered necessary accessories to the buildings already built and planned, I will scare up the money and send it to you.[57]

Wright responded in his inimitable fashion, "My dear Mr. Martin: You are incorrigible,—but I love you just the same. Send the money."[58]

By November 16, 1906, the Martin House was sufficiently completed for the Martins to hold a formal reception. The *Buffalo Courier* reported on the event:

RECEPTION GIVEN
Mr. and Mrs. Darwin D. Martin of Jewett Avenue gave a delightful

reception last evening from 8 until 11 o'clock. The host and hostess received with Mr. Frank Lloyd Wright of Chicago. Chrysanthemums of many colors adorned the various rooms, pink ones being used in the receiving room, red flowers in the drawing room and yellow in the library. Supper was served in the basement from a buffet table adorned with yellow and white chrysanthemums.

Mrs. Martin wore a gown of white lace. Among the friends assisting were Rev. and Mrs. Thomas B. Berry, Mr. and Mrs. W. R. Heath, Mr. and Mrs. Louis Wright Simpson, Mrs. Bertha C. Hubbard, Miss Crawford, Mr. and Mrs. James F. Foster, Mr. and Mrs. E. J. Barcalo, Mr. and Mrs. F. C. Deming, Mr. and Mrs. Edward J. Harvey, and Mr. and Mrs. A. H. Morey.[59]

As a final gesture of closure, Wright presented Isabelle Martin with a set of Japanese wood-block prints, purchased with $250 of her own money during his 1905 journey to Japan.

Owing to the passage of time and to periods of neglect and vandalism the experience of the Martin House as it existed shortly after completion in 1907 is difficult to recapture today. The photographs taken by Clarence Fuermann for the March 1908 *Architectural Record* constitute an invaluable visual record of the buildings, but the photographs are black and white and they represent the Martin House in a particular way that Wright wanted the house to be experienced by the readers of that periodical. Fuermann took more than thirty photographs throughout the property, from which Wright selected thirteen images—six exterior and seven interior—for publication. These were accompanied by the Martin House floor plan | see *fig. 53* as Wright redrew it for the occasion. Fuermann made several attempts to capture the full expanse of the complex from elevated positions in buildings across Jewett Parkway, but only one of these images, "D. D. Martin House—General View" | *fig. 80*, was published, and in it the main house and the dependencies are obscured by trees. The remaining twelve photographs present the complex as a series of unconnected vignettes. We are not led through the house in a systematic way. The living room fireplace and a typical pier cluster

fig. 80

are prominently featured, but obscure corners of the house heavily encumbered with foliage are also included. It is possible to understand the relationship of the photographs to the floor plan only with considerable effort; consequently, the Martin House is presented in the *Architectural Record* as intriguing and mysterious.

The experience of the Martin House by an actual visitor in 1907 would very likely have involved a delayed reaction rather than a sudden, dramatic impact. It is true the complex is vastly more ambitious in scale and cost than anything else in the neighborhood, but as unfamiliar as Wright's rectilinear design vocabulary was at that time, it was softened by the warmth of the Roman brick, the blurring of the distinction between building and foliage, and the easy, layered horizontality of the buildings' principal lines. The hypothetical visitor would soon recognize that the main house and its dependencies were full of ambiguities, as well. For instance, at a maximum of 32 feet, the buildings are modest in height but monumental in feeling | *fig.* 81; the skeletal construction of the main house is radical in its openness, and yet the obscurity of its entrances and its surrounding parterres and parapet wall suggest inaccessibility; the buildings are symmetrical in some elevations and asymmetrical in others; the main house is large, with sixteen rooms, but its spaces are intimate; the detailing of the house is primitive in the Semperian nakedness of its structure but highly sophisticated in the interpenetration and transparency of its spaces.

The interior of the Martin House is dark and gladelike by contemporary standards, but it evinced a burnished, glowing ambience achieved by Wright's use of an autumnal palette flecked with gold. Wright used color and chiaroscuro architectonically to advance the experiences of movement and repose within the web of structure and space of the Martin House interior. It is easy to understand how Isabelle Martin, with her diminished eyesight,[60] would not have appreciated the subtleties of the Martin House. But what of Darwin Martin? How did a notion of portraiture exist in all of this?

previous pages
| *fig.* 80
Darwin D. Martin House.
"Martin House, General
View"

| *fig.* 81
Darwin D. Martin House,
kitchen. Entrance

fig. 83

| *fig.* 82

Darwin D. Martin House,
west entrance to conser-
vatory (left) and pergola
(right)

| fig. 83

Darwin D. Martin House,
raking view along pergola
and conservatory

overleaf
| fig. 84
Darwin D. Martin House,
garage/stable

| fig. 85
Darwin D. Martin House,
rear yard facing pergola,
conservatory, and
garage/stable

fig. 84

fig. 85

fig. 86

|fig. 87

previous pages
|fig. 86
Darwin D. Martin House,
reception room

|fig. 87
Darwin D. Martin House,
dining room, looking
toward east porch

|fig. 88
Darwin D. Martin House,
conservatory

fig. 88

Chapter Six
ARCHITECTURE AS PORTRAITURE

FROM FRANK LLOYD WRIGHT'S initial iteration of the home-as-portrait idea in 1894 to his reiteration in 1908, a change occurs that parallels the development of the prairie house and attests to the architect's growing conviction that architecture could be more than just a matter of style. When in 1894 Wright wrote, "It is the individuality of the occupants that should give character and color to the buildings and furnishings,"[1] it was already evident that he was concerned with something beyond the programmatic accommodation of a client's needs and desires. In 1900 he compared his architecture to the portraits painted by the celebrated artist John Singer Sargent: "A Sargent might paint a hundred portraits without a signature, and the moment we see the work we might recognize it as Sargent's."[2] In the *Architectural Record* of March 1908, Wright again invoked Sargent and referred to the architect as "the individual to whom [the client] entrusts his characterization." He added:

> Then, if the architect is what he ought to be, with his ready technique he consciously works for the client, idealizes the client's character and his client's tastes and makes him feel that the building is his as it really is to such an extent that he can truly say that he would rather have his own house than any other he has ever seen.[3]

Thus, over time, Wright arrived at a distinction between depicting the client with "the insight of a great craftsman" and idealizing the client with "the insight of the true poet."[4] The implication, of course, is that Wright himself would provide the great poetic insight that would idealize the character of the client through the art of architecture. Thus he not only introduced the idea that his buildings would portray his clients, but he suggested that his works would do so at the uppermost level of artistic achievement.[5] In doing so he was offering the client an opportunity to be associated with a timeless work of art. Such a notion might verge on the preposterous if it were not for the comprehensiveness and supreme self-confidence that Wright brought to his work. It is as though Wright were the personification of Emerson's "transparent eyeball,"[6] channeling the energies of the universe into his work.

In what ways, then, does the Martin complex constitute a portrait of Darwin D. Martin? It is already apparent that Martin's approach to the project was extremely cautious, both in terms of expenditure and artistic vision. The Barton House is a slightly modified version of the J. J. Walser House; the Martin House is an enlarged and elaborated version of Wright's "Home in a Prairie Town" | cf. *figs.* 7 AND 61, and *figs.* 48 AND 31. Both the "Home in a Prairie Town" and the Martin House plans are cross-axial and have identically placed fireplaces, dining rooms, living rooms, libraries, reception halls, porches, porte cocheres, and principal entries. Their facades are strikingly similar, despite the larger size, richer materials, and greater skeletality of the Martin House. Wright was far more daring and original on behalf of his other major prairie clients—Susan Dana, Frederick C. Robie, and the Coonleys. The Dana House of 1902 contains three monumental spaces: a two-story entrance hall | *fig.* 89 and barrel-vaulted dining and music rooms, each with small, elevated balconies for musicians and for other entertainment purposes. For the Coonley House of 1908, Wright elevated the main living spaces a full story above grade along the south face of an elaborate U-shaped plan | *fig.* 90, with a special corridor that allowed Mrs. Coonley to see her Christian Science clients without interrupting the private life of the family within the house. The Coonley living room | *fig.* 91 is Wright's most masterful synthesis of structure, space, and decoration, about which he wrote "[It was] the best I could then do in the way of a house."[7] For the Robie House of 1909, the budget and lot of which were considerably more limited than those of Dana, the Martins, and the Coonleys, Wright created a tour de force of hovering planes | *fig.* 92 in a design that so transcended conventional notions of domestic architecture as to resemble a magical brick ship moored alongside East Fifty-eighth Street in Chicago.

Darwin Martin's choices of modified versions of the Walser and "Home in a Prairie Town" plans placed certain constraints upon Wright's creativity with regard to structure and space.[8] Unlike the other major prairie houses, the main floor of the Martin House lies close to the ground and its plan is tightly disciplined by a multiple overlay of grids: that of the 3/4-inch floor tile (which runs throughout the house and onto the porches); the 4-foot-square grid that Wright published in the *Architectural Record* of January 1928[9] | *fig.* 93; the tartan grid | *fig.* 94 formed by the interlacing of living spaces with pier clusters, as revealed by Richard

| *fig.* 89
Frank Lloyd Wright,
Susan Dana House,
Springfield, Illinois,
1902. Entrance hall

| *fig.* 90
Frank Lloyd Wright,
Avery Coonley House,
Riverside, Illinois, 1908.
Main floor plan

| *fig.* 89

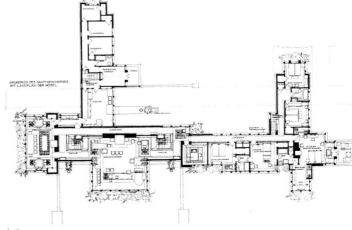

| *fig.* 90

|*fig.* 91

Avery Coonley House,
living room

| fig. 92

Frank Lloyd Wright,
Frederick Robie House,
Chicago, 1908–09.
Elevation

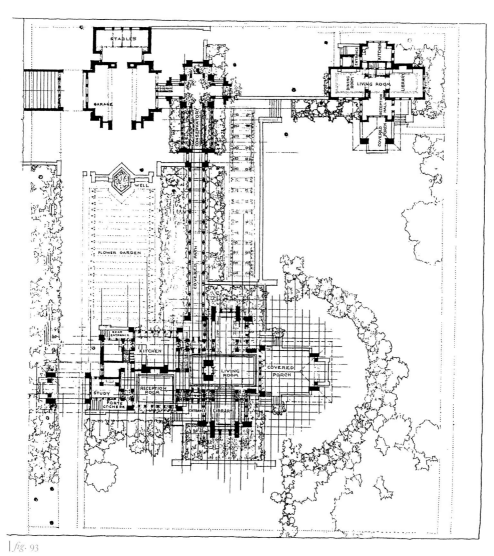

| *fig.* 93

| *fig.* 93
Darwin D. Martin
House. Plan with 4' grid,
Architectural Record,
January 1928

| *fig.* 94
Darwin D. Martin
House. Plan with tartan
grid superimposed

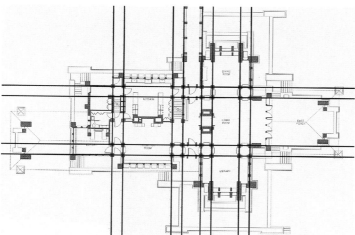

| *fig.* 94

176

fig. 95

Darwin D. Martin House,
view from entrance hall
through pergola toward
conservatory

C. MacCormac[10]; and the metagrid of the earth's longitude and latitude to which the cross-axial Martin plan, and most of the prairie houses, so comfortably conform. Surely the meticulous Martin was at home in the hyperordered, ledgerlike organization of the plan of his house. Owing to the deep horizontal raking of the Roman brick joints and the proliferation of other horizontals (flared tops of tables and stanchions, moldings above and below windows, the caming of the wisteria patterned windows), the interior of the Martin House reads as a stratification of horizontal grids, as opposed to vertical grids, such as those employed by Josef Hoffmann and other architects.

The interior of the Martin House is intimate rather than grandiose. Its principal spatial drama unfolds horizontally in the arresting entrance view down the length of the pergola | *figs. 95, 96* and in long axial views through the unit room and the reception room eastward through the living room and onto the east porch, with only modest vertical counterpoints in the form of subtly shifted ceiling heights and the (would-be) sky-lit stairway in the entrance hall. The house is scaled to Darwin's and Isabelle's (and Wright's) diminutive heights,[11] and its lack of grandiose spaces suggests a preference on their part for an intimate, homey environment rather than a lavish or showy one. The Martins rarely gave parties and, as teetotalers, preferred to entertain small numbers of friends or relatives over dinner.[12] It is impossible to imagine Darwin Martin living in the Dana House, for instance, the voluminous rooms of which would be alien to his ideal of home.

Within its conservative conceptual framework, however, the Martin House is distinguished by an intensity of structural elaboration, densely woven spaces, and detailing that has no parallel in Wright's other prairie houses.[13] In a sequence of changes from the initial plan sketch of May 1903 to the as-built plan of August 1905, Wright gradually eliminated walls from the Martin House in favor of pure pier construction: there are no conventional walls on the first floor of the house. In the process, he transformed the house into a diaphanous pavilion, nested under its capacious roofs in a landscape of shielding shrubs and trees | see *fig. 97*. Wright never again made a house quite this skeletal. The Robie House appears to be so, but the floating planes of its extraordinary southwest elevation are made possible by a rear elevation that is a solid brick wall; hence the drama at Robie is concentrated on the front elevation at the expense of the rear.[14]

| *fig. 96*
Darwin D. Martin House, view halfway along pergola toward conservatory

overleaf
| *fig. 97*
Elevated view of Darwin D. Martin Complex

fig. 97

In addition to its plan fragmentation, the Martin House is detailed with a delicacy bordering on fussiness that appears to be a manifestation of Darwin's nervous intensity, his passion for detail, his exacting nature, and his love of numbers—Wright's response to a man who would write him, on occasion, as many as three letters a day. This intensity is evident in the detailing of the furniture and moldings | *fig.* 98, but it is especially obvious in the signature tree-of-life window, which, in its most frequently employed dimensions (51 inches by 25 5/8 inches) | see *fig.* 69, is comprised of 750 individual pieces of glass, two hundred more than were deployed in comparable windows in the Dana, Robie, and Coonley houses.[15] In short, the cumulative evidence of the fragmented plan, the thin Roman brick, the finely detailed moldings, and the art-glass windows points inevitably to Darwin D. Martin— "D.D.M.," to Wright—a man of details and data. With the detailing and furnishing of the house completed in 1905 and 1906, Wright had by this time had two years to become acquainted with Darwin Martin's character before undertaking this work.

The success that enabled Darwin Martin to build his home was a result of his passion for learning and his excessive devotion to work, both of which are manifested in the design of the Martin House. An avid reader in his childhood and throughout his adult life, Darwin eventually became a collector of rare books.[16] Isabelle shared Darwin's love of literature despite her eye affliction and was a charter member of the Highland Park Literary Club, which periodically met at the Martin House. Wright made the library, which projects forward toward Jewett Parkway | see *figs.* 54, 55, a prominent part of the Martin House. However, he did not limit the display of Martin's books to a traditionally masculine, wood-paneled, leather-chaired, cloistered library. Instead, he distributed Darwin's fine book collection throughout the house on shelves located within the pier clusters | see *fig.* 50 that frame and define the principal living spaces of the main floor.

Additional book shelving was provided in each of the second floor bedrooms.[17] Thus Darwin's books were thoroughly integrated into his life in the house and, metaphorically, with the very structure of the house, omnipresent and yet unobtrusive, a perfect environment for an avid bibliophile whom a colleague characterized as a student all his life.[18] The pier clusters proved insufficient in accommodating all of Martin's volumes: additional bookshelves were built into the stanchions of the living room sofa, a matched set of small books

| *fig.* 98
Darwin D. Martin House.
Interior oak trim detail

|*fig.* 99

Darwin D. Martin House.
View into east alcove of
living room

was placed atop the library table in the east alcove of the living room, and in the corner of that same space stood a 5-foot-tall, Wright-designed book cabinet glazed on two sides (and possibly four) | *fig.* 99. Wright also designed a freestanding bookshelf | *fig.* 100 with individual shelves for each volume of Darwin's prized eleventh edition of the *Encyclopaedia Britannica*. Dorothy Martin Foster maintained that her father often took a volume of the encyclopedia to read on the Belt Line Railroad on his way to work at the Larkin Company,[19] and Everett Martin (William's son) recalled that when his family visited Buffalo, his uncle Darwin often quizzed the children on various topics, and if they didn't have an answer he directed them to look it up in his encyclopedia.[20]

The Martin House also contains numerous accommodations for and expressions of Darwin's compulsive attitude toward work. It is one of the few among Wright's sixty prairie houses designed to include an office: the small bursar's office on the west end of the house, an inner sanctum where Darwin could focus his attention on his numerous financial dealings outside of the Larkin Company. The office was equipped with horizontally arranged rectangular windows placed high on the wall so as to minimize distractions. A specially placed entrance through the westernmost pier cluster, gained by a separate stairway, ensured that business associates and tradesmen could meet with Darwin without intruding on the private life of his family | *fig.* 101. In this room Wright inserted a three-sided desk between two structural piers, creating a cubicle effect. Through the skylight descended illumination that passed through the lower roof, down a 4-foot shaft, and through an art-glass panel.[21]

Numerous similarities between the Martin House and the Larkin Administration Building suggest that Wright consciously related the two designs in recognition of the importance of work and of the Larkin business in Darwin's life. Both buildings had conservatories | *figs.* 102, 104, both contained statues of Nike prominently displayed at their entrances | *figs.* 102, 103, both had light shafts | *figs.* 105, 106 and sun traps located alongside their principal entrances,[22] each employed a decorative motif based on a sprig of chevrons exfoliating from a square base | *fig.* 107; see *fig.* 69, and both facades employed colossal piers flanking smaller piers—a motif that, for all of its Wrightian familiarity, is not duplicated precisely in any other Wright design. These similarities connected Darwin's work and his home life.[23]

| *fig.* 100
Darwin D. Martin House. *Encyclopaedia Britannica* bookshelf

| *fig.* 101
Darwin D. Martin House, bursar's office. Detail of plan

| *fig.* 102
Darwin D. Martin House, conservatory. Replica of Nike of Samothrace

| *fig.* 100

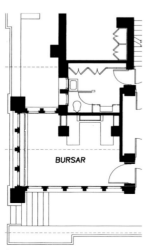

BURSAR

| *fig.* 101

| *fig.* 102

| *fig.* 103

| *fig.* 103

Larkin Administration
Building, Annex.
Drawing of Nike above
reception desk

| *fig.* 104
Frank Lloyd Wright,
Larkin Administration
Building, Buffalo,
New York, 1903–06.
Conservatory, on the
sixth floor

| *fig.* 104

| fig. 105

| fig. 106

| fig. 107

| fig. 105
Darwin D. Martin House.
Light shaft in entrance
hall

| fig. 106
Larkin Administration
Building. Light court

| fig. 107
Larkin Administration
Building. Pier-capital
model

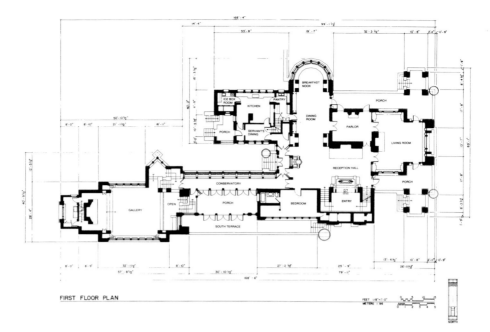

FIRST FLOOR PLAN

| fig. 108

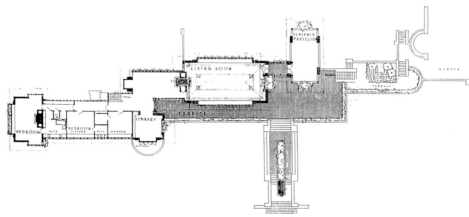

| fig. 108
Susan Dana House,
Springfield, Illinois,
1902–04. Plan

| fig. 109
Frank Lloyd Wright,
Francis Little House,
Wayzata, Minnesota,
1912. Plan

| fig. 109

Isabelle Martin is strikingly absent in all of these design features. Her children both complained that she had to beg Wright for a proper storage closet on the second floor. By 1910 the proliferation of books throughout the house meant much less to her, nearly blind, than to Darwin (who usually read to her). The interior of the house was distressingly dark to Mrs. Martin, the angles and edges of its furniture, even dangerous. In his zeal to capture Darwin Martin in the design, Wright failed to consider his client's wife.[24]

THE MEANING OF THE PLAN

The deepest personal concerns of Darwin Martin are most fully manifested in the plan of the Martin complex. According to Edgar Tafel, who joined Wright's Taliesin Fellowship in 1932, its first year, and remained for nine years,[25] the plan of the Martin House was Wright's personal favorite: he published it frequently (on five occasions during his lifetime), and he pinned it up over his drafting table and made frequent reference to it in discussions with his apprentices.[26] In comparison with Wright's other major prairie-house complexes—most notably those for the Dana | *fig.* 108, Coonley | see *fig.* 90, and Little houses | *fig.* 109 —the plan enjoys an incomparable formal elegance.

In fact, the plan of the Martin complex can only be fully understood and appreciated in light of the events and experiences that shaped Darwin Martin's life, especially the untimely death of his mother, his early separation from his father and his siblings, and his many lonely years in boardinghouses. These experiences apparently fueled an ambition to succeed in business and to acquire the wealth and power that would enable him to somehow transcend his painful past. The epicentral motif of this ambition was a home, one that would reunite the dispersed Martin family. Darwin's persistent efforts during the 1880s and 1890s—abundantly documented in his diaries—to establish a home with his father and to lure his siblings to Buffalo were repeatedly frustrated; but with his success in business in the 1890s and the fortuitous appearance of Frank Lloyd Wright in 1902, he was able to begin to formulate a plan to build a housing complex of such transcendent beauty and tranquility that it would draw his siblings to him, where together they could live out the rest of their lives in luxury and blissful reminiscence.

Very little documentation exists to tell us precisely what Darwin communicated to Wright regarding his personal history and his ambitions, but it is evident that the two men spent substantial amounts of time together (including a ten-hour train ride from Chicago to Buffalo and occasional overnight stays at each other's homes) and were close enough that Wright could write to Darwin, in his disarming way, that he loved him, and to another client that he regarded Darwin Martin as his "best friend."[27] Wright's plea to Darwin to expand his vision for the Martin House to make it "[a] real something to show for [your] years of hard work, and a translation of those hard, faithful years into a permanent record that will proclaim [you] to subsequent generations as a lover of the good! the true! the beautiful!"[28] is the best written documentation of Wright's intentions regarding Darwin's personal aspirations.

A metaphorical interpretation of the Martin plan would hold that the buildings are shiplike. Darwin and Wright employed the nautical term "midships" in discussing the house, just as Wright would subsequently use the German word *Dampfer* (steamship) to describe the Robie House.[29] Indeed, it may be that Wright's term "prairie house" has its origins in the term "prairie schooner," so often ascribed to the wagons of westward-moving pioneers. Understood as a vessel, the Martin House "steams" eastward, "driven" by Darwin's office at the west end of the main floor, its bow (the east porch) breasting a wave of flowers (the floricycle designed by Walter Burley Griffin, later redesigned as a semicircular pool) in the vast "sea" of lawn in the southeast quadrant of the lot.[30] The destination of Darwin's metaphorical vessel is the village of Clayville in central New York, the site of Darwin's fondest childhood memories and of his mother's grave. Delta's house is poised, tuglike, to assist, just as she had assisted Darwin through his most difficult early years in Buffalo, and as he had always envisioned her in his life.[31] Such an interpretation is rooted in Darwin's fierce sentimentality regarding his familial past and gains credence from the fact that, to complete the landscaping of the Martin House, Darwin had a tree uprooted in Bouckville, his birthplace 175 miles away, and transplanted on his lawn in Buffalo.[32]

The plan of the Martin complex is distinguished from those of the Dana, Coonley, and Little houses in that it was conceived as a family compound, rather than as a main house with elaborate dependencies, that would accommodate not only Darwin Martin and his family and the Bartons, but other Martin siblings who might be persuaded to move to Buffalo. The well-known Wasmuth version of the plan | see *fig. 46* should be understood, then, as a graphic representation of one man's hopes and ambitions, suspended between the moment (the houses for Darwin and Delta) and the future, with the potential for further development in the form of additional houses for Darwin's other siblings, Frank, Alta, and William.

Evidence that Wright was aware of Darwin's desire to reassemble his siblings around him has come to light in the form of an undated drawing | *fig.* 110, held in the Archives of the Frank Lloyd Wright Foundation, for an additional Martin House for the site just north of the Barton House on Summit Avenue. The drawing is not signed by Wright and there is no reference to it in the Martin-Wright correspondence,[33] but the building on its left (south) bears a strong resemblance to the Barton House, the roof of its single-story kitchen wing here adjusted upward a full story to elevate it above the connector wall leading to the new house to the right (north). (A similar wall connected the conservatory to the Barton House.) Grant Manson, who examined Wright's drawings several times in Wright's presence in preparation for his book *Frank Lloyd Wright to 1910*, inscribed "Barton House 1903" on this drawing under the left-hand image and "Additional house on Summit Ave. for Martin? c1905 (G.C.M.) [Manson's initials]" under the proposed new building to the right.

This drawing suggests that the Martin plan as we know it was a partial scheme awaiting further development, a truly organic possibility.[34] Such an interpretation brings the conservatory, with its life-sized replica of the Nike of Samothrace | see *fig.* 102, more fully into play. Wright used miniature versions of the Nike in several of his prairie-period buildings, including the Dana House, but here, at its full 9-foot 3-inch height, bathed in the bright natural light of the conservatory, and standing as the centerpiece of a compound of Martin houses, it becomes a discreet reference to Darwin's mother—a winged, headless, and idealized representation of the mother he hardly knew, as well as a perfect centerpiece around which the Martin family could gather.

The Nike vista also carried a powerful personal message for Darwin Martin, one that is key to the experience of the Martin House. Upon passing through the principal entrance to the house, one's vision was immediately drawn to the distant Nike, the ancient Greek personification of Victory, brilliantly realized by its anonymous sculptor as a synthesis of human and animal forms caught at the moment of alighting on the prow of a ship at sea. By placing Nike at the vanishing point of the long pergola, Wright transformed into

| *fig.* 110
Barton House and "Additional House for Martin?" Elevation drawing with annotations by Grant C. Manson

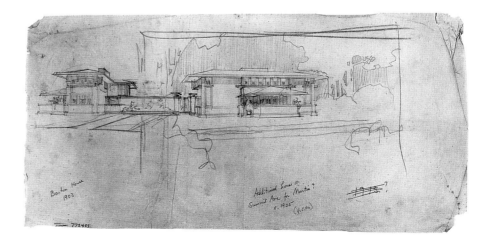

architectural and sculptural terms a narrative of Darwin Martin's life—the long and difficult journey fraught with loneliness and adversity that culminated in wealth, prestige, a splendid home, and a stable family.

Was Nike intended as Mother or as Victory? It is very likely that Wright intended it to be both; forever oscillating between the two themes it would remain fresh and engaging to Darwin. For anyone else entering the front door of the Martin House, the Nike was an arresting visual experience, beckoning and yet distant, too far beyond the immediate living spaces of the house to be a realistic goal. Hence the imagination was engaged and drawn forward—set in motion—while the conscious mind sought more practical paths of movement. The Nike vista establishes the Martin House as a place of axes and movement, where spaces made palpable stream past other spaces in a rush to connect with the world beyond. How appropriate to Darwin Martin, who couldn't stop working and learning, and how different from the serenity of the Coonley House interior.

Since no body of documentation on a Wright prairie house has come to light that is comparable to the breadth and depth of the Darwin D. Martin papers, the task of testing Wright's portrait claim with respect to other prairie clients is problematic. Nevertheless, the differences among the prairie houses—once one begins to look for them—are pronounced, and in several cases there is sufficient client information available for informed conjecture. The Susan Dana House in Springfield, Illinois, and the Coonley House in Riverside, Illinois, each represent a case in point.

THE SUSAN DANA HOUSE

Susan Lawrence Dana could hardly have been more unlike Darwin Martin. In addition to the difference of gender, she was at the time of her involvement with Wright recently widowed, she had neither siblings nor children of her own, and her considerable wealth (said to amount to $3 million) was entirely inherited from her father. There is only one letter known to exist between Wright and Dana,[35] but Susan Dana was sufficiently prominent in Springfield society that many of the major events of her life, and some personal insights, are recorded in newspapers and local histories.[36] These sources indicate that Susan married Edwin Dana in 1883; that they lived in Minneapolis for about a decade, during which time they had two children who died at birth; and that they returned to Springfield in the early 1890s, where they lived with Susan's parents in the family's imposing italianate mansion on Aristocracy Hill. In an essay entitled "Susan Dana, Feminist," Richard C. Taylor writes that Dana helped to create the Springfield Woman's Club in 1894, chaired its Art Department and its Home and Domestic Department in consecutive years, and gave occasional lectures on domestic issues.[37] In short, Susan Dana seems to have lived a fairly conventional life as a wealthy woman of the late nineteenth century in midwestern America.

All of this changed with the sudden death of Susan's husband in a mining accident in 1900 and with the passing away of her father, Rheuna Lawrence, to whom she is said to have been very close (even to a point of significant physical resemblance), a few months later. Susan's immediate reaction to this double tragedy is not recorded, but her actions are telling. She immediately proceeded to have her father's will removed from probate so that she, with her mother's consent, could administrate the estate, including the $3 million that he had put in trust.[38] She then hired Frank Lloyd Wright to build a lavish new house on the site of the traditional family home.

Dana's Wright-designed house was built at a point of transition in her life from a conventional role as wife and daughter of men of wealth and power to sudden independence. It is not possible to fathom her motives precisely, but in view of her status as a single woman and the enormous size and splendor of the house, it is apparent that she wanted to assert her independent self in a grand manner in Springfield society. The house was designed to accommodate large groups of people in voluminous spaces and to impress them with its scale and its lavish display of sculpture, furniture, murals, and art glass.

Dana's aspirations were tempered, however, by a strong vein of sentimentality. At the outset of the commission she asked Wright to preserve something of the original Lawrence homestead |*fig.* 111 within the new building.[39] Drawings for the project suggest that Wright nibbled away at the heirloom house until all that remained was a small sitting room with its original Victorian fireplace |*fig.* 112, which he deftly tucked away among the tall chimney mass and soaring spaces of the dining room, entrance hall, and Dana's officelike living room. It is not certain how Wright managed to persuade Susan Dana to allow him to reduce the original house to the extent that he did, but based on the evidence of his interactions with

|*fig.* 111
Original Lawrence House, Springfield, Illinois, 1901

|*fig.* 112
Frank Lloyd Wright, Susan Dana House, Springfield, Illinois, 1901–02. Room from old Lawrence House placed within new structure,

|*fig.* 111

|*fig.* 112

Darwin Martin and the importance he attached to his portrait claim, it is likely that he convinced her that he would embody her deepest concerns—her grief for her deceased father and husband, her wish to memorialize the older family house, and her desire to assert herself as a person of social and intellectual significance in Springfield society—in the new house. To achieve this Wright appropriated the butterfly motif from the original Lawrence House fireplace | *fig.* 113 and made it a thematic emblem of the entire commission. In his hands the butterfly, well known as a symbol of metamorphosis, appears in varying degrees of specificity throughout the house, in art-glass windows | *fig.* 114, in chandeliers | *fig.* 115, and even in the upturned gable ends of the eaves. The old house was metamorphosed into the new, just as Dana herself was undergoing a profound change in her relationship to Springfield society. Thus the butterfly simultaneously symbolizes both the client and her house, a notion that is summarized at the principal entrance in the form of a sculpted female figure | *fig.* 116. With this highly discreet representation of Susan Dana, sculptor Richard Bock pairs an abstract geometric stalactite closely resembling the patterns of art glass in a nearby door, and hence the house itself. The female figure and the abstraction emerge from a common pyramidal base suggesting a simultaneous metamorphosis of the house and its owner, as though they were one.

Susan Dana's aspirations seem, in a general way, to account for the lavish nature of her house, but two additional insights, subsequent to the design and construction of the house, warrant further consideration. Sometime during 1902 or 1903, Dana began to embrace the occult, and in 1904 she began to write "spirit letters" to her father, her husband, and, later, her mother (who died in 1905). These letters reveal tremendous grief but also a yearning for an unspecified fulfillment. "Shall I enter public life?" she asked her father, "If so, how soon and on what subject shall I lecture?...What field will fill the great big craving of my heart[?]"[40] These letters and the Wright-designed house were the first steps in a new life that would later be characterized as "eccentric" and "unconventional" and that would include two more marriages, one in 1912 to a Danish singer who was twenty-four years her junior, and another, in 1915, to a family friend with whom she lived for only two years. Thereafter her life was focused on spiritualism, especially theosophy and New Thought, and in 1924 she established the Lawrence Metaphysical Center in her home.

| *fig.* 113
Susan Dana House.
Detail of butterfly motif
from fireplace mantel of
original Lawrence House

| *fig.* 6.25

In "Wright and Dana: Architect and Client," Mark Heyman writes, "I suspect that Dana's spiritualism would have repelled Wright."[41] He maintains that Wright was not entirely happy with the Dana House design, which he described in his 1910 Wasmuth portfolio as "a home designed to accommodate the art collection of its owner and for entertaining extensively, somewhat elaborately detailed."[42] Despite the great size and elaboration of the Dana House, Wright never again published the plans after 1910.[43] Heyman's comments, coupled with those of Edgar Tafel and others who believe that Wright worked better with male clients than with women,[44] suggest that there may have been a deeper, darker side to this architect–client relationship that accounts for the clamorous nature of the Dana House. But this is purely speculation. Heyman writes, "Susan Dana was more satisfied with the house than her architect was. In the almost Victorian character of some of its detailing, the house reflects Dana as well as Wright, although there is no evidence that [it] is not entirely Wright's design. The client was clearly not a 'guest of the architect' in this house."[45]

Darwin Martin and Susan Dana shared a sentimental view of their families' pasts and an attraction to religious spiritualism, but otherwise it is the differences in their personalities that are striking and that are manifested in their respective prairie houses. Among these differences there exists a curious reversal of traditional male-female roles. Whereas Martin sought domesticity, privacy, and intimacy for himself and his family, Dana apparently wanted stridency, public attention, and monumentality. As a result, the Martin House is refined and delicate in its detailing, and its exterior elevations convey a kind of serenity—qualities that have traditionally been ascribed to femininity. The Dana House, on the other hand, seems to burst the confines of its lot; there are touches of bombast in its arched entrance, of clamor in the crowding and upward thrust of its gables, and of gaudiness in its colors and windows—qualities that might be described as aggressive and hence masculine.[46] These differences suggest that in his quest for a portraitlike resemblance in his commissions Wright was not bound by convention. His buildings were not only innovative with structure, space, materials, and technology but with the very idea of what a house might represent.

| *fig.* 114
Susan Dana House.
Art-glass transom detail

| *fig.* 115
Susan Dana House.
Chandelier

| *fig.* 116
Susan Dana House.
Richard Bock with
Frank Lloyd Wright,
"Flower in the Crannied
Wall"

| *fig.* 114 | *fig.* 115 | *fig.* 116

The Avery Coonley House | *fig.* 117 ; see *figs.* 90, 91, is the largest and is generally regarded as the finest of all of Wright's prairie houses, based on Wright's comment to that effect.[47] Its plan is U-shaped, organized around a spacious courtyard, with its principal living spaces ranged along the bottom (southern) axis of the U, the kitchen and servant's wing reaching up on the left (west) side of the court, and the guest wing extending similarly on the right (east) side. Much of the grandeur of the Coonley House derives from the elevation of its principal living spaces a full story above grade. The tan stucco walls of its first floor give way on the second to bronze-colored tiles and art-glass windows that glow and scintillate from within the shadows of the overhanging eaves. All of the spaces on the principal living floor are given shaped, trim-articulated ceilings that derive from the various roof configurations of the house. Moreover, each of the major living spaces—dining room, living room, and master bedroom—takes the form of a discrete pavilion projected off the long, broken corridor that defines the east-west spine of the plan. The largest of these spaces, the living room, is further distinguished by a large reflecting pool below. As a result, the Coonley House projects an unprecedented combination of aloofness, unassailability, and serenity.

In his autobiography Wright attributed much of the success of the Coonley House to his clients:

> About this time Mr. and Mrs. Avery Coonley came to the Oak Park workshop to ask me to build a home for them at Riverside, Illinois.
>
> They had gone to see nearly everything they could learn that I had done before they came.
>
> The day they finally came into the Oak Park workshop Mrs. Coonley said they had come because it seemed to them they saw in my houses "the countenance of principle." This was to me a great and sincere compliment. So I put my best into the Coonley house. Looking back upon it, I feel now that the building was the best I could then do in the way of a house.[48]

fig. 117

Avery Coonley House,
Riverside, Illinois, 1908.
Garden elevation

Grant Manson, in a masterful discussion that makes the experience of the Coonley House almost palpable, twice alludes to the importance of the architect–client relationship in this commission. He begins, "The Coonley house is the product of that rare set of factors in architectural history, a liberal client, a great designer, and perfect trust between the two"[49] and he concludes,

> The word "harmonious" constantly comes to mind in connection with the Coonley house. It emerges first in the harmonious relation of client and architect and culminates in the perfectly harmonious relation of house to site—the poetic statement of innermost meaning of that entire segment of Wright's creativity for which the term Prairie House has come to stand.[50]

Leonard K. Eaton probed deeper into the lives of the Coonleys and found them typical of most of Wright's prairie clients in their political, religious, and educational progressivism and in their musicality, but exceptional in that they were both born to wealth and educated at elite schools—Queene Ferry Coonley, at Vassar, and Avery Coonley, at Harvard and MIT. Eaton described their style of life as aristocratic rather than middle class and noted that Queene Coonley's lead in seeking out Wright and commissioning the house from him was unique among the male-dominated prairie client couples.[51] About their house Eaton noted:

> The Coonleys' house presents one generally unnoticed paradox. Almost any visitor would assume that its large, superbly modulated spaces were intended for entertainments on a lavish scale. The fact of the matter is that the house was decidedly a family-centered structure. The Coonleys entertained very seldom, and then only for relatives and close friends. One is tempted to conclude that [Wright] intuitively sensed the pleasure which these particular clients would take in this kind of environment.[52]

Theodore Turak carried Eaton's work further in an interview with Elizabeth Coonley Faulkner (daughter of the clients) and her husband, from which it is evident that Mr. and Mrs. Coonley enjoyed a harmonious and complementary marital relationship.[53] Mrs. Faulkner emphasized the congeniality of the relationship between Wright and her parents, as well, and ventured that Wright's reputation for being "high-handed" with clients resulted from the clients' uncertainties, whereas her parents "knew what they wanted. They started out with a preconceived appreciation of him and they didn't mind speaking up. . . . I think if Mr. Wright's clients had stepped up and spoken as frankly, but as genially, as father did, there wouldn't have been so many incidents."[54]

Beyond biographical data and a sense that the Coonleys were pleasant, urbane people, neither Eaton nor Turak were able to offer much insight into the individual personalities of the two clients. Eaton maintains that Mrs. Coonley was Wright's client, but in the Turak interview Mrs. Faulkner suggests that while her mother took the lead and her father initially wanted a more traditional house, "once he embraced the idea, he and Mr. Wright had just as many spirited and amiable conversations as my mother and Mr. Wright. So in the end they were both his patrons."[55]

Turak attempted to elicit from Mrs. Faulkner some idea as to how Mrs. Coonley's and Wright's "intellectual convergence" influenced the character of the house itself:

> *Mrs. Faulkner:* Yes, Mr. Wright said that when she [Mrs. Coonley] came to him, she found in his work "the countenance of principle." This was part of her Christian Science in which the concept of God is a much more abstract idea than in conventional religions.

> *Turak:* How did this philosophy or view influence the house?

> *Mrs. Faulkner:* I don't know that I could really say. I think for one thing she had very definite ideas about the practical uses that she wanted to make of the house. She liked the Prairie architectural idea—she was willing to have it extended. There was no basement.

It was all aboveground. The only basement rooms or first-floor rooms were my play room and the root cellar—the heating and the storage. They wanted the second floor for family life—they did very informal entertaining.[56]

Mrs. Faulkner then described how the staircases and hallways of the south or main axis of the house were arranged so that members of the Christian Science faith could enter the house, visit Mrs. Coonley, a Christian Science practitioner, in her study, and depart without encountering one another.

Turak expanded on Mrs. Faulkner's remarks in his introduction. "In expressing Principle...Wright's houses symbolized the divine order of things. The Unitarian [Reverend William C.] Gannett sought in domestic architecture the moral values that Mrs. Coonley, the Christian Scientist, found in Wright's work. In developing infinite variations from absolute principles, Wright created a kind of temple to her ideals."[57]

Taken together, the findings of Manson, Eaton, and Turak contain the essence of the elusive subject portrayed by Wright in the Coonley House. The "undeniable grandeur" and "moneyed ease" described by Manson, the intimately scaled "family-centered structure" noted by Eaton, and Turak's "temple to [Mrs. Coonley's] ideals" to which Christian Science members were regularly admitted, can only have materialized with the full and harmonious cooperation of both clients—clients who shared a powerful commitment to the Christian Science faith.[58] Indeed, in the Coonley House Wright achieved that which Norris Kelly Smith deemed impossible when he denied that a house could portray a client because it "is not built for a single person but for a family group, the members of which will not possess the same traits of character and will themselves change with the passage of time."[59]

Frank Lloyd Wright's portrait concept was an expression of something fundamental and integral to his way of thinking about architecture. In speaking and writing of the individuality of every client, he was invoking the ideals of Emerson and Thoreau and the Lloyd Jones family traditions with which he had himself been raised and of which he was an outstanding example. Furthermore, there is abundant evidence in Wright's writings to indicate that he personalized and animated pure geometric forms and buildings in ways that suggest that he made no firm distinctions among the personal, the inanimate, and the abstract.[60] He made Sullivan's "As you are, so are your buildings; and, as are your buildings, so are you" an integral part of the process of creation. The success of any given commission, and thus the success of the portrait, was contingent upon many variables—financial resources, relationships between clients and between the client(s) and the architect, the client's preconceptions about the commission, etc.—but Wright seems to have responded best when the client offered something concrete to portray—a strong personality, a specific vision, or a theme. Susan Dana was remaking herself as Springfield's leading social hostess; the Coonleys expressed harmony and solidarity in their commitment to Christian Science and to each other; Darwin Martin was seeking to rectify a childhood of loss and deprivation. All three of these major clients were committed to new forms of spiritualism and all were founders of neighborhood schools, which in the cases of the Martins and the Coonleys were kindergartens. To Wright, whose architecture was an expression of principle, these were highly principled people.

The Dana, Coonley, and Martin houses were Wright's three large-scale, nearly unbudgeted, multiple-building prairie masterpieces. Other clients, with whom Wright enjoyed less intense relationships, fared less well. The Bartons, if they can be considered clients, were not portrayed at all. William E. Martin, whose relationship with Wright was tempestuous, whose own son described him as "high strung" in nature and "subject to occasional temperamental outbursts," received a house that Wright once characterized as "the worst house that [he] ever designed."[61] Walter V. Davidson, handicapped with a pronounced limp as a result of polio and possessed of a volatile temperament, was given a two-story design of the Isobel Roberts type, with five different floor levels for Davidson to manage.[62]

By introducing the specter of human psychology into his buildings, by seeking a meaningful thematic content based on the client, Wright separated his work from that of the leading European modernists whose machine-inspired abstractions made for greater demands on the clients to accommodate themselves to their buildings. But in doing this, Wright sometimes gave too much of himself, with the result that his involvement with the client became protracted, as was the case with Queene Ferry Coonley (who was persuaded to invest in Frank Lloyd Wright, Inc. many years after the completion of her house), and more to the point of this larger investigation, with Darwin Martin.

CONCLUSION

ON FEBRUARY 14, 1929, Darwin Martin wrote a letter to Frank Lloyd Wright, prompted in part by the death of George Barton the previous day:

> We do not know what Mrs. Barton's future plans will be. She is likely to go to Swarthmore Pa. and live with her daughter. Mrs. Martin has said, that with strangers in the Barton house she would willingly give up our house, as we could pay a handsome rent and save two-thirds of the present cost of maintaining the home. It would be a financial saving of current expenses if we gave it away.
>
> I have cudgeled my brain for a thought of how it could be used. Can you think of any public or quasi-public use that could be made of it, in its location?[1]

Wright responded:

> I don't know how serious you are concerning giving up your home,—probably a feeling of loss and depression controlling you at the moment. I can think of nothing worse for you and Mrs. Martin than to have that beautiful establishment cut out of your lives just for a handsome rent which you don't really need. It adds a great dignity and has more value to your lives subconsciously than you may imagine.
>
> Of course there are many public or semi-public uses that could be made of it in its location. I could suggest several but I won't.[2]

Twenty-three years had passed since the Martins first moved into their home on Jewett Parkway. During that time, significant changes had occurred in their lives and in the world around them. The Martin children, Dorothy and Darwin R., had married and no longer lived at home. Darwin had retired from the Larkin Company in 1925. Both he and Isabelle were beginning to experience health problems: Darwin suffered a mild stroke in 1928, and

Isabelle, her eyesight steadily deteriorating, had recently fallen and injured herself in the shadowy interior of the Martin House. George Barton's death must have been a vivid reminder of their own vulnerability. Nevertheless, in view of the extraordinary amount of time, financial resources, and emotional energy expended in the creation of the Martin House, Darwin's letter is stunning in its seeming indifference to Wright's work, and it raises questions concerning the differing intentions and expectations of Wright and Martin in the creation of the house.

The philistine overtones of Darwin's letter are consistent with his attitude toward the project from its earliest days: first, the struggle to save $500 in the construction of the Barton House, when the whole project would eventually exceed $173,000; then, his request for "a good plain middle-of-the-road design"3 for a Martin House table in 1911; later his request for a new wing for the Martin house that would be "as plain, humdrum, middle of the road stock architecture as you can,"4 and finally the commission in 1926 for Graycliff, the Martin summer house, for which Darwin requested that Wright "omit every fillet and non-working feature, reducing the job to the barest simplicity."5 These constraints suggest that Darwin was forever conflicted about the goals of Wright's art versus the cost of achieving them and that perhaps he never fully appreciated the depth and subtlety of Wright's creations. In fact, nowhere in their voluminous correspondence does Darwin offer more than a cursory appreciation of the Martin complex. If the play of sunlight filtered through art glass onto the walls or Wright's architectonic uses of color delighted him, he never wrote about it. What, then, did Darwin Martin want and how did Wright accommodate him?

Martin had strong motives for commissioning the Martin complex. The status it would bring, its modernity, the portrait element, its investment value, and a certain defiance of convention, all were important; but perhaps the strongest motive resided in the person of Frank Lloyd Wright. Darwin Martin's involvement with Wright was, in a significant way, its own reward. Darwin had driven himself from his earliest years to learn, to compete, and to succeed, often at a cost to his health. These drives seem to have been fueled by a life punctuated by depression-inducing events and circumstances, not only the untimely death of his mother and the dispersal of his siblings, but the physical and emotional remoteness of his father; the aloofness of John D. Larkin; the premature deaths of Dan Robins, George Korn,

Isabelle's father, Alexander Reidpath, and sister, Nettie Reidpath; the loss of Elbert Hubbard; and Darwin's frustrations with the Larkin Company.[6] Even Isabelle seems to have grown apart from him, as is evident in her departure from the master bedroom, her summers in distant resorts, her frequent lengthy illnesses, and her need for a live-in companion.

Coupled with this inner void, and perhaps as a result of it, Darwin was drawn toward such prominent personalities as Elbert Hubbard, Booker T. Washington, Andrew Carnegie, Theodore Roosevelt, and Julius Rosenwald. While each of these men had distinguished himself nationally, Frank Lloyd Wright would have stood out among them, even in the early 1900s, as a singular person, already widely regarded as a genius, actively engaged in redirecting the very nature of American life through architecture. Moreover, to Darwin, Wright was the embodiment of the artist, driven not by an inner emptiness or a need to accumulate wealth for its own sake but instead by a marvelous if mysterious will to create. Wright was fully aware of his unique abilities, and comported himself accordingly in his eccentric garb, lordly strut, handsome mien, and air of utter infallibility. Darwin Martin was an easy mark: Wright drew him in with a combination of innovative work and adroit psychological manipulation. Dorothy Martin Foster proclaimed that "that man mesmerized my father," adding on one occasion, "my father was a fool— spelled P-H-O-O-L—for that man."[7] But was he? Considering that Darwin experienced an intimate, thirty-two-year-long relationship with a man who has been characterized as "the greatest artist this country has ever produced"[8] and that his home will forever be identified with one of the iconic works of early modernism, it appears that Darwin Martin derived a great deal from his relationship with Frank Lloyd Wright.

While Darwin Martin's motives for commissioning the Martin House are readily apparent, the picture is entirely different from Wright's side of the client–architect equation; it is less about motives than about a vision or an enterprise so ambitious in scope that Lewis Mumford once wrote of a retrospective of Wright's work (at the Guggenheim Museum) that it "seemed the work not of a single individual over a limited period of time but almost of a whole culture, over a century-long span."[9] Wright's vision had its genesis in the Unitarian-Transcendentalist thought that permeated his family life during his formative years and remained with him throughout his career. From Unitarianism came Wright's understanding of the home and its owner as integral parts of the grand universal unity that lies at the heart of the Unitarian conception of God.

Transcendentalism, in combination with the Unitarian ideal, provided Wright with the impetus to create a home that would be something greater than the sum of its functions cloaked in a veneer of historicism. A transcendent home—a prairie house—must be conceived as part of a continuum comprised of the client, the structure, the space, the landscape, nature, and the universe. The essential, generative element in this ideal is the client. Wright's challenge in each commission was to fashion a living environment wherein the client would experience a personal continuity with the transcendent and the universal. In this effort, Wright was striving for an essentially spiritual environment.

Darwin Martin was doubly valuable to the realization of Wright's vision. Whereas the other major prairie-house clients—Susan Dana, Queene Ferry and Avery Coonley, and Frederick Robie—were born into wealth and privilege, Darwin Martin's life story had all the dimensions of an American epic. Furthermore, Darwin possessed the wealth, the persistence, and just enough infatuation with Wright to allow the architect the freedom to pursue his vision in ways that few clients ever would. The result, for all its formal rigor, is deeply personal—a testament to Wright's conviction that architecture at its highest level can achieve the condition of portraiture.

|*fig.* 118

Darwin D. Martin House,
from Summit Avenue

POSTSCRIPT

IN THE YEARS following the completion of the Martin House the interactions between Frank Lloyd Wright and Darwin Martin fell off precipitously.[1] The Martins settled into their house and lived rather quietly, occupying themselves with raising their children, occasionally entertaining guests for dinner, reading, working on behalf of the Christian Science church, and taking automobile excursions in western New York | *fig.* 119. They shunned social clubs but enjoyed entertaining prominent visitors to the city.[2] Isabelle was often ill and spent most of the summers at distant resorts. In 1912 she hired a live-in companion named Cora Herrick. The Martin children, Dorothy and Darwin, went to private schools in Buffalo and eventually attended Smith and Yale colleges, respectively. Darwin's net worth reached one million dollars in 1907 and continued to rise steadily in the years that followed, though his diaries and memoranda reflect a less frantic involvement with the Larkin Company on his part.

At the height of his creative powers between 1907 and 1909, Frank Lloyd Wright completed more than thirty-five commissions, among them the Robie and Coonley houses, Unity Temple, and the City National Bank Building and Hotel in Mason City, Iowa. He also obtained his first significant national recognition in the form of the copiously illustrated, sixty-four-page article in the *Architectural Record* of March 1908. These successes notwithstanding, Wright wrote to Darwin Martin in September of 1909, "I am leaving the office to its own devices [and] deserting my wife and children for one year, in search of spiritual adventure."[3]

Wright and Mamah Borthwick Cheney, the wife of an Oak Park client, traveled to Europe, where Wright had arranged to produce the large-format lithographic edition of his work for the Berlin publisher Ernst Wasmuth. The couple was discovered by a newspaper reporter, and a scandal followed in the American press.[4] Following a year of work on the portfolio, Wright returned to Chicago on October 8, 1910, and promptly called William E. Martin to request a ride home to Oak Park from the station. William was embarrassed but acceded. He reported back to Darwin in Buffalo, "He is as winning in his ways as ever, when he wants to be."[5]

Wright was immediately beset by seemingly insurmountable problems: he had to provide a home and financial support for himself, his wife, and six children; presumably he wished to provide similarly for Mrs. Cheney and possibly for her three children; and he owed his publisher approximately $10,000 before his lithographic portfolio could be delivered to him in America for distribution and sale.[6] Moreover, his architectural practice was moribund and was likely to remain so in the wake of the scandal surrounding him and Mrs. Cheney. Under these constraints Wright and Darwin Martin resumed their correspondence, Darwin assuming the role of friendly adviser.

Wright obtained a small number of commissions in 1911, including a large prairie house for Francis Little in Wayzata, Minnesota, and the six-building Ravine Bluffs development and the Sherman Booth House in Glencoe, Illinois. In 1912 he occupied himself with building Taliesin, a home for himself and Mrs. Cheney, in Spring Green, Wisconsin, financed in part by a loan from Darwin Martin. In 1913 Wright obtained the commission for Midway Gardens, a large-scale entertainment and dining complex in Chicago.[7] He also published *The Japanese Print: An Interpretation*, and traveled to Tokyo in pursuit of the commission for the Imperial Hotel.[8] Upon his return the architect resumed working feverishly on Midway Gardens, which was scheduled for completion on June 11, 1914. The Martins were not entirely forgotten, however.

THE MARTIN HOUSE REVISITED

Indications that Isabelle Martin was not happy with the Martin House began to surface not long after the Martins began their occupancy in November of 1905. In many of his letters to Wright during these years, Darwin couched his requests for alterations to the house in terms of Isabelle Martin's needs.[9] Her dissatisfaction was related, in part, to the chronic eye affliction that had troubled her since childhood.[10] Her requests for changes in the house often involved the enhancement of the interior lighting, but it is likely that Isabelle Martin's dissatisfaction with the house was exacerbated by other personal feelings as well.[11] In 1904, before the house was even completed, an article in the *Illustrated Buffalo Express* had emphasized the unorthodox nature of the house.[12] The Martin House was, after all, the result of Darwin's unbridled enthusiasm for Wright—the product of a pact between two men from which Isabelle was all but excluded. Moreover, she must have suffered considerable embarrassment as a result of her family's association with Wright, whose personal life had become so publicly scandalous. It is likely that she shared the sentiments of Winifred Martin, William's

| *fig.* 119

The Martin family,
behind the Martin
House, circa 1907

wife, who "refused to be seen with [Wright] in the auto" when the architect first returned to Oak Park from Europe in 1910.[13]

Isabelle Martin's dissatisfactions precipitated a series of proposals for alterations to the Martin House over the course of a decade. In the first, in 1909, Wright provided the Martins with plans and elevations | *fig.* 120 for a second floor balcony that would circumscribe the entire west end of the second floor of the house and would include heavy plate-glass deck panels that allowed additional light penetration into the first floor spaces below. Nothing came of this scheme, however.

In August 1913 Darwin notified Wright that "Mrs. Martin wants to move the windows of the south [reception] room to the south edge of the sill course eliminating the basement lights [sun traps] and lowering part of the radiator enclosure to form a seat all to get more light."[14] Again, nothing resulted.

A third scheme involving the east porch was developed in January 1914. Darwin wrote: "It won't do at all to expect to accomplish Mrs. Martin's objectives by sketches and correspondence. The veranda is not the only thing she wishes to discuss with you. She won't have a glass roof on the veranda. We must make a sun parlor and conservatory of it by subterranean means. So come at your earliest convenience."[15] Wright came to Buffalo in mid-February 1914 to discuss the completion of the hall skylight, the living room verandah, and alterations to the south wall of the reception room, but he again failed to follow through.

Darwin wrote in April 1914 urging Wright to complete the work while Mrs. Martin was away for the summer, but Wright failed to produce any drawings. His anger rising, Darwin wrote on July 2, 1914: "I must have the skylight details at once....[O]nly six weeks remain to do the work. Words fail me to express my resentment at the scurvy treatment you are according me."[16] On August 5, 1914, Darwin received blueprints for the change to the south wall of the reception room but nothing regarding the hall skylight and drawing.[17] Wright's office manager wrote to Darwin on August 6 to say that the skylight drawing was missing,[18] to which Darwin responded in a letter addressed to Wright, "I have no language at my command to express my disgust at the treatment Mr. Wright has accorded me."[19]

These were the circumstances of the Wright–Martin relationship when, on August 14, 1914, while Wright was working in Chicago on Midway Gardens, Mamah Borthwick Cheney,

fig. 120

Darwin D. Martin House.
Altered photograph
showing balcony
proposed for west end
of second floor

her three children, and several of the Taliesin employees were murdered by a deranged member of the household staff.[20] Wright was devastated. Just as his life seemed to be sorted out and on track, all was destroyed.

The multiple murder was reported on the front page of the *Buffalo Courier* on August 16, 1914, under the heading "WRIGHT IS PROSTRATED," with the subheading "Chicago Architect receives news by Long-Distance—Declines to Comment."[21] The reaction of the Martin family can only be imagined as no letters have surfaced between Isabelle, who spent that summer in Scituate, Massachusetts, and Darwin, who remained at home. Darwin traveled to Scituate ten days after the murder, closed up the vacation house, and returned with his family to Buffalo on September 5.[22] Shortly after their return home the Martins were visited overnight by Mrs. (Catherine) Wright and her two youngest children, Frances and Llewellyn, an indication of the Martins' close association with Wright's family.[23]

Wright did not resume his correspondence with Darwin Martin until two months after the murder, at which time he apologized for "abusing [Martin] shamefully." He added,

> You have been a good friend of mine and at bottom I have a sincere affection for you and a respect too that makes the consciousness of my neglect — (it is no more than neglect) — really painful to me. Of course you may imagine, I haven't cared much whether things went on or not for some months past. I have been hard hit — how hard only God alone knows, although that is no concern of yours as a creditor although it might be as a friend.[24]

Wright also included a request for financial assistance in his letter.[25]

In the year following the tragedy in Spring Green, Wright immersed himself in rebuilding Taliesin, obtained new work through Sherman Booth, and pursued the commission for the Imperial Hotel in Tokyo. Darwin, busier at work than he had been for many years due to the impact of the war in Europe, kept a distance. From April 1915 to April 1916, the only interaction between Wright and Martin concerned the disposition of Wright's Home and Studio in Oak Park. In 1915 Darwin reported to Catherine Wright that her husband was indebted to him for a total of $31,000.[26]

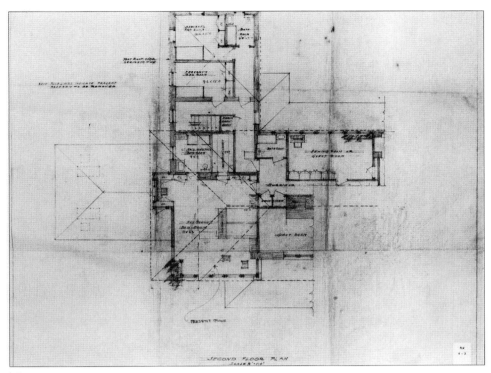

| *fig.* 121

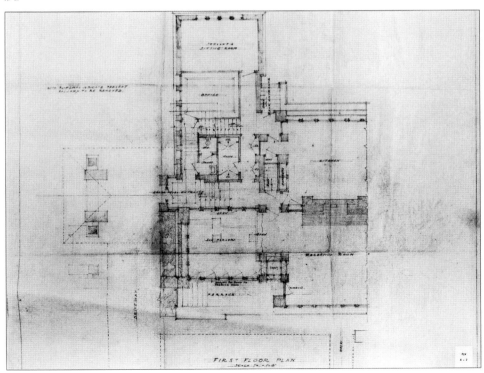

| *fig.* 122

| *fig.* 121
Darwin D. Martin House,
proposed west wing.
Second floor plan

| *fig.* 122
Darwin D. Martin House,
proposed west wing.
First floor plan

ALTERATIONS of RESIDENCE of D.D. MARTIN Esq BVFFALO N.Y ∞ FRANK LLOYD WRIGHT, ARCHITECT · TALIESIN ·

| *fig.* 123

Darwin D. Martin
House, proposed west
wing. Watercolor
elevation

Finally, in June 1916, Darwin proposed a major alteration to the Martin House, conceived by Isabelle Martin. The reworking of the design would involve the demolition of the west end of the house and the porte cochere to make way for the construction of a new two-story wing parallel to the unit room, which would contain a sun parlor ("a delightful light room"), a bedroom for Mrs. Martin, and some servants' quarters.[27]

Inexplicably, Wright provided a scheme on June 23, 1916, that entirely ignored the Martins' request and instead proposed converting the conservatory into a "Garden House," a place to have tea, play billiards, lounge, dance, or serve refreshments from a kitchen below.[28] Darwin rejected Wright's scheme out of hand and asked him again to design the new west wing.[29] Wright complied at the end of June with drawings for a new wing that would extend from the present location of the bursar's office northward and would contain the spaces required by Mrs. Martin | *figs.* 121, 122, 123.[30] Isabelle was in Lake Placid, New York, and unable to see the drawings, but she objected to Darwin's narrative description of the revised plan and wrote to Wright asking for a wing that would project southward as well as northward in close imitation of the cross-axial alignment of the unit room. Wright argued, "It is a serious error to make the additional wing balance the present one. The whole will become very stiff—formal like a hotel.[31] Then, on August 30, 1916, for reasons that are not clear, Darwin abruptly terminated the discussion of changes to the Martin house.[32]

Wright and Martin interacted very little between 1916 and 1925. Wright was in Japan for an average of seven months a year during much of that period, and when he returned he was occupied with commissions in Southern California, with financial problems, and with personal problems regarding his relationship to Miriam Noel—a companionship that began soon after the death of Mrs. Cheney in 1914. From June 28, 1917, until January of 1918, Darwin Martin took a leave from the Larkin Company in order to assist Julius Rosenwald, the president of Sears, Roebuck & Co., on the Committee on Supplies of the Council of National Defense in Washington, as part of the national war effort—a sign, perhaps, that Darwin's role in the Larkin Company was diminishing.

In 1920, in Wright's absence, the Martins hired Andrew Willatzen, a former draftsman in Wright's office, to make some of the changes that had been discussed with Wright in 1913 and 1916. Willatzen moved the south wall of the second floor of the Martin House 3 feet outward from its original position, thereby diminishing the extent of the eaves and moving the interior spaces of bedrooms Nos. 5 and 6 closer to natural light. Willatzen also added a trunk room to the northeast corner of the second story of the house by walling in the deep cantilever of the projecting eaves.

Darwin Martin continued to work on Wright's behalf during the Tokyo years, and on the architect's return to the United States in 1922, Darwin led the effort to keep the architect solvent and working by establishing Frank Lloyd Wright, Inc., and selling shares in Wright's future earnings.[33] Darwin commissioned a house for his daughter on the occasion of her marriage to James Foster in 1923, but Dorothy rejected it as "a pagoda"—a reference to its Japanese-inspired decoration—which she claimed to have torn up.[34]

In 1925 Darwin Martin retired from the Larkin Company, and in 1926 Isabelle Martin, no longer willing or able to travel to distant resorts and in anticipation of having grandchildren to entertain, commissioned Wright to design a summer house in Derby, New York, eighteen miles southwest of Buffalo on the shore of Lake Erie. Graycliff, as the house was known, was the only commission Wright was able to complete during 1927 and one of the few in the decade from 1925 to 1935. Other Martin-related commissions—a school for black children for Julius Rosenwald, a mausoleum for the Martins, a design for a gas station in Buffalo—were discussed between Martin and Wright but never realized.

The stock market crash of 1929 hit Darwin Martin very hard. Worth $2.5 million in 1929, he informed Wright that he did not have $6 to purchase a copy of the architect's autobiography.[35] Darwin suffered a series of strokes between 1928 and 1934, the last one rendering him withdrawn and without the ability to speak. Upon hearing of Darwin's fate, Wright wrote to a letter to Isabelle that uniquely expresses the nature of the relationship between these two men, as Wright understood it:

My dear Ms. Martin: I am terrified by what you say of dear D-D-M.

I feel as though a strong sane comradeship had ended for me and as though all might end like wise.

This must be the supreme trial of your strength and I wish Olgivanna and I might be of some help. You and he were always ready to help our rather hopeless ship to come to port. Be sure our deepest gratitude and love is yours and if we in our own helplessness have anything more helpful to give do not hesitate to ask it of us.

I should like to see him again—or should I try to see him?

It is good to know that he does not suffer—that all his burden of worry is gone—and that he still haunts the familiar scenes and is a physical presence still although his mind has gone away from him. Perhaps ahead of him, waiting for him!

Neither Olgivanna nor I could understand why we had no word from either of you but of course we understand, now.

In the retrospect I am sure only human values have any value—and on that intrinsic basis Darwin D. Martin and his wife and Frank Lloyd Wright and his Olgivanna have a blessed relationship to treasure and travel on.

I only wish I had been less taking and more Giving where he was concerned but character is fate and mine got me into heavy going—and no safe harbor yet in sight.

Olgivanna will write—meantime feel my sympathy—my love for you both.

Affectionately,

Frank Lloyd Wright

TALIESIN: SPRING GREEN WISCONSIN: DECEMBER 6th, 1935

My secretary referred to a plaster model; of a scheme for your cemetery lot in which D. D. was interested and which was sent on to him at his request. It is probably around here somewhere.

F. L. L.W.[36]

On December 17, 1935, Darwin was stricken by a massive stroke and died at home just as Isabelle returned from shopping.[37] She remained in the Martin House, accompanied by Cora Herrick, for two years, after which time she was unable to afford the taxes. She relocated to 800 West Ferry, a lavish neo-Gothic apartment building built by her son in 1929. The Barton House and the gardener's cottage were sold to new owners in the 1930s. The principal Martin House stood empty until the City of Buffalo took it over for back taxes in 1946. Architect Sebastian Tauriello purchased the main Martin House in 1954 and converted it into a three-unit apartment house with an office for his practice in the basement. In 1960 Tauriello sold the lot behind the house to a developer, who demolished the pergola, conservatory, garage/stable, and greenhouse, and constructed three two-story apartment buildings on the site. In 1966 the main house was purchased by the University at Buffalo Foundation as a residence for its in-coming president, Martin Meyerson, a distinguished city planner. Edgar Tafel, one of Wright's original Taliesin apprentices, was employed to convert the house back to single-residence status.[38] With Meyerson's departure in 1971, the Martin House was converted into offices for the University at Buffalo Foundation and the University Archives. When these functions were removed to new facilities on the Amherst Campus of the State University of New York at Buffalo, the future of the house became uncertain.

Preservation efforts were begun under the cochairmanship of Lorelei Z. Ketter, wife of Robert Ketter, Meyerson's successor as president of the University, and the author, but little progress was made owing to the constraints imposed by the educational mission of the State University system. This juggernaut was broken when, in 1991, under the enlightened leadership of university president William Greiner a unique three-way partnership was created between the State University of New York at Buffalo, the New York State Office of Parks, Recreation, and Historic Preservation, and the Martin House Restoration Corporation, a group of leading citizens who had come to believe that the Darwin D. Martin House is one of the city's greatest assets. At the present, $25 million have been raised toward the restoration of the house, the Barton House and the Gardener's Cottage have been acquired, the intrusive apartments have been purchased and demolished, and the restoration of the entire complex is well underway.

It now appears that the house that William E. Martin once predicted would be "the envy of every rich man in Buffalo…talked about all over the east" will soon regain its golden aura, and Nike will resume her vigil over Frank Lloyd Wright's sensitive portrait of Darwin D. Martin.

APPENDIX

Adam and Westlake
(location unknown)
lighting

Akron Roofing Tile Company
Akron, Ohio

American Monolith
Milwaukee, Wisc.
magnesite flooring

Ashtabula Manufacturing Company
Ashtabula, Ohio

Assembled Tile and Slab Company
Pittsburgh, Pa.

W. T. Ayers and Company
Chicago, Ill.
wood trim

Barrows Lock Company
Lockport, N.Y.

Becker Glass Company
Buffalo, N.Y.

(Mr.) Bown, Buffalo, N.Y.
masonry

Buffalo Cement Company
Buffalo, N.Y.

Buffalo Paragon Wall Plaster
Buffalo, N.Y.

Buffalo Sanitary Company
Buffalo, N.Y.

Buffalo Wire Works
Buffalo, N.Y.
vine trainer

Burrows Window Screens
Portland, Maine

P. P. Caproni Bros.
Boston, Mass.
Manufacturers of plaster casts

Carnegie Steel Company
Pittsburgh, Pa.
structural steel

Cockburn Brothers
Buffalo, N.Y.
cement walks

P. and F. Corbin
11–13–15 Murray Street
New York, N.Y.
hardware

Dohn, Fischer and Beyer
Buffalo, N.Y.
woodwork

Expanded Metal Floor Company
(location unknown)

(Mr.) Farmer
Buffalo, N.Y.
cement mixing

John Flacker and Beyer
(location unknown)
window and door screens

C. B. Foster
Chicago, Ill.
furnace and heating

Foster and Glidden
Oak Park, Ill.
bathroom fixtures

P. H. Frank
(location unknown)
masonry

Giannini and Hilgart
Chicago, Ill.
glass and mosaic art

Robert Gruber and Company
Buffalo, N.Y.
gutters

William Henrich's Sons
193 Spring Street
Buffalo, N.Y.
lumber, planing mill, interior finish

George H. Howard
Hoyt Street
Buffalo, N.Y.
slate and tile roofing

Introstile and Novelty Company
Marietta, Ohio
weather stripping

Jewett Refrigerator Company
Chandler Street
Buffalo, N.Y.

Jones Iron Works
Terrace Street
Buffalo, N.Y.

Robert A. Keasbey & Company
Pearl Street
Buffalo, N.Y.
heat and cold insulating material

J. B. King and Co.
Genesee Street
Buffalo, N.Y.
asbestos cement, plaster, marble dust manufacturing

Ira Lake
Buffalo, N.Y.
(recommended to Wright by Lang)
sculptor

(Mr.) Larsen
(location unknown)
cement

O. D. Levering
Columbus, Ohio
capital wall ties and nail grip

Limited Glazing Company
(location unknown)

Linden Glass Company
Chicago, Ill.
art glass

F. P. Little Electrical Company
Main Street
Buffalo, N.Y.

Lord and Burnham
Irvington-on-Hudson, N.Y.
horticultural architects and builders

Wilfred Lumley
Pittsburgh, Pa.
electrical fixtures

George W. Maltby
Buffalo, N.Y.
sculptor (finials or birdhouses)

Matthews Brothers (Crosby)
Milwaukee, Wisc.
furniture manufacturer

Mixer and Company
Buffalo, N.Y.
cartage

Mosaic Tile Company
Zanesville, Ohio

National Regulator Company
Chicago, Ill.
automatic temperature controls

W. G. Palmer
North Tonawanda, N.Y.
sashes, doors, blinds, moldings, flooring, shingles, and lumber

A. B. Penfield and Co.
Terrace Street
Buffalo, N.Y.
agents for Keasbey & Mattison Co.

Penn-American Plate Glass
Company
Pittsburgh, Pa.

Persian Rug Manufacturing Company
New York, N.Y.

Pfanschmidt and Quincy
Chicago, Ill.
window shades

Pierson-Sefton Company
Jersey City, N.J.
horticultural structures

Pittsburgh Air Tight Door Sill
Company
Pittsburgh, Pa.

Pittsburgh Reduction Company
Pittsburgh, Pa.
aluminum manufacturers

Queen City Wire Works
Buffalo, N.Y.

Robertson Electric Company
Main Street
Buffalo, N.Y.

Rupert Greenhouse & Co.
(location unknown)

Herbert I. Sackett
Pearl Street
Buffalo, N.Y.
electrical contractor

W. W. Savage
Buffalo, N.Y.
electrical wiring

Sherwood Manufacturing Company
Elmwood Avenue
Buffalo, N.Y.
engine and boiler supplies

Silver and Company
(location unknown)
kitchen furnishing goods manufacturer

Soss Invisible Hinges
150 Nassau Street
New York, N.Y.

Robert C. Spencer
Chicago, Ill.
window adjusters

Stearns and Sons
Warren Street
Syracuse, N.Y.
fireplace goods

Sterns Electric Equipment Company
Buffalo, N.Y.

Tuttle and Bailey Manufacturing
Company
Beekman Street
New York, N.Y.
bronze register plates

Wadsworth Harland and Company
Boston, Mass.
brick and cement coating for horse stalls

Walbridge and Company
Main Street
Buffalo, N.Y.

The Waterproofing Company
147 East 35th Street
New York, N.Y.

Winslow Brothers Company
West Harrison
Chicago, Ill.
iron work

DDM	Darwin D. Martin
DDM Autobiography	Darwin D. Martin's unfinished, unpublished autobiography, written in the early 1930s. Martin Family Papers, Archives of the University at Buffalo
DDM Daily Reminder	Martin Family Papers, Archives of the University at Buffalo
DDM Diaries	Personal diaries maintained by Darwin D. Martin between 1882 and 1892. Martin Family Papers, Archives of the University at Buffalo
DDM Index	A typed index of Darwin D. Martin's diaries and other autobiographical materials prepared by him in the early 1930s for the purpose of writing his autobiography. Martin Family Papers, Archives of the University at Buffalo
DDM Letterpress Book	Letterpress book containing nearly three hundred letters written by Darwin D. Martin to members of his family between May 1880 and June 1882. Martin Family Papers, Archives of the University at Buffalo
DDM *Memorandum*	Darwin D. Martin, *Memorandum of Events in the Life of Darwin D. and Isabelle R. Martin,* a notebook containing a chronology of Martin's life from 1865 to 1934. Martin Family Papers, Archives of the University at Buffalo
FLW	Frank Lloyd Wright
IRM	Isabelle R. Martin
JDL	John D. Larkin
SU-WMP	Wright-Martin Papers, Stanford University
UB-MCC	Martin Contractor Correspondence, Archives of the University at Buffalo
UB-MFP	Martin Family Papers, Archives of the University at Buffalo
UB-WMP	Wright-Martin Papers, Archives of the University at Buffalo
WBG	Walter Burley Griffin
WEM	William E. Martin

NOTES

1 *Illustrated Buffalo Express*, 9 October 1904, 6.

2 The numbers are approximate because, in some cases, Wright remodeled buildings or added a new structure such as a garage or a gatehouse. In addition to houses, he designed apartment buildings, boathouses, a bank, several religious buildings, a hotel, and clubhouses, among other things.

3 The plan of the Martin House that Wright originally created for the *Architectural Record* of March 1908 and subsequently had reworked for *Ausgeführte Bauten und Entwürfe von Frank Lloyd Wright* in 1910 is perhaps the most frequently published of his plans. It appears in *Frank Lloyd Wright: Ausgeführte Bauten* (Berlin: Ernst Wasmuth, 1911); H. de Fries, *Frank Lloyd Wright: Aus dem Lebenswerk eines Architekten* (Berlin:Verlag Ernst Pollak, 1926); Henry-Russell Hitchcock, *In the Nature of Materials* (New York: Duell, Sloan and Pearce, 1942); Frank Lloyd Wright, *A Testament* (New York: Horizon Press, 1957); Grant C. Manson, *Frank Lloyd Wright to 1910: The First Golden Age* (New York: Reinhold Publishing Corporation, 1958); Vincent Scully, Jr., *Frank Lloyd Wright* (New York: George Braziller, Inc., 1960); Peter Blake, *Frank Lloyd Wright: Architecture and Space* (Baltimore and Harmondsworth, Middlesex: Penguin Books, 1964); Edgar Kaufmann, Jr., *The Rise of an American Architecture* (New York: Praeger Publishers, 1970); Frederick Gutheim, ed., *In the Cause of Architecture: Frank Lloyd Wright* (New York: Architectural Record, 1975); Edgar Tafel, *Apprentice to Genius* (New York: McGraw-Hill Book Company, 1979); David P. Handlin, *The American Home: Architecture and Society, 1815–1915* (Boston: Little, Brown and Company, 1979); Leland M. Roth, *A Concise History of American Architecture* (New York: Harper and Row, 1979); Kenneth Frampton, *Modern Architecture: A Critical History* (London: Thames and Hudson, 1980); Marcus Whiffen and Fred Koeper, *American Architecture, 1607–1976* (Cambridge, Mass.: MIT Press, 1981); Frank Lloyd Wright, *The Early Work of Frank Lloyd Wright: The "Ausgeführte Bauten" of 1911* (New York: Dover Press, 1982); William Allin Storrer, *The Frank Lloyd Wright Companion* (Chicago: University of Chicago Press, 1983); H. Allen Brooks, *Writings on Wright* (Cambridge, Mass.: MIT Press, 1984); idem., *Frank Lloyd Wright and the Prairie School* (New York: George Braziller, Inc., 1984); Jean Castex, *Le Printemps de la Prairie House* (Liege and Brussells: Pierre Mardaga Editeur, 1985); Thomas Doremus, *Frank Lloyd Wright and Le Corbusier: The Great Dialogue* (New York: Van Nostrand Reinhold, 1985); Brendan Gill, *Many Masks: A Life of Frank Lloyd Wright* (New York: G.P. Putnam's Sons, 1987); Bruce Brooks Pfeiffer, ed., *Frank Lloyd Wright Monograph, 1902–1906* (Tokyo: A.D.A. Edita, 1987); Robert McCarter, ed., *Frank Lloyd Wright: A Primer on Architectural Principles* (New York: Princeton Architectural Press, 1991); Bruce Brooks Pfeiffer (text) and Yukio Futagawa (ed. and photographer), *Frank Lloyd Wright: Selected Houses* 1 (Tokyo: A.D.A. Edita, 1991); Terrance Riley and Peter Reed, eds., *Frank Lloyd Wright, Architect* (New York: Museum of Modern Art, 1994); Donald Hoffmann, *Understanding Frank Lloyd Wright's Architecture* (New York: Dover Press, 1995); Thomas A. Heinz, *The Vision of Frank Lloyd Wright* (Edison, N.J.: Chartwell Books, Inc., 2000); and Jean Lamarche, *The Familiar and the Unfamiliar in Twentieth Century Architecture* (Urbana and Chicago: The University of Illinois Press, 2003).

When Wright created the plan of the Martin complex for the *Architectural Record* in 1908, neither the Robie nor the Coonley houses were sufficiently completed for formal photographs to be taken.

4 These include the pioneering Wright scholars Henry-Russell Hitchcock, *In the Nature of Materials: The Buildings of Frank Lloyd Wright, 1887–1941* (New York: Duell, Sloan and Pearce 1942); Grant C. Manson, *Frank Lloyd Wright to 1910: The First Golden Age* (New York: Reinhold Publishing Corporation, 1958); and Vincent Scully, Jr., *Frank Lloyd Wright* (New York: George Braziller, 1960).

5 William J. R. Curtis, *Modern Architecture since 1900* (Upper Saddle River, N.J.: Prentice Hall Publishers, 1987), 93, figs. 7.2 and 7.3.

6 Grant C. Manson, *Frank Lloyd Wright to 1910: The First Golden Age* (New York: Reinhold Publishing Corporation, 1958).

7 FLW, "The Architect and the Machine," a talk presented to the University Guild in Evanston, Illinois, in 1894, published in Bruce Brooks Pfeiffer, *Frank Lloyd Wright, Collected Writings*, vol. 1, 1894–1930 (New York: Rizzoli, 1992), 23.

8 FLW, "Art, Architecture, and the Client," a talk presented to the University Guild in Evanston, Illinois, in 1896, published in Pfeiffer, *Frank Lloyd Wright*, vol. 1, 27–38. Wright wrote:

These homes in themselves will be biographies and poems instead of slanderers and poetry crushers, appealing to the center of the human soul through perceptive faculties as potent as those that made the book....The opportunity to characterize men and women in enduring building material for their betterment and the edification of their kind is really one of the world's fine opportunities. A great responsibility. An Architect has had a rare chance to read the souls of man and woman when he has finished building a home. What they are, what they hope to be, is all there in highlight to be easily read.

Wright first published the portrait idea in an essay entitled "Art and the Home," in *Arts for America* 7, nos. 9 and 10 (June 1898): 579–88:

Go, then, to an architect; state your case to him clearly and frankly, give him an understanding of your condition and an opportunity to know you as you live, to study you enough to characterize you rightly, then go away and let this trained artist who is an experienced planner and accomplished designer, and who respects himself and his ideal, work out your salvation in bricks, stone and mortar, which are technic to him, but nothing less than mortar, stone and bricks to you.

9   FLW, "A Philosophy of Fine Art," a talk presented to the Architectural League of the Art Institute of Chicago in 1900, published in Pfeiffer, *Frank Lloyd Wright*, vol. 1, 41.

10   FLW to Mr. and Mrs. Avery Coonley, 24 September 1906, Archives of the Frank Lloyd Wright Foundation.

11   FLW, "In the Cause of Architecture," *Architectural Record* 23, no. 3 (March 1908): 162. Wright published an additional reference to the portrait theme in his introduction to *Augeführte Bauten und Entwürfe von Frank Lloyd Wright* (Berlin: Ernst Wasmuth, 1910), but Sargent is omitted, perhaps because Wright believed he would have been less well known to a German-speaking audience.

12   DDM to JDL, 20 March 1903, UB-WMP. Just what Wright said to the Martins in regard to the house-as-portrait idea, how they understood it, and whether Wright continued to promote the idea beyond the prairie period are called into question in a letter from Isabelle Martin to Frank Lloyd Wright dated March 16, 1929 (UB-WMP) concerning the garage at Graycliff, the Martins' summer house designed by Wright with Mrs. Martin as client. Isabelle concludes her letter with the enigmatic postscript, "P.S. 1. Everyone in the family calls this "Mother's house" so you see that really you and I have got to do something to make it look like us—or rather like you!"

13   Wright pays ample tribute to his principal mentor, Louis Sullivan, in *An Autobiography* (New York: Longmans, Green and Company, 1932). Wright also acknowledges the importance of Ruskin in his autobiography and in his essay "The Art and Craft of the Machine," which he read publicly twice in 1901 and again in 1902 and published in the *Catalogue of the Fourteenth Annual Exhibition of the Chicago Architectural Club* in the spring of 1901.

14   John Ruskin, *Seven Lamps of Architecture* (New York: Farrar, Straus and Cudahy, 1961), 173. I am indebted to Donald Hoffmann, who called my attention to this and the following quotation from Sullivan.

15   Louis Sullivan, *Kindergarten Chats and Other Writings* (New York: George Wittenborn, Inc., 1968), 234.

16   According to Hilde Heynen in *Architecture and Modernity: A Critique* ([Cambridge, Mass: MIT Press, 1999], 73), Bahr's essay was entitled "Secession" and was published in Vienna in 1900.

17   Sigmund Freud, *The Interpretation of Dreams* (Leipzig and Vienna: Franz Deuticke, 1899–1900), *On Dreams* (Wiesbaden: J. F. Bergmann, 1901); *The Psychopathology of Everyday Life* (Berlin: Karger, 1901); and "Three Essays on the Theory of Sexuality," *Monatsschrift für Pschyiatrie und Neurologie* 18, nos. 4 and 5 (October and November 1905), 285–310 and 408–467.

18   Phrenology was founded by the Viennese physician Franz Joseph Gall (1758–1828), who believed that each faculty of the mind is located in a discrete organ in the brain that may be larger or smaller according to its individual power. Gall was convinced that he could determine an individual's character by measuring the various contours of the skull.

Orson Squire Fowler's phrenological report to Darwin Martin is dated January 16, 1886 and begins:

Your brain Sir, is large in size and extra good in quality and these conditions in conjunction render you a decidedly smart man and too smart for your own good for you are a little top heavy. Have more brain than body to support it, and must take extra care of your body or it will break down and break down your head with it. Are remarkably tough and can recuperate readily after exhaustion or disease; and if you will take advantage of this native hardihood you will be able to put forth an immense amount of life functionality without breaking down, but you must not dare to shingle over today's fatigue upon tomorrow, but must keep well rested up and slept out.

Phrenological Description of Darwin D. Martin, 1886, UB-MFP.

19 FLW, "In the Cause of Architecture," 155.

20 See Chapter One, n.20.

21 FLW, "In the Cause of Architecture," 87.

22 Hugh Downs interview with FLW, NBC TV, 1 December 1957, transcribed and published in Patrick Meehan, *The Master Architect: Conversations with Frank Lloyd Wright* (New York: John Wiley and Sons, 1984), 55.

23 Norris Kelly Smith, *Frank Lloyd Wright: A Study in Architectural Content* (Watkins Glen, N.Y.: American Life Foundation, 1979), 73–74.

24 Smith, *Frank Lloyd Wright*, 73–77, from a chapter subsection entitled "Portrait Painting." In his gossipy *Many Masks: A Life of Frank Lloyd Wright*, Brendan Gill reiterates Smith's sentiment when he writes, "[T]he Martins were the fortunate custodians of a work of art that had sprung from [Wright's] brain and was his in all but ownership" (150). This comment has no basis in fact.

25 Smith, *Frank Lloyd Wright*, 75.

26 The conditions under which the Bartons lived in their house are not known. In a letter to Wright on August 18, 1903 (UB-WMP), Darwin Martin writes, "The Bartons say they could not be happy in a house on which the rent would bear no comparison with a fair interest on the investment." In an interview conducted by archivist Shonnie Finnegan and Lorelei Z. Ketter on December 5, 1972, Dorothy Martin Foster, daughter of Darwin Martin, was asked what George Barton's position in the Larkin company was. She replied, "Very humble." Tape and transcript held in the Archives of the University at Buffalo. In a response to a letter of inquiry about the Bartons, Priscilla M. de Forest (daughter of Laura Barton) wrote, "And regarding 'their special interests, abilities or characteristics,' they were gentle, intelligent, good people, much loved by friends and family, and by those business associates of Mr. Barton, at the Larkin Co., who affectionately addressed a gift 'to Daddy Barton' on his retirement." Priscilla M. de Forest to author, November 9, 1980.

27 Smith, *Frank Lloyd Wright*, 75.

28 Ibid., 76.

29 Dorothy Martin Foster recalled, "Mr. Wright had built a chest of drawers about that square on each side of that room and they were drawers [?], they were for my father, there was very little for my mother and the result was that all this stuff was taken out of there. And eventually my mother went out because of grandfather's [?] snoring. But he had wonderful cupboard space, closet space, she had very little." Dorothy Martin Foster, interviewed by Sue Greenwood, November 1971, UB-MFP.

30 DDM to FLW, 19 August 1903, UB-WMP.

31 DDM to FLW, 20 August 1904, UB-WMP: "Mrs. Martin objects to the refrigerator location"; DDM to FLW, 15 January 1904, UB-WMP: "Barton suggested that the women should be consulted on the colors of the glass, but I ejaculated for you your 'Gott in Himmell.' The architect has the right of way on this."

32 DDM to FLW, 5 May and 11 May 1926, SU-WMP. Additional evidence of Isabelle Martin's position in the creation of the Martin House appears in Wright's *An Autobiography* (1943 ed.), 253: "Tell, especially of the lifelong interest and loyalty of Darwin D. Martin and the building of several houses for him—under fire from Mrs. Martin—who finally joined us."

33 Darwin Martin mentions the larger complex in a letter to Wright on March 26, 1903 (UB-WMP), just a week after the trip to Chicago during which Darwin selected the design of the J. J. Walser house for the Bartons: "Wouldn't it be a great scheme to heat two houses, a greenhouse, poultry house and barn from a boiler in the barn?"

1   DDM to WEM, 30 August 1902, UB-MFP.

2   On August 8, 1902, Darwin offered to lend William money toward a new home; on August 18, 1902, William outlined the places on the periphery of Chicago where he would like to live; and on August 30, 1902, Darwin agreed to come to Chicago to help William look for property.

There is a total of thirteen letters dating from 1899 to 1902 and exchanged between Darwin and William Martin in the Archives of the University at Buffalo.

3   See for example, DDM to WEM, 30 August 1902, UB-MFP.

4   Through his marriage to Mary Hubbard, William R. Heath, was also a brother-in-law of Mrs. John D. Larkin (née Frances Hubbard), hence John Larkin's willingness to add him to the staff of the Larkin Company in the late 1890s.

Heath's relationship to Andrews is substantiated in a letter written by William Martin to his brother [10 October 1910; UB-MFP] to describe the occasion of Wright's return to Oak Park from his sojourn in Europe with Mamah Borthwick Cheney: "I tried to drive streets home where I was least known. Mr. Heath's brother-in-law, Mr. Andrews, was walking down Washington Street Blvd as we went by, but I didn't toot my horn for him to look up. Perhaps he did not see us."

5   William R. Heath is quoted by Darwin Martin in a letter to William Martin dated August 30, 1902 (UB-MFP):

> Mr. Heath, perhaps, does not attach as much importance to geographical advan-
> tages as you do, and possibly therefore, is better contented with any neighborhood
> that has nice people. He says however, that he summered in Winnetka—the next
> station north of Wilmette and that is the first place on high ground.

This account of the Martin brothers' discovery of Frank Lloyd Wright's work differs substantially from that in Grant Manson's seminal work, *Frank Lloyd Wright to 1910: The First Golden Age* (New York: Reinhold Publishing Corporation, 1958). It is likely that Manson's account came directly from Wright, who was not in Oak Park the day the Martin brothers first arrived, some thirty-five years after the fact.

6   Hasbrouck Peterson Associates, "An Historic Structure Report: Condition Survey and Preliminary Restoration Plan, The Darwin D. Martin House, Buffalo, New York, Frank Lloyd Wright, Architect, 1904" (December 1990), 11. The authors have reproduced the page of Darwin Marin's own copy of the Chicago Architectural Club catalog of 1902 in which Frank Lloyd Wright published a revised version of the plan, elevation, and bird's-eye view of the "Home in a Prairie Town," previously published in the *Ladies' Home Journal* of February 1901. Three-sided bays have been added to the two ends of the unit room (the dining room to the north; the library to the south) in pencil, so as to extend the shorter axis of the plan considerably. A scenario in which this was done during the Martin brothers' initial meeting with Walter Burley Griffin at the Oak Park studio is plausible.

7   DDM to Elbert G. Hubbard, 19 September 1902, UB-MFP.

8   Ibid.

9   Elbert G. Hubbard to DDM, 20 September 1902, UB-MFP. Hubbard did not commission a building from Wright for the Roycroft campus. A Wright building would have been radically at odds with the medieval stone and half-timbered buildings of Hubbard's Roycroft. No architects's names have surfaced in connection with the construction of most of the Roycroft buildings. The Roycroft Inn, begun in 1905, represents a departure from the other buildings. It has a nearly flat roof, extruded pilasters, and recessed spandrel-like shingled walls that seem to echo the exterior flanks of Wright's Larkin Administration Building. The inn is attributed to James Cadzow, a local builder-architect.

10   WEM to DDM, 22 October 1902, UB-MFP. Wright was actually thirty-five at the time.

11   Ibid.

12   Ibid.

13   DDM to WEM, 29 October 1902, UB-MFP.

14   Ibid.

15   DDM *Memorandum.* Darwin describes the *Memorandum* as follows in his unpublished autobiography (UB-MFP):

A thankful Boston gentleman, by name J. Mathison, had prepared and offered to
the public at about that time his life diary. I bought one, the cover stamped in gilt,
'Memorandum of Events in the Life of Darwin D. and Isabelle R. Martin' with
spaces for seventy-five years. Mine dates from January 1865, therefore, at this writing, 1934, the pages ending December 1939, are awfully thin and I am constantly
reminded by them that though the little book exceeds the biblical three score and
ten, I must get along if I am to leave an adequate biography.

16   DDM to JDL, 20 March 1903, UB-WMP.

17   "I selected a plan of Wright's for a simple, inexpensive house which he can furnish blueprints of with no work on his part—only some modifications by his draughtsmen, which therefore, should be ready for me in a few weeks and which I will proceed at once to build, probably by day's work. In a few months, therefore, we will all be able to better judge the consistency and practicability of Wright's ideas in so far as a little house can exemplify them." Ibid.

In regard to Wright's first sketches for the Larkin Administration Building, Darwin Martin reported to John Larkin, "He said that he should have made a much larger sketch and brought it to us himself, and I think this is what he will immediately proceed to do. As he reiterated when he was here, he has not had tentative work to do and he didn't know how to do it." Ibid.

18   Biographical studies by Robert Twombly, Brendan Gill, and Meryle Secrest have each contributed new insights into Frank Lloyd Wright's complex life and personality, although none has been illuminating in regard to Wright's architecture. The best account of the early development of his architecture remains Manson's *Frank Lloyd Wright to 1910*, wherein Japanese art and architecture, the Froebel kindergarten experience, nature, music, Wright's engineering training, and his years with Adler & Sullivan are set forth as the principal influences on his artistic formation. Anthony Alofsin's *Frank Lloyd Wright: The Lost Years, 1910–1922* (Chicago: University of Chicago Press, 1993) considers the impact of Wright's sojourns in Europe in 1909 and 1911 on the Europeans and the impact of Europe upon Wright himself. The first full study of Wright's architecture in the context of his life and thought and in the broader context of the modern movement is Neil Levine's *The Architecture of Frank Lloyd Wright* (Princeton, N.J.: Princeton University Press, 1996). Robert McCarter's *Frank Lloyd Wright, Architect* (London: Phaidon Press, 1997) provides a spatial-structural analysis of more than one hundred Wright buildings, organized by type, and includes an exceptionally incisive discussion of the Martin House.

The biographical sketch and discussion of the prairie house that follow will adumbrate the nature of Wright's achievement up to the point at which the Martin brothers first encountered his work in the fall of 1902.

19   FLW, *An Autobiography* (New York: Duell, Sloan and Pearce, 1943), 10–11.

20   Wright's maternal uncle, Jenkin Lloyd Jones, was a leading Unitarian minister in the American Midwest, and Wright's father, originally a Baptist minister, became a Unitarian as well. The history and significance of the Lloyd Jones family's involvement in the Unitarian faith in their native Wales and subsequently in Chicago and Wisconsin is treated extensively in Meryle Secrest, *Frank Lloyd Wright: A Biography* (New York: Alfred A. Knopf, Inc., 1992), 3–77. Joseph M. Siry has written extensively about Wright's involvement in Unitarianism in *Unity Temple: Frank Lloyd Wright and Architecture for Liberal Religion* (Chicago: University of Chicago Press, 1996), chapter one and passim.

Wright's sister, Maginel Wright Barney, provides an insightful recollection of Ralph Waldo Emerson's role in the life of her family in *The Valley of the God-Almighty Joneses* [(Spring Green, Wisc.: Unity Chapel Publications, 1965), 59–60]:

Most impressive was the gleaming square piano at the end of the room. My brother always claimed it was a Steinway, but I know very well that it was an Emerson,
because I remember the awe and admiration I felt, believing a man of that name
could build pianos and write books, too—books that one's mother, father, aunts
and uncles were always quoting: 'As Mr. Emerson says....'

According to Raymond H. Geselbracht ("Transcendentalist Renaissance in the Arts: 1890–1920," *New England Quarterly* 48 [December 1975]: 463–86), there was a Transcendental renaissance in the arts in the United States during Wright's prairie period. Relevant evidence of that includes Darwin Martin's admonishing comment in a letter to Wright of October 28, 1910, among the Wright-Martin Papers, Archives of the

227

University at Buffalo, "Do not forget Emerson. He gave it to us straight"; Elbert Hubbard's publication of an edition of Emerson's *Nature* at the Roycroft Press in East Aurora in 1905; and the weekly meetings to read and discuss Emerson's writings at the home of William R. and Mary (Hubbard) Heath.

21   This account of Darwin Martin's life is derived from his unfinished, unpublished autobiography, written in the early 1930s; a letterpress book containing nearly three hundred letters written by Darwin Martin to members of his family between May 1880 and June 1882; diaries maintained by Darwin Martin between 1882 and 1892; a small notebook entitled *Memorandum of Events in the Life of Darwin D. and Isabelle R. Martin*; and some letters to Darwin from family members. All of these sources are held in the Martin Family Papers, Archives of the University at Buffalo.

The *Memorandum* is dated 1896, hence Darwin must have backdated the chronology of his life to 1865 from memory and from some of the sources listed above. The chronological accounts of events continue through 1934, when Darwin suffered a severe stroke.

22   DDM Autobiography, 17.

23   According to Darwin's autobiography, Hiram knew Ann Winyard in his youth in nearby Cazenovia, New York.

24   Darwin Martin's siblings were L. F. "Frank" Martin, born 1852; Alpheus Erwin "Alta" Martin, born 1855; and Delta Louise Martin, born 1859. William E. Martin was born in 1862.

25   Darwin later recalled, "Willie and I were rather frequent victims of the blues in those years and often cried ourselves to sleep." DDM Autobiography, 25. In a letter to his brother William of May 18, 1880 (UB-MFP), Darwin referred to his stepmother as "a dirty greasy bitch."

26   Darwin's unpublished autobiography is filled with accounts of his misadventures with rattlesnakes, swarms of mosquitoes, an angry turkey, sunstroke, and runaway sheep. DDM Autobiography, 20–40.

27   Ibid., 40.

28   Ibid., 4.

29   DDM to Frank Martin, 11 December 1882, Letterpress Book. "I wish I could live with you. Wouldn't that be nice? I am sick of hashmills. I have never been homesick until lately. I have been wishing awfully that we had a home here." Also, DDM Diaries, 11 November 1885. "I am so tired of bachelor's hall; it is a most wretched manner of living."

30   DDM Autobiography, 45–46.

31   This brief history of the Larkin Company was derived from J. D. Larkin, Jr., "Our Pioneers," *Ourselves* 13, no. 5 (May 1921); Mildred B. Schlei, "The Larkin Company: A History," unpublished master's thesis (University of Buffalo, 1932); DDM letter to Crate Larkin outlining the history of the Larkin Company, 3 November 1924, UB-MFP; and from numerous conversations with Daniel I. Larkin, grandson of John D. Larkin.

32   Beginning in 1881 Hubbard tried including premiums with soap (the first was a chromolithographic card). Next he solicited storekeepers directly by mail, and then he tried soliciting customers directly by mail. By 1885 the Larkin Company succeeded in eliminating middlemen entirely. In 1881 the first Creme Oatmeal soap, with bits of mildly abrasive oatmeal in each bar, was sold with immediate success. Creme Oatmeal soap was the product of two other Buffalo industries: meat processing and grain milling.

33   DDM to WEM, 7 January 1881, DDM Letterpress Book. "I said in my last [letter] that I was through with the nights but I take it all back. I haven't been off a night for nearly 2 months except holidays. I worked 1/2 day New Year's Day, none on Christmas."

34   DDM to Belle Baker, 23 March 1881, DDM Letterpress Book. "I tell you I am just at home in the soap business. I am a soap maker from the ground up. We have over 100 hands in the factory. And I am the head bookkeeper." Darwin was deeply ambivalent about his situation. Although he carried his responsibilities well, part of him yearned for the nurtured childhood that had eluded him after his mother's death. When a cousin addressed him as "Mr. Darwin Martin," he protested, "I don't want you to put 'Mr.' on my envelopes any more. I don't like to be called 'Mr.' and I don't like to have my envelopes addressed that way. I don't want to be a man at 15 because that would make me gray haired at 35. I had rather be called 'sonny' or 'Johnny.'" DDM to Belle Baker, 3 June 1881, DDM Letterpress Book.

35   For a fuller picture of John D. Larkin, see Daniel I. Larkin, *John D. Larkin: A Business Pioneer* (Amherst, N.Y.: Daniel I. Larkin, 1998).

36   Darwin wrote to his father, "About two weeks ago Mr. Hubbard (one of the firm) took me up town to the best hatter in the city and bought me a three dollar straw hat and made me a present of it! Don't you think they are v[ery] kind?" DDM to Hiram Martin, 8 June 1880, DDM Letterpress Book. To his sister, Delta, Darwin wrote, "Yes, Mr. Hubbard is as good looking as his picture. He is a 'boss' looking gentleman." DDM to Delta Martin, 24 June 1880, DDM Letterpress Book.

37   Darwin wrote at some length about his railroad housemates in a letter to Delta. DDM to Delta Martin, 7 March 1882, DDM Letterpress Book.

38   DDM Diaries, 19 August 1883. Even after Delta was married and visited Darwin in 1886, he wrote, "My darling sister, would that we might live together." DDM Diaries, 27 January 1886.

39   DDM Diaries, 21 October 1883.

40   DDM Diaries, 4 September 1883.

41   In a letter to Belle Baker of May 18, 1882 (DDM Letterpress Book), Darwin admits that he had himself measured with his boots on. It is unlikely that he ever grew much taller.

42   DDM Autobiography, 72.

43   Ibid.

44   Darwin wrote, "It does not seem possible that I shall never see him anymore…when I go up to our room I cannot control my feelings." DDM Diaries, 9 January 1883. It is typical of Darwin that fifty years later he would seek out Dan Robins's grave in Welland, Ontario. In 1888, Korn also met an untimely death, in Leadville.

45   DDM Diaries, 1881, 1882, 1883, 1884.

46   DDM Autobiography, 81.

47   Ibid., 82.

48   DDM Diaries, May, July, and August 1884.

49   DDM Diaries, November 1883.

50   DDM Diaries, 4, 16, and 18 January 1884.

51   Darwin wrote, "I really enjoy keeping 'bachelor's hall,' our den seems a great deal more like a home than the boarding house did." DDM Diaries, 27 January 1884.

52   Darwin Martin's visits to the Larkin's summer camp and to the Hubbard home in East Aurora are recorded in his diary entries for 1884 and 1885.

53   DDM Autobiography, 97. "I finished Monte Cristo and began 'Tour of the World in Eighty Days.' I was also reading such books as 'Orange Blossoms' and 'The Brain and the Bible,' poetry from Mr. Hubbard's library, 'Thanatopsis' and that sort of thing."

54   DDM Diaries, 14 October 1885.

55   DDM, *The First to Make a Card Ledger* (Buffalo, N.Y.: n.p., 1932), unpaginated, Collections of the Buffalo and Erie County Historical Society

56   DDM, *Card Ledger*, last page.

57   DDM Diaries, 10 February 1886.

58   For a good summary of the early history of the Larkin Company and Hubbard's marketing ideas, see Darwin Martin's letter to Crate Larkin, son of John Larkin, Jr., 3 November 1924, UB-MFP; see also Schlei, *The Larkin Company: A History*.

59   DDM, *Card Ledger*.

60   Isabelle's shyness contrasted with the behavior of the brazen factory girls about whom Darwin had this to say, "Most girls are such liars. Every girl in our office has told us the biggest lies about themselves or their folks so people would have a good opinion of them that I ever heard. I begin to lose faith in the general run of girls." DDM to Delta Martin, 23 February 1882, DDM Letterpress Book.

61   DDM Diaries, 13 June 1885. Darwin noted this sad event with words forged from his own experience, "Saw Bella [Isabelle] and Mrs. R[eidpath] at noon. They are very very lonely. I sympathize with them more deeply than I ever did with anyone else."

62   DDM Diaries, 22 June 1885.

63   According to a partial list of works drawn from architectural periodicals between 1881 and 1893, C. R. Percival designed thirty-seven houses, three churches, nine stores, a school, and several other structures. I am grateful to Martin Wachadlo for sharing his research with me.

64   DDM Diaries, 9 December 1887.

65 According to his diary entry of September 4, 1888, Darwin budgeted the house at $2,500. His total expenditure on the house of $3,580.92 is mentioned in diary entries for January 1889. (DDM Diaries).

66 DDM Diaries, 24 March 1889.

67 DDM Diaries, 31 December 1890. This comment was added to the diary in 1934 when Darwin was writing his autobiography. "In this 1 1/2 years of first married life I have omitted most of the detailed records I made of our maladjustments thereof, recorded when they were painful and seemed so important; but they are among things all passed and I hope they did not leave on our characters any adverse impress."

68 DDM Diaries, 2 August 1889.

69 Regarding his father's departure Darwin wrote, "Father removed remainder of his goods & left our roof and table today. Sorry, v. sorry to have him do so, but he seems v. happy & his face is aglow. Poor old man, Poor old Father." DDM Diaries, 18 September 1890.

70 See DDM Diaries, 24 September 1883, 29 August 1884, 14 January 1885, 1 March 1886, 18 February 1887, 4 June 1890, 15 January 1891, and 18 January 1892.

71 Frank Martin functioned as the principal salesman while Darwin (and Isabelle) assumed the tasks of writing and mailing hundreds of circulars, setting up a laboratory, and hiring assistants—all on weekends and evenings. Darwin earned an extra $1,400 in 1890 and 1891, but Isabelle became exasperated with him, and Elbert Hubbard again cautioned him about his responsibilities to the Larkin Company. Darwin wrote, "Frank isn't v.[ery] pleasant; so extremely nervous he communicates unrest to all. Belle doesn't like him." DDM Diaries, 5 October 1890.

72 DDM Autobiography, 185.

73 According to DDM *Memorandum*, Alta Martin died on August 5, 1910, at the age of fifty-five.

74 DDM Autobiography, 181. William complained to Darwin that George Barton lacked enterprise (DDM Diaries, 3 April 1888), and Delta complained that William was abusive to George (DDM Diaries, 15 March 1888).

75 The first mention of the stove-polish business occurs in a letter from Darwin Martin to his brother William on February 20, 1882 (UB-MFP).

76 DDM Diaries, 7 January 1888.

77 Winifred Kirby's father owned the building in which Hiram Martin operated his Mount Ayr, Iowa, cobbler shop in 1875–76, and above and behind which he, William, and Darwin lived. William worked in the Kirby store until he became a soap slinger in 1881.

78 DDM to WEM, Letterpress Book, 4 April 1881.

79 DDM Diaries, 2 August, 14 September, and 22 September 1886, and 6 August and 23 August 1887.

80 DDM Diaries, 23 August 1887.

81 DDM Autobiography, 175. According to correspondence between Donna Duncan Mann, a descendant of William E. Martin, and Jack Lesniak, author of the tour notes to the William E. Martin house for "Wright Plus 1995," George Barton tripped the mechanism that severed William's fingers. This would account for the transfer of George and Delta from Chicago to Buffalo.

82 DDM to IRM, 24 April 1894, UB-MFP.

83 The culminating idea, after the initial creation of the "Combination Box," was the "Larkin Club of Ten," an idea that the company attributed to an anonymous housewife in Pennsylvania, which involved a single customer soliciting nine other customers to each contribute $1 per month for ten months toward the purchase of ten combination boxes and ten premium certificates. Each month the ten customers would draw straws to see who got the premium certificate. In effect, customers began to function as Larkin sales personnel. The Larkin Company recognized the significance of this by honoring them with annual meetings at the home office in Buffalo and by recognition in the company's customer publication, *The Larkin Idea*. The company's motto became "Factory to Family: Save All Cost which Adds No Value."

84 Schlei, "The Larkin Company: A History," 1932, 12–13.

85 DDM Diaries, 20 December 1888.

86 DDM Diaries, 3 December 1892.

87 DDM Diaries, 7 July 1891.

88 Regarding Hubbard's affair with Alice Moore, see Charles F. Hamilton, *As Bees in Honey Drown: Elbert Hubbard and the Roycrofters* (Cranbury, N.J.: A. S. Barnes and Company, Inc., 1973).

89 DDM Diaries, 20 September 1892. Hubbard deceived his partner in saying this; he subsequently told Darwin that he would study writing at Harvard, and he did so.

90 DDM Diaries, 28 October 1892. "Mr. Larkin told me that Mr. Hubbard has agreed to sell him 13,000 shares of his stock at $2.00. On Oct. 5 I bought 2,000 shares new corp. stock at $4.00 though book value was but $2.00."

91 DDM Diaries, 7 January 1893. On January 9, 1893, Darwin wrote in his diary, "A sad, lonesome day, home with a heavy heart." The following day he wrote, "Mr. Larkin is such a trifler and is so inclined to fritter away with little details and to leave nothing to my authority he makes me heartsick." This is probably an unconscious expression of the loss of Hubbard from the office.

Hubbard eventually wrote and published a thinly veiled tribute to Darwin Martin entitled *The Boy from Missouri Valley* (East Aurora, N.Y.: Roycroft Press, 1904).

92 DDM Autobiography, 184. "When Mr. Hubbard left the corporation, in 1893, he held Mr. Larkin's notes for over $50,000 and was proportionately INTERESTED in our success."

93 DDM Autobiography, 74. "I am so very literal because unimaginative." For descriptions of the development of the Larkin business, see DDM to Crate Larkin, 3 November 1924, UB-MFP, and M. Schlei, "The Larkin Company: A History," 176. Schlei quotes Martin's comment, "I was always for sticking to a demonstrated success."

94 Office and especially filing space became a problem, however, and led to the commission for the Larkin Administration Building from Frank Lloyd Wright in 1903.

95 DDM to IRM, 7 May 1894, UB-MFP. "My little darling:...I was so blue yesterday (first moments I haven't been busy). I felt too awful to write my little wifey. Didn't do a thing....Darling I wouldn't want to live without you. I couldn't live alone again and unloved again as I used to." The following summer, Darwin's letters included a word coined from his boyhood experiences. "Am awful lonesick. House seems like a grave. Come home! to your poor old lonesome husband that loves you and tried to show it but some ways don't succeed always very good." DDM to IRM, 31 July 1895, UB-MFP.

96 According to notes taken by Daniel I. Larkin from Larkin Company minute books, William R. Heath's salary was $5,000 in 1899 and was raised to $7,500 in 1901. Harry Larkin, Jr., Collection, Buffalo and Erie County Historical Society.

97 Darwin Martin's autobiographical manuscript abruptly ends in 1898, very likely because Darwin sustained a stroke in the early 1930s that made it impossible for him to continue beyond that point.

98 DDM Autobiography, 184. "In 1894 my salary was $2,500, in 1895 $3,000, and in 1896 $4,000. On December 8, 1895 I asked by note to Mr. Larkin an increase of my salary to $5,000, which was Mr. Hubbard's and his own salary in 1892. In 1896 my salary was $5,000, and I think Mr. Larkin's $10,000."

99 DDM *Memorandum*, September 1899.

100 "Assets reached a million for first time." DDM *Memorandum*, December 1907. "Net assets $2,229,752.07." DDM *Memorandum*, December 1912.

101 William Martin agreed on November 23, 1903, to furnish the Larkin Company with liquid stove polish. DDM Daily Reminder.

102 WEM to DDM, 17 November 1900, UB-MFP. "Frank tells me that...Darwin Jr has been having a hard time making a go of it in this world and we are very sorry to hear it. Hope he is O.K. now & will grow healthy. Our boy is so big—fat—healthy—that I call him "mogul" puts me in mind of a freight engine." In this same letter, William comments on the quality of the printing of the Larkin company premium list. "I wonder that you can accept such work"—harsh criticism in view of the dependence of William's own business on the Larkin Company and his reliance upon Darwin for significant loans.

103 Ibid.

104 DDM to WEM, 8 August 1902, UB-MFP.

105 WEM to DDM, 18 August 1902, UB-MFP.

106 DDM to WEM, 22 and 25 August 1902, UB-MFP.

1   On the evolution of Wright's prairie house, see Grant C. Manson, *Frank Lloyd Wright to 1910: The First Golden Age* (New York, Reinhold Publishing Corporation, 1958).

2   These figures were derived from a chronologically arranged list of Wright's projects by assigned number compiled by Bruce Brooks Pfeiffer, in Anthony Alofsin, ed., *Frank Lloyd Wright: An Index to the Taliesin Correspondence* (New York, Garland Pub., 1988), vol. 1, *Chronological Index, 1885–1946*.

3   Additional incentive for the Larkin commission existed in the form of a prior commission. Wright had spent considerable time and effort between 1895 and 1902 designing the Abraham Lincoln Center, a multi-storied, multipurpose building for his uncle Jenkin Lloyd Jones. In 1902 it was apparent to Wright that this commission, which contained many ideas that would be further developed in the Larkin Administration Building, was slipping through his fingers. On the Abraham Lincoln Center, see Joseph Siry, "The Abraham Lincoln Center in Chicago," *Journal of the Society of Architectural Historians* 50 (September 1991): 235–65.

4   Dorothy Martin Foster commented to the author in 1975 that she thought her parents had been "mes-merized by that man."

5   Orson Squire Fowler, Phrenological Description of Darwin D. Martin, 1886, UB-MFP; and DDM Diary, 31 December 1886, UB-MFP, respectively.

6   Edgar Tafel captured something of Wright's attitude toward his associates in *Apprentice to Genius* (New York, McGraw-Hill Book Company, 1979), 210, in writing about George Cohen, a specialist in concrete construc-tion, who applied to Wright in person at the Plaza Hotel, New York, to build the Guggenheim Museum. "At 11:00 a.m. George rang Mr. Wright's doorbell. 'So you are the expert in concrete?' 'No, Mr. Wright, I have come to learn from you.' Mr. Wright said, 'You are my man.'"

7   Leonard K. Eaton, *Two Chicago Architects and Their Clients: Frank Lloyd Wright and Howard Van Doren Shaw* (Cambridge, Mass.: MIT Press, 1969), 254.

8   Arthur Heurtley was a banker; Nathan Moore a real estate lawyer; Frank Thomas a stock broker.

9   WEM to DDM, 22 October 1902, UB-MFP.

10   Darwin Martin's letter of March 20, 1903, to John D. Larkin (UB-WMP) indicates that Larkin initial-ly expressed an interest in having the Larkin Administration Building designed by Louis Sullivan, whose Guaranty Building of 1894 is a prominent feature of downtown Buffalo. In view of this preference it can be argued that John Larkin set in motion the forces that would lead to Wright's Buffalo work. See J. Quinan, *Frank Lloyd Wright's Larkin Building: Myth and Fact* (Cambridge, Mass.: The Architectural History Foundation/MIT Press, 1987), chapter one and Appendix C.

11   Beginning in 1892 the Larkin Company purchased large quantities of goods from manufacturers at reduced prices, a practice that enabled the company to "give away" these items as premiums. As manufac-turers realized that they were undercutting their own profits and began to resist bulk sales to the Larkin Company, the company began to develop its own subsidiary manufacturers. When the premium catalogue reached its maturity in the early 1900s, the offerings included, among other things, baby carriages, shot-guns, curtains, dresses, tableware, baseball gloves and bats, fishing tackle outfits, tents, and a variety of wooden and wicker furnishings. The more expensive items required the customer to collect multiple pre-mium certificates over time. As secretary of the Larkin Company, Darwin Martin supervised the Larkin buyers and was constantly involved in the acquisition of new premium items. For this reason he wrote about the Manufacturer's Building at the World's Columbian Exposition of 1893 in Chicago, "Saturday we put in the whole day in the Manufacturers building. We remember many, many features of that building. I doubt if the world has ever seen such a wonderful aggregation, and we were much impressed by the fine personnel in charge of the foreign exhibits. We have never ceased talking of what we saw there." DDM Autobiography, 172.

12   DDM to JDL, March 1903, UB-MFP. One wonders where Darwin obtained this means of describing the value of a Wright house—from Walter Burley Griffin, from one of Wright's Oak Park clients, or from his own imagination?

13   DDM Diaries, 4 September 1883.

Darwin Martin had a distinctly unconventional side. He was uncomfortable socially among his peers in Buffalo society: he did not drink or smoke, and he did not join clubs of any kind. He was drawn to phrenology, to Christian Science, and to African American causes. He enjoyed inviting interesting people to his home, including Theodore Roosevelt, the artist Henry Ossawa Tanner, and Booker T. Washington. His distinction from his peers would be manifested in his choice of Wright as his architect and in his decision to build not on fashionable Delaware Avenue but in a neighborhood on the eastern side of Delaware Park, where his house cost twenty times those of most of his neighbors.

14   Ibid.

15   DDM to FLW, 26 March 1903, UB-WMP.

16   Ibid.

17   Delta wrote Darwin an average of twenty letters per year in 1882, 1883, and 1884. DDM Diaries, 1882, 1883, 1884.

18   DDM to Hiram Martin, 13 December 1881, DDM Letterpress Book.

19   DDM to Hiram Martin, 12 April 1880, DDM Letterpress Book.

20   DDM to WEM, 21 July 1903, UB-MFP. William Martin would have had to travel about ten miles out from Chicago to Oak Park in order to keep abreast of the work on his house, whereas Darwin lived close by the site of his buildings on the corner of Jewett and Summit avenues in Buffalo.

21   DDM to FLW, 21 March 1903, UB-WMP.

22   DDM to FLW, 26 March 1903, UB-WMP.

23   FLW to DDM, 27 March 1903, UB-WMP.

24   Ibid.

25   Ibid.

26   Wright visited Buffalo twice in April 1903 to negotiate with Larkin Company executives over the Administration Building commission. It was probably during one of these visits that he obtained verbal permission to go ahead with the construction drawings for the Barton House and allayed whatever lingering concerns the Martins may have had.

27   FLW to DDM, 11 May 1903, UB-WMP. The rest of the letter pertains to the Larkin Administration Building. Wright's references to the Larkin Building in this letter are unusual in that Darwin, always concerned with the organization of data, asked Wright to keep the correspondences concerning the two buildings separate. While the Wright-Martin correspondence concerning the Martin House is more or less intact, according to Daniel I. Larkin, grandson of John Larkin, the Larkin correspondence was apparently kept in the library of the Administration Building, and following the demise of the Larkin Company during the Great Depression, it was moved to a garage in Ontario where a fire destroyed it.

28   DDM to FLW, 14 May 1903, UB-WMP. "All the lot side lines are parallel. Houses stand parallel to the side lines. The curves of the street are entirely ignored."

29   DDM to WEM, 21 July 1903, UB-WMP. According to this letter, John Larkin agreed to pay half of Wright's requested $2,000.

30   DDM to FLW, 4 August 1903, UB-WMP.

31   DDM to IRM, 14 August 1903, UB-WMP.

32   Ibid.

33   FLW to DDM, 17 August 1903, UB-WMP.

34   DDM to FLW, 19 August 1903, UB-WMP.

35   FLW to DDM, 22 August 1903, UB-WMP.

36   DDM to FLW, 25 August 1903, UB-WMP.

37   FLW to DDM, 28 August 1903, UB-WMP. Wright would omit the fireplace on the second story in subsequent drawings.

38   DDM to FLW, 2 September 1903, UB-WMP.

39   FLW to DDM, 27 October 1903, UB-WMP. According to Ted Lownie, the architect of the restoration of the Barton House, no beam was put in. The wide flat arch that forms the opening between the reception hall and the adjoining space is constructed of wood framing members, the largest of which is 3"x 6". This relatively light support carries a section of Roman brick wall, its coping, five windows, and some of the roof load. Until restoration, it sagged noticeably.

40   FLW to DDM, 5 November 1903, UB-WMP.

41   The centrifugal motif is more fully developed in the plan of the Ward Willits House, in Highland Park,

Illinois, also of 1901: the overall plan is cross-axial but the living room and dining room are juxtaposed at right angles—a synthesis of the two plan types.

42 It is characteristic of Wright's organicism that these prototypes are also archetypal prairie forms: the T-shaped and closely related cross-axial planes derive their axiality from the four cardinal directions sacred to Native Americans of the Plains and are fundamental to the basis of the grid that organizes the Midwestern prairie. The pinwheeling plan evokes the tornado, the counterforce of order on the prairie, the wind that activates it.

43 The Barton House living room is labeled as such on Wright's Martin Complex plan as it was published in the March 1908 *Architectural Record*. In the redrawn version published two years later, in *Ausgeführte Bauten und Entwürfe von Frank Lloyd Wright*, the entire unit space is labeled *Wohnzimmer* (living room) and the space previously identified as the living room is labeled *Bücherei* (library).

CHAPTER THREE

1 Wright showed respect for very few architects, but among the few Louis Sullivan, Wright's mentor, ranked the highest. Nevertheless, Wright wrote about Sullivan's "sentimentality" in *An Autobiography*, 2nd ed. (New York, 1943), 103–04:

> He had just written [the essay] "Inspiration." He read it to me. I thought it was a kind of baying at the moon. Again too sentimental....Whenever the Master would rely upon me for a detail I would mingle his sensuous efflorescence with some geometric design, because, I suppose, I could do nothing else so well. And, too, that way of working to me seemed to hold the surface, give needed contrast, be more architectural. Again—less sentimental. But I couldn't say this to him and I wasn't sure.

2 Ibid., 141–42. "In this sense I was working away at the wall as a wall and bringing it towards the function of a means of opening up space which, as control of building materials improved, would finally permit the free use of the whole space without affecting the soundness of the structure."

In an interview with William MacDonald on WTTW-Chicago Television in late October 1958, Wright had this to say about the box of conventional architecture. "The box was a containment. It contained within everything. Whereas the new idea was to eliminate the box and let everything that was in go outward and associate with its environment. So environment and interior and life itself became as one." Quoted in Patrick J. Meehan, ed., *The Master Architect: Conversations with Frank Lloyd Wright* (New York: John Wiley and Sons, 1984), 90.

3 Edgar Kaufmann, Jr., had this to say about the Ward Willits House in "Frank Lloyd Wright at the Metropolitan Museum of Art," *The Metropolitan Museum of Art Bulletin* (Fall 1982), 15. "However commodious and restful, the Willits house lacks the conciseness of its model ["A Small House with 'Lots of Room in It'"] and the walls and spaces are lax, but much about Wright's ideas can be learned from it." When queried by the author about this rare critical comment, Kaufmann replied, enigmatically, "Isn't it obvious?" Certainly, if any space in the Willits first-floor plan could be considered "lax" it would be the boxy living room.

4 DDM to FLW, 26 August 1904, UB-WMP.

5 DDM to FLW, 29 September 1904, UB-WMP. When Wright redrew the Martin House complex for the *Architectural Record* of March 1908, the gardener's cottage was not yet built. When he drew the complex again for the Wasmuth portfolio of 1910 he did not add it, probably because the additional building would have changed the entire nature of his plan from an L-shape to a T-shape, and the impact of the main Martin House would have been reduced.

6 FLW to DDM, 31 October 1904, UB-WMP. The commercially designed greenhouse survives only in a few photographs, and there is no evidence that Wright applied any design features to it.

7 DDM to FLW, 14 May 1903, UB-WMP.

8 DDM to FLW, 26 December 1903, UB-WMP.

9 The difference between the east and west gardens suggests the possibility of an entirely different drafting hand within Wright's Oak Park studio.

10 FLW to DDM, 2 January 1904, UB-WMP. Wright's design for William Martin's house in Oak Park was then under construction.

11   On the left side of the entrance hall to the Martin House, alongside the stairway to the second floor, Wright opened a slot of space into the basement protected by a low parapet. Together with the skylit shaft visible in | *fig. 105*, this constituted a vertical spatial axis connecting all three floors of the house.

12   DDM *Memorandum*, 8 and 11 May 1904.

13   DDM *Memorandum*, 16 May 1904.

14   WEM to DDM, 20 May 1904, UB-WMP. For another perspective on Wright's studio practices, one that includes additional insights into the production of the Martin House, see Nancy K. Morris, ed., "Letters, 1903–1906, by Charles E. White, Jr. from the Studio of Frank Lloyd Wright," *Journal of Architectural Education* 25 (Fall 1971), 104–12. Darwin Martin's telegram to his brother is lost.

William chafed somewhat under his brother's demands:

> It has been a mighty big job for *one* fellow to look after the completion of a house, (on which nearly every contractor has "*laid down*" or "*gone broke*") and to move, and to sell the *old* house, and to run his legs off until there is nothing left but stumps, trying to find a factory location, and to plan for new machinery, and to experiment with shoe polish, and to crowd Mr. Wright for plans, and to look after his own business, which requires more or less attention,—and at the same time, to keep good natured and to keep you thoroughly posted.

WEM to DDM, 29 April 1904, UB-WMP.

William must have felt a heavy obligation to Darwin, who, in addition to lending him funds for the new house, also made an arrangement whereby the Larkin Company would purchase large quantities of William's stove and shoe polishes. See WEM to DDM, 29 April 1904, UB-WMP.

Regarding his loans to William, Darwin wrote on 2 May 1906, (UB-MFP):

> You jar me most awful when you say you still expect me to put up $12,000. You started to build a factory to cost, I think, $18,000, and I agreed to finance it. Then you proposed a power plant to cost some $5,000 and I agreed to finance that; say $23,000. I have sent you $22,750. I need about $4,000 at once for my own affairs, and am today about $500 in the hole. Please advise me by return mail about how you will call for the $12,000 and how it happened and I will arrange for your needs and mine.

15   DDM to FLW, 23 May 1904, UB-WMP

16   FLW to DDM, 20 May 1904, UB-WMP.

17   DDM to FLW 23 May 1904.

18   DDM to FLW, 25 May 1904, UB-WMP. The "blow out" to which Darwin refers is his and Isabelle's anniversary. Apparently William Heath's comment refers to the following Christmas, five months beyond Martin's deadline. It is impossible to tell whether Heath was being sarcastic, but his prediction was only off by one month.

19   DDM to FLW, 27 May 1904, UB-WMP.

20   DDM *Memorandum*, 20 June 1904.

21   FLW to DDM, 14 July 1904, UB-WMP. Presumably Wright refers here to the steel I beams that were eventually laid atop the major piers as supports for the roofs and especially for the cantilevered eaves that give the house its character. These are, of course, still in place.

22   DDM to WEM, 1 August 1904, UB-WMP.

23   WEM to DDM, 4 August 1904, UB-WMP.

24   Darwin explained to William that he wanted the house completed for the celebrations of his wedding anniversary on June 26 and of Dorothy's birthday the following day, both events to be combined with a neighborhood housewarming, and that Wright's failure to provide information and drawings in a timely fashion was causing unnecessary, expensive delays.

> I am not trying at all to unduly rush the part of the house, which to rush would injure it, i.e., to finish. It is to avoid that very thing that I am trying to obtain intelligence requisite for the carrying on of the mason work, and putting in the windows. Mr. Wright has advised having the celebrated Milwaukee cabinet maker, Matthew Bros. put in the trim, and I am disposed to do it, and to lend myself in every way

possible to make for him a monumental job, but in withholding data, which we
know he can easily give, and this after his promises when I was writing a check to
be prompt with information, is exceedingly exasperating as well as expensive.

DDM to WEM, 5 August 1904, UB-WMP.

25 DDM *Memorandum*, 8 and 11 May 1904. "Visit from Mr. Wright. Plan of our new house practically settled."

26 DDM to FLW, 12 August 1904, UB-WMP.

27 FLW to DDM, 17 August 1904, UB-WMP.

28 DDM to FLW, 19 August 1904, UB-WMP.

29 FLW to DDM, 28 August 1904, UB-WMP.

30 Wright created a similar site plan for the Ward Willits House in Highland Park, Illinois, in 1901. See Bruce Brooks Pfeiffer, ed., *Frank Lloyd Wright Monograph, 1887–1901* (Tokyo: A.D.A. Edita, 1986), fig. 392.

31 FLW to DDM, 17 August 1904, UB-WMP.

32 In the library and dining room of the Martin House, Wright employs a similar spatial configuration vertically; i.e., the ceiling height in the center of these two spaces (and the living room as well) is nine feet, but at the outer east and west extremities the ceiling is lowered to six feet, five inches. These lowered ceiling zones function as traffic spaces in some instances and lend intimacy in others, but the taller central space can also be read as jetted upward from the lowered ceiling plane. By these means Wright achieves ambiguity—is the space expanding upward or contracting downward?—and thus dynamism.

33 In 1904 Wright was also working on the H. J. Ullman house, an unrealized T-shaped plan in which the terminals of the building were resolved in a system of twin piers juxtaposed at right angles with glazing between them. It is impossible to know for which commission, Ullman or Martin, Wright first developed this idea.

CHAPTER FOUR

1 The complex was complete except for the gardener's cottage, the installation of the art-glass windows, the pouring of cement walkways, and the placement of many landscape elements.

Six of Darwin Martin's photographs feature the interior, although they are not very revealing. Darwin occasionally used photographs to show Wright problems in construction.

2 The abundance of dimensions and factual details in the article suggests that Lang was interviewed at length, although there are two quotations ("like corded silk" and "we mortify our staircases") that appear to come from Wright.

3 The bowling alley under the pergola, along with various other ideas, were never realized

4 This figure was apparently derived by multiplying the total number of pier clusters—eight—by the number of sides on each pier—four—to bring the total number of openings between piers of the same width and distance apart to thirty-two. The piers framing the stairway are not part of a pier cluster, but they have the same dimensions and hence would qualify as the thirty-third opening. Of course, these figures do not account for the fact that the outer piers of some of the pier clusters are in the plane of the exterior wall and hence do not read or function as openings, except for small casement windows.

5 The Wright-Martin Papers in the Archives of the University at Buffalo contain a list of over fifty-six pieces of Carnegie Steel used in the construction of the Martin House.

6 I owe this observation to Ted Lownie of Hamilton Houston Lownie, Architects, P.C., the architect charged with the restoration of the Martin complex.

7 Fumed oak was used everywhere except for bedrooms five and six, where Isabelle Martin requested mahogany to match the furniture she brought from the 1888 house. A finer grade of quartersawn oak was used in the main Martin House than in the Barton House.

8 Approximately 225 sheets of drawings and blueprints exist today in various archives: the Archives of the University at Buffalo have 52; the Deutsches Architekturmuseum in Frankfurt, Germany, has 49; and the Frank Lloyd Wright Foundation in Scottsdale, Arizona, has 125.

9 O. S. Lang, letterpress book, 6 June 1905–20 February 1906, UB-WMP.

10 DDM Contractor (O. S. Lang) Correspondence, 1904–09, UB-MCC.

11   W. L. Krause to Oscar Lang, 17 June 1905, UB-MCC.

12   DDM to Linden Glass Company, Memo, 5 June 1905, UB-MCC.

13   In 1917 Martin left the Larkin Company for a year in order to work with Julius Rosenwald, the president of Sears, Roebuck & Company, in supervising the production and organization of materials for the United States effort in World War I.

14   Martin, a militant teetotaler, ordered the job dry on August 23, 1904, against the better judgment of the chief mason, Mr. Frank, who feared a mass exodus from the site. Only one man left the job, however.

15   DDM to OSL, Memo, 6 June 1905, UB-MCC.

16   OSL to DDM, 6 June 1905, UB-MCC. Emphasis in the original.

17   DDM to FLW, 24 May 1904, UB-WMP.

18   FLW to DDM, 25 August 1904, UB-WMP.

19   DDM to FLW, 27 August 1904, UB-WMP.

20   DDM to FLW, 12 October 1904, UB-WMP.

21   Ibid.

22   FLW to DDM, 13 October 1904, UB-WMP.

23   DDM to FLW, 14 October 1904, UB-WMP. Wright used sun traps at the Martin House and on the Larkin Administration Building. At the Martin House, these consisted of a series of heavy-gauge glass plates laid horizontally within a ledge just outside the south-facing reception room windows. The sun trap allowed light to penetrate into the basement below but also reflected light upward into the reception room.

Wright's exuberant promises to Darwin Martin did not sit well with William R. Heath, to whom Martin must have shown the letter. Heath wrote:

> DDM
>
> I'm mad—hot mad—I didn't draw any "domestic symphony" and my commission
> didn't bring forth any such over flow of over soul.
>
> It beats all what money'll do.—but—business is business.
>
> If the physical construct don't capture, he tries his intellectual and if this
> don't *fetch* he rings in his *oversoul*. He's *got you*!
>
> H[eath] 10/04

W. R. Heath to DDM, 15 October 1904, UB-WMP.

24   DDM to FLW, 2 November 1904, UB-WMP.

25   DDM to FLW, 23, 27, 28, and 31 January 1905, UB-WMP.

26   FLW to DDM, 26 January 1905, UB-WMP.

27   "Mr. Wright starts 14th with Mrs. W[right] for Japan." DDM *Memorandum*, 11 February 1905.

28   DDM to FLW, 28 January 1905, UB-WMP.

CHAPTER FIVE

1   For a definitive study of Wright's art glass, see Julie L. Sloan, *Light Screens: The Complete Leaded-Glass Windows of Frank Lloyd Wright* (New York: Rizzoli International Publications, Inc., 2001).

2   The source of the names for these windows, in use since the 1960s, remains unknown. Neither the term "tree-of-life" nor "wisteria" appears anywhere in the Wright-Martin correspondence.

3   WBG to DDM, 22 February 1905, UB-WMP.

4   WBG to DDM, 9 March 1905, UB-WMP.

5   That William Martin's windows have a similar but much heavier series of horizontals suggests that Wright wanted to create a certain affinity between the two houses.

6   There is a parallel between Wright's use of the tree-of-life pattern on the second floor of the Martin House and the vigorous upward splay of Louis Sullivan's angel sculptures at the top of the Bayard Building in Manhattan.

7   DDM to WBG, 10 March 1905, UB-WMP.

8   DDM to FLW, 28 May 1906, UB-WMP.

9   FLW to DDM, 16 September 1909, UB-WMP.

10   DDM to WBG, 10 April 1905, UB-WMP.

11   WBG to DDM, 11 April 1905, UB-WMP.

12   FLW to DDM, 18 May 1905, UB-WMP.

13   Curiously, there is no mention of beds in Darwin's letter to Wright of May 19, 1905 [UB-WMP], or in Wright's additions to the list.

14   DDM to FLW, 19 May 1905, UB-WMP; Wright's response and a listing of additional pieces of furniture are written directly on Martin's letter. The client did not make a written reply to Wright's additions to his letter.

15   "Mr. Bown assures me that if we use glass mosaic on the chimney that when it settles the mosaic will crack and we will be sorry ever after. Have you considered this point? Do not all chimneys settle?" DDM to FLW, 3 June 1905, UB-WMP.

16   FLW to DDM, 7 June 1905, UB-WMP.

17   Ibid.

18   DDM Index.

19   Darwin wrote, "Please reply to my letter of May 18th....Please reply to my letter of May 19th....We don't want our investment [to] stand idle." DDM to FLW, 5 June 1905, UB-WMP.

20   DDM to FLW, 17 July 1905, UB-WMP.

21   FLW to DDM, 28 July 1905, UB-WMP.

22   DDM to FLW, 26 August 1905, UB-WMP. Emphasis in the original.

23   Ibid.

24   Ibid.

25   The reason for the three-year delay in the construction of the Martin gardener's cottage is not known.

26   DDM to FLW, 31 August 1905, UB-WMP.

27   There is no document to indicate why this date was chosen. It may have been to allow the family to settle in for Christmas.

28   DDM to FLW, 23 October 1905, UB-WMP.

29   FLW to DDM, 25 October 1905, UB-WMP.

30   Currently the walls of the Martin House are painted throughout with what appears to be a cream-colored latex, but test patches indicate that the walls were originally washed with pigment while the plaster was still wet and then glazed after it had dried. The original plaster surface was roughly textured and the color(s) were uneven. The palette was autumnal, with greens and golds predominating.

31   DDM to FLW, 30 October 1905, UB-WMP.

32   FLW to DDM, 2 November 1905, UB-WMP. Wright may have written this letter before receiving Darwin's letter of October 30, 1905.

33   DDM Index, "Wright, Frank Lloyd—Nov. 8–9, '05 Here."

34   DDM to FLW, 14 November 1905, UB-WMP.

35   DDM to FLW, 16 November 1905, UB-WMP.

36   FLW to DDM, 21 November 1905, UB-WMP.

37   Ibid.

38   DDM to FLW, 11 November 1905, UB-WMP.

39   DDM to FLW, 23 November 1905, UB-WMP.

40   FLW to DDM, 5 December 1905, UB-WMP. Emphasis in the original. Wright had already designed all of the furniture for the Susan Dana House in Springfield, Illinois, prior to the Martin commission.

41   Ibid.

42   A letter instructing Lang how to best place the Nike into position in the conservatory was sent by its manufacturer, P. P. Caproni & Bros. of Boston, on October 20, 1906, UB-MCC.

43   Oscar Lang to FLW, 24 December 1905, UB-WMP.

44   FLW to DDM, circa 25 December 1905, UB-WMP

45   On Edward C. Waller, Wright's most important early client, see Leonard K. Eaton, *Two Chicago Architects and Their Clients: Frank Lloyd Wright and Howard Van Doren Shaw* (Cambridge, Mass.: MIT Press, 1969), 91–95.

46   DDM to FLW, 26 December 1905-A, UB-WMP.

47 Wright's penchant for three-legged chairs has never been explained. Wright designed a three-legged metal office chair for the Larkin Administration Building that became known as the "suicide chair" among the office staff, according to Harry Larkin, Jr., in an interview with the author in 1980. Wright also designed another, in tubular metal, for the Johnson's Wax Company headquarters in 1937.

48 DDM to FLW, 1 February 1906, UB-MCC.

49 DDM to FLW, 26 December 1905, UB-WMP.

50 Ibid.

51 FLW to DDM, 28 December 1905-B, UB-WMP.

52 Ibid.

53 Ibid.

54 DDM to FLW, 26 December 1905, UB-WMP.

55 FLW to DDM, 2 January 1906, UB-WMP.

56 DDM Index, "Wright, Frank Lloyd—May 10 '06 Here."

57 DDM to FLW, 22 May 1906, UB-WMP.

58 FLW to DDM, 28 May 1906, UB-WMP.

59 *The Buffalo Daily Courier*, 17 November 1906.

60 In an interview conducted by archivist Shonnie Finnegan, Lorelei Z. Ketter, and Jack Quinan on October 18, 1976, Darwin R. Martin stated that his mother suffered from scleritis, an ulcerative condition of the eye related to tuberculosis. She underwent eye surgery in 1893. Mrs. Martin lacked focal power and depth perception, saw color well, but could not endure bright light.

CHAPTER SIX

1 FLW, "The Architect and the Machine," a talk presented to the University Guild in Evanston, Illinois, in 1894, published in Bruce Brooks Pfeiffer, *Frank Lloyd Wright, Collected Writings*, vol. 1, 1894–1930 (New York: Rizzoli, 1992), 23.

2 FLW, "A Philosophy of Fine Art," a talk presented to the Architectural League of the Art Institute of Chicago in 1900, published in Pfeiffer, *Frank Lloyd Wright, Collected Writings*, vol. 1, 41.

3 FLW, "In the Cause of Architecture," *The Architectural Record*, 23, no. 3, (March 1908): 162.

4 Wright took a big risk in making this claim. If it were merely a sales pitch—or if, as Norris Kelly Smith put it in *Frank Lloyd Wright: A Study in Architectural Content* [(Watkins Glen, N.Y.: The American Life Foundation, 1979) 73–74], the idea was "farfetched" and that in actuality, "each commission presented him with an opportunity for solving afresh a problem that was essentially his own"—it would soon become evident and the news would quickly spread that he was a charlatan.

5 FLW, "A Philosophy of Fine Art," in Pfeiffer, *Frank Lloyd Wright*, vol. 1, 42.

6 Ralph Waldo Emerson, *Nature* (Boston: James Munroe and Company, 1836).

7 FLW, *An Autobiography* (New York: Duell, Sloan and Pearce, 1943), 161.

8 There is an interesting parallel here between Darwin Martin's aforementioned approach to the Larkin business after the departure of Elbert Hubbard, wherein he simply expanded the business by adding new catalogue items, and his approach to his home, wherein he took preexisting designs and had Wright elaborate on them. See Chapter One for this discussion.

9 FLW, "In the Cause of Architecture," *Architectural Record* 13 (March 1908) (New York: Architectural Record Books, 1975), 157.

10 Richard C. MacCormac, "The Anatomy of Wright's Aesthetic," *Architectural Review* 143 (February 1968), 143–46.

11 According to an interview with Dorothy Martin Foster conducted by Sue Greenwood in November 1971 [tape and transcript, Archives of the University at Buffalo], Dorothy stated, when asked if her father was about as tall as Wright, "I haven't any idea. My mother was about my height and I am 5′ 1 1/4″. I don't think my father was over 5′ 7″ or 5′ 8″ if he was that." Clearance beneath the lowered ceilings between the entrance hall and the unit room and the reception room is 6′ 5″.

12   DDM to FLW, 23 August 1904, UB-WMP. "We turned the job [Martin House construction] absolutely dry yesterday, substituting ice water and clean glasses for the bottled beer that was strewn all over the place...."

In an interview conducted on December 5, 1972, by Shonnie Finnegan, archivist of the State University of New York at Buffalo, and Lorelei Z. Ketter, Dorothy Martin Foster, when asked about her parents' friends, replied, "My father was a very peculiar person. He was very scornful of what he called 'Delaware Avenue.' And he was once enticed to a dinner party with a group of Delaware Avenue people and he sat, one lady removed, from, I think, Norman Mack. Father refused the wine and he refused the cigarettes and finally Norman Mack leaned over and said, 'What the hell do you do for a good time?' But you see he was not popular with that group at all. He read Lyon's *History of the World* in two volumes riding on the trolley car to the Larkin Company."

In an interview conducted on October 4, 1976, by the author, Darwin R. Martin said that his father was a teetotaler and that there was never any liquor served in the house.

13.   For an incisive analysis of the structure and space of the Darwin Martin House, see Robert McCarter, "The Fabric of Experience: Frank Lloyd Wright's Darwin Martin House," in Jack Quinan, ed. *Frank Lloyd Wright: Windows of the Darwin D. Martin House* (Buffalo, N.Y.: Burchfield-Penney Art Center/Buffalo State College Foundation, Inc., 1999), 21–29.

14.   Donald Hoffmann, *Frank Lloyd Wright's Robie House: The Illustrated Story of an Architectural Masterpiece* (New York: Dover Publications, Inc., 1984), 37, figs. 54, 55. The same can be said of the design for Fallingwater, the Edgar J. Kaufmann House in Mill Run, Pennsylvania, of 1937.

15.   The chevron pattern in the tree-of-life window can be read as an "M," that is, as a monogram for the house's patron.

16.   Darwin kept a record of his readings in his diaries. As he became wealthy he purchased rare books, such as the 1842 edition of John James Audubon's *Birds of America,* and first editions of Mark Twain's books, which he gave to the family as Christmas presents. DDM *Memorandum,* 25 December 1911 and 25 December 1916.

17   DDM to FLW, 19 May 1905, UB-WMP. DDM lists furniture desired. "BOOKCASES 1st Bed room 2 2nd Bed room 1 3rd Bed room 1 4th Bed room 1."

18   DDM Autobiography, 69.

> In the course of all the years, I have picked up a smattering of education, probably the equivalent, finally, of the best high-school courses; but for lack of proper ideals, nothing ever prompted me to seek to learn any of the sciences, for which I seem to have had no natural taste. When I apologetically said to William R. Heath that, "I never went to school," he quickly rejoined, "You've been in school all your life!"

19   Dorothy Martin Foster, interview with author, 14 December 1975. In the Ketter-Finnegan interview of December 5, 1972, Dorothy said, "We had to have an encyclopedia in the dining room and an encyclopedia in the library. If any controversial subject arose at the dining table he [Darwin D. Martin] would hop up and get the proper volume of the encyclopedia, which was right here."

20   Everett K. Martin, interview with author, 5 August 1981.

21   Darwin recorded the cutting of the skylight into his office ceiling in DDM to FLW, 18 May 1905, UB-WMP. "Mr. Lang began cutting the hole for the bursar skylight Monday morning."

22   Wright's "sun traps" are thick, horizontally laid glass plates that allow daylight into basements and simultaneously reflect light upward into adjacent rooms. They occurred alongside the entrance stairs to the annex of the Larkin Administration Building and along the base of the south-facing elevation of the annex. See Jack Quinan, *Frank Lloyd Wright's Larkin Building: Myth and Fact* (Cambridge, Mass.: The Architectural History Foundation/MIT Press, 1987), 78, fig. 77, and 126, fig. 117. Sun traps appear in a similar position in the Martin House, just outside the windows of the reception room, alongside the entrance stairs. There are also references to sun traps in Oscar Lang's letters to Wright of October 6 and 10, 1904 [UB-WMP].

23   A long-standing rumor holds that the four birdhouse finials on the roof of the Martin house conservatory are marten houses. Although this has not been substantiated, Wright seemed to enjoy assigning playful titles to some of his projects. Franklin Toker was the first to observe that the name "Fallingwater" contains Wright's initials. The Hanna "Honeycomb," in addition to its alliterative qualities, is a reference to the building's hexagonal planning module, and "Hollyhock" is a play on Hollywood, the location of the Barnsdall House.

The marten, distinguished ornithologically for consuming five times its weight in insects every day, is an apt metaphor for Darwin Martin's voracious appetite for work.

24 Darwin R. Martin is quoted in *The Buffalo Evening News* of July 2, 1952. "And it was only after hysterics that mother got closets in the house. No original space was provided for storage except in the basement." Regarding the quality of light in the house he stated, "As a child I resented the house....[T]here was no light for my mother, who was partially blind."

In an interview conducted by Lorelei Z. Ketter, Shonnie Finnegan, and Fred Tamalonis with Dorothy Martin Foster on December 5, 1972 (Archives of the University at Buffalo), Dorothy reported, "Mr. Wright would not permit a linen closet big enough to have even the family sheets and towels in it. And my mother finally wept and got a linen closet that was about a quarter or a fifth the size of the linen closet that my brother provided when he built [800 West Ferry, a luxurious apartment building in Buffalo]."

25 Edgar Tafel, *Apprentice to Genius: Years with Frank Lloyd Wright* (New York: McGraw-Hill Book Company, 1979), 84, 85, 174, 176. Tafel supervised the construction of Fallingwater and the Johnson's Wax Company Building, Racine, Wisconsin, of 1937 for Wright and visited the Martin House with Wright during the 1930s, after Darwin Martin's death but before Mrs. Martin left the house.

26 Tafel, *Apprentice to Genius*, 91.

27 FLW to Aline Barnsdall, 29 December 1935, Archives of the Frank Lloyd Wright Foundation.

28 FLW to DDM, 13 October 1904, UB-WMP.

29 Frank Lloyd Wright, *An Autobiography*, 2nd ed. (New York, 1943), 252.

30 A drawing dating from circa 1910 exists in the Archives of the Deutsches Architekturmuseum in Frankfurt, in which Wright proposes wrapping the east end of the east porch of the Martin House with a shallow pool, thus furthering the vessel-in-water analogy. D.A.M. acc. no. 283-001-023.

31 See Chapter One, 38–39, and Chapter Two, page 55, regarding Darwin's relationship with Delta.

32 DDM *Memorandum*, 12 May 1905.

33 There is no mention in the correspondence, either, of Wright's drawing for the Grace Fuller design of 1907 or for the Rosenwald Negro Children's School of 1927. References to Wright's designs for a summer cottage for the Martins at Bay Beach, Ontario, of 1909 and the house for Dorothy Martin Foster of 1923 only occur in passing, several years after the fact. It is possible that there were relevant letters but they were removed from the Wright-Martin correspondence at some point prior to their sale in 1981 when, unfortunately, some forty to fifty drawings were separated from the rest of the purchase.

34 It is impossible to attribute this house to a specific Martin with any certainty. Because it is large, it might have served Darwin as a means of tempting William away from Oak Park. Because Frank Martin had some business connections to Buffalo through the sachet-powder business that Darwin had established for him, he is also a candidate. Alta seems less likely.

35 Wright's brief, undated letter (probably written in 1902) to Susan Dana [UB-WMP] introduces Darwin Martin.

36 For an excellent discussion of Susan Dana and her house, see Mark Heyman and Richard Taylor, *Frank Lloyd Wright and Susan Lawrence Dana: From the Town and the Prairie Conference* (Springfield, Ill.: Sangamon State University, 1985).

37 Ibid., 1–4.

38 Ibid., 4.

39 Ibid., 6.

40 Spirit letters, Dana Papers, Illinois State Historical Library, ibid., 4–5.

41 Ibid., 32.

42 Frank Lloyd Wright, *Ausgeführte Bauten und Entwürfe von Frank Lloyd Wright* (Berlin: Ernst Wasmuth Verlag, 1910).

43 I am grateful to Mark Heyman for calling my attention to Wright's refusal to publish the Dana house after 1910.

44 "But the contractor and workmen weren't the only villains. Sometimes the client's wife was a villain in disguise. Mr. Wright's buildings were always the result of a relationship between men, and Mrs. Client was too often in the way. He often said, 'Only fools and women criticize half-done work.'" Tafel, *Apprentice to Genius*, 64–65.

45 Heyman and Taylor, *Frank Lloyd Wright and Susan Lawrence Dana*, 31.

46 Wright was not averse to defining some of his work, such as the Larkin Building and the Johnson's Wax Company Building, as masculine and feminine, respectively. See FLW, *An Autobiography*, 2nd ed. (New York, 1943), 474.

47 Ibid., 161.

48 Wright, *An Autobiography*, 161.

49 Grant Manson, *Frank Lloyd Wright to 1910* (New York: Reinhold Pub. Co., 1958), 187.

50 Ibid.

51 Leonard K. Eaton, *Two Chicago Architects and Their Clients: Frank Lloyd Wright and Howard Van Doren Shaw* (Cambridge, Mass.: MIT Press, 1969), 83.

52 Ibid., 85.

53 Theodore Turak, "Mr. Wright and Mrs. Coonley: An Interview with Elizabeth Coonley Faulkner," in Richard Guy Wilson and Sidney K. Robinson, eds., *Modern Architecture in America: Visions and Revisions* (Ames: Iowa State University Press, 1991), 144–63.

54 Ibid., 156.

55 Ibid., 155.

56 Ibid.

57 Ibid., 154.

58 In addition to Mrs. Coonley's activities as a Christian Science practitioner, her husband was a member of the publications committee for the State of Illinois Christian Science Church, a position that led him to move the family to Washington, D.C., in 1912, where his involvement with the church expanded.

59 Smith, *Frank Lloyd Wright*, 76.

60 In his spirited defense of the unadorned surfaces of the Larkin Administration Building, Wright wrote,

> I confess to a love for a clean arris; the cube I find comforting; the sphere inspiring. In the opposition of the circle and the square I find sufficient motives for architectural themes with all the sentiment of Romeo and Juliet: combining these with the octagon I find sufficient materials for symphonic development. I can marry these forms in various ways without adulterating them, but I love them pure, strong, and undefiled.

Jack Quinan, "Frank Lloyd Wright's Reply to Russell Sturgis," *Journal of the Society of Architectural Historians* 41 (October 1982): 242.

To Walter V. Davidson, a Buffalo client, Wright wrote on December 29, 1908 [author's collection], "It is always a satisfaction to have one's work in appreciative hands. I think you will wear this new garment of yours gracefully—to get the best out of it. With best wishes to you and the soul and the center of the new home to be, I am...Yours Sincerely."

To Paul and Jean Hanna, clients of a house in Palo Alta, California, based on a hexagonal planning grid, Wright wrote, "You look so well in the bee cells that were made to imprison you in sunlight." The letter is reproduced in Paul R. and Jean S. Hanna, *Frank Lloyd Wright's Hanna House: The Clients' Report* (Cambridge, Mass.: The Architectural Foundation/MIT Press, 1982), 75.

In his discussion of the Larkin Administration Building in *An Autobiography* [(New York: Duell, Sloan, and Pearce, 1943), 151], Wright writes, "Rebellious and protestant as I was myself when the Larkin Building came from me," as though he had given birth to the building.

61 Frank Lloyd Wright, as paraphrased by Everett Kirby Martin, in an interview with the author, 5 August 1981.

62 A substantial number of letters exist between Wright and his office staff and Charles W. Barnes of McCook, Nebraska, regarding a Walser-Barton type house for Barnes that was never realized. Walter Burley Griffin wrote most of the letters from the Oak Park studio. The few Wright letters are businesslike and have none of the warmth and engagement of the Martin correspondence. It would appear that Wright saw little promise in McCook, although the Barnes project did lead to the Harvey Sutton House there in 1906. The Sutton commission is also documented in a series of letters between the Oak Park studio and Mr. Sutton and again, few are from Wright's own hand. On the Sutton House, see W. R. Hasbrouck, "A Wright House on the Prairie," *Prairie School Review* 2 (third quarter 1965): 5–19. On the Barnes House, see Randy G. Stramel, "Frank Lloyd Wright's Charles W. Barnes Residence (Project of 1903)," master's thesis (Graduate College of the University of Nebraska, Lincoln, December 1995).

1   DDM to FLW, 14 February 1929, SU-WMP.

2   FLW to DDM, 5 March 1929, SU-WMP.

3   DDM to FLW, 4 January 1911, UB-WMP.

4   DDM to FLW, 16 June 1916, SU-WMP.

5   DDM to FLW, 21 April 1926, SU-WMP.

6   John D. Larkin, Jr., began to take control of the Larkin Company during the 1910s. His older brother, Charles, left the company in 1918; William R. Heath retired in 1922; and Darwin Martin retired in 1925, at the age of sixty.

7   Dorothy Martin Foster, interviewed by the author, 14 November 1975. Dorothy and Darwin R. Martin were both aware that their father had loaned Wright substantial sums of money during the years prior to the Great Depression. Wright never returned any of the money. The Martin family struggled throughout the 1930s. After Darwin Martin died, Isabelle was all but forgotten as Wright moved on to new clients and projects that brought him a resurgence of fame.

8   Robert Campbell, "This May Be the Year of Wright," *The Boston Globe*, 23 January 1990.

Campbell continues, "I suppose it's controversial to make that claim for the architect Frank Lloyd Wright. But really it shouldn't be. America's other great artists—our best painters, sculptors, composers—don't really rank with the tops of all time. They're just not Rembrandt or Michelangelo or Beethoven. Wright alone has that kind of standing. By common consent of those qualified to judge, he's among the greatest architects who ever practiced."

9   Lewis Mumford, *Sketches from Life: The Autobiography of Lewis Mumford, The Early Years* (New York: The Dial Press, 1982), 437–38.

POSTSCRIPT

1   After having written 277 letters between 1904 and 1906, Martin and Wright managed just nine letters in the following three years.

2   Darwin R. Martin, interview with the author, 18 December 1976. Guests of the Martin family included Booker T. Washington, Henry Ossawa Tanner, Gertrude Stein, and Theodore Roosevelt.

3   FLW to DDM, 16 September 1909, UB-WMP. This letter included a separately enclosed bill for drawings for the Martin gardener's cottage.

4   Wright's involvement with Mamah Borthwick Cheney has been extensively documented by his biographers Robert C. Twombly, Brendan Gill, and Meryle Secrest.

5   WEM to DDM, 10 October 1910, UB-MFP.

6   This, according to letters between Wright and Martin of 12 November and 17 November 1910, and from Ernst Wasmuth to Wright of 3 November 1910, UB-WMP.

7   See Paul Kruty, *Frank Lloyd Wright and Midway Gardens* (Urbana and Chicago: University of Illinois Press, 1998).

8   Kathryn Smith, "Frank Lloyd Wright and the Imperial Hotel: A Postscript," *The Art Bulletin* 67 (June 1985), 296–310.

9   Darwin Martin wrote, "Why can you not design for Mrs. Martin a dining room table to entirely replace the one we are using?" [DDM to FLW, 9 January 1911, UB-WMP]; "Mrs. Martin has jury-rigged light for playroom, she wants you to design ceiling lights and trim." [DDM to FLW, 9 December 1911, UB-WMP]: A memo from Darwin to his gardener is especially revealing: "We must <u>do</u> things to make this place more attractive to Mrs. Martin, winter and summer. It depends on you!" [DDM to Thomas Skinner, 20 April 1911, UB-WMP]. Emphasis in the original.

10   Both Martin children called their mother's ailment "scleritis" and spoke of her difficulties with the house, with some bitterness, in interviews with the author in the late 1970s. According to the Grant C. Manson Papers, held in the Oak Park, Illinois, Public Library, Mrs. Martin told Manson in April 1940, when he

visited her in Buffalo, that she found the house dark and uncomfortable. In a presentation to the Martin House docents on July 19, 1997, Margaret Foster, daughter of Dorothy (Martin) Foster, described her grandmother as "vision impaired" and recalled having to assist her in various ways during summers at the Martin summer house, Graycliff, in the early 1940s.

11   During interviews with Darwin R. Martin, Dorothy Martin Foster, and Evelyn Heath Jacobsen, children of Darwin Martin and William Heath, conducted by this author in the late 1970s and early 1980s, an undercurrent of disapproval bordering on distaste for Wright was evident. This seems to have been a result of Wright's notoriety, the unconventional nature of his houses, and—in the case of the Martins—a conviction that Wright owed the family a large sum of money. Nevertheless, these three people all grudgingly admired his work.

12   "A House of Many Oddities," *Illustrated Buffalo Express*, 9 October 1904. The phrase "Chinese puzzle" appears as the caption under a photograph of the foundations of the conservatory and garage/stable.

13   WEM to DDM, 10 October 1910, UB-WMP.

14   DDM to FLW, 28 August 1913, UB-WMP.

15   DDM to FLW, 21 January 1914, UB-WMP. There are no drawings in the Martin Papers regarding alterations to the veranda of the Martin House. A drawing does exist, however, among the Martin House drawings in the Archives of the Deutsches Architekturmuseum in Frankfort [D.A.M. no. 283-001-023].

16   DDM to FLW, 2 July 1914, UB-WMP.

17   DDM to FLW, 5 August 1914, UB-WMP. According to a letter from Harry Robinson, Wright's office manager, to Darwin Martin dated July 9, 1914 [UB-WMP], "For some reason the Linden Glass co. does not care to make your skylight. I have tried time after time to get a figure from this concern but without success."

18   Harry Robinson to DDM, 6 August 1914, UB-WMP.

19   DDM to FLW, 10 August 1914, UB-WMP.

20   For a vivid, detailed account of the murder, see Merle Secrest, *Frank Lloyd Wright: A Biography* (New York: Alfred A. Knopf, 1992), 216–22.

21   *The Buffalo Courier*, 16 August 1914.

22   DDM *Memorandum*, entries for August and September, 1914.

23   DDM *Memorandum*, September 1914.

24   FLW to DDM, 20 October 1914, UB-WMP.

25   Ibid.

26   DDM to Catherine Wright, 3 December 1915, SU-WMP. Seven pages (untitled) summarizing Darwin Martin's financial holdings as of 1 Jan. 1916 — $1,947,715.59 in stocks (mostly Larkin Company), $133,703.73 in bonds, and $270,294.85 in real estate. [UB-MFP]

27   DDM to FLW, 16 June 1916, SU-WMP.

28   FLW to DDM, 23 June 1916, SU-WMP.

29   DDM to FLW, 29 June 1916, SU-WMP.

30   FLW to DDM, 31 June 1916, SU-WMP.

31   FLW to Isabelle Martin, undated (circa 19 August 1916), SU-WMP.

32   Darwin Martin wrote: "The question of remodeling a portion of the house is again very unsettled, so that it will not be worth while for you to allow your other engagements to be affected by a possible call from Buffalo. Will write you more definitely when I am able to do so." DDM to FLW, 30 August 1916, SU-WMP. Darwin may have been motivated by the uncertainty caused by the war in Europe, or by the prospect that Wright would be in Japan for extended periods. Darwin may have been becoming less certain about the future of the Larkin Company, the control of which was shifting toward John D. Larkin, Jr. Or, it may have been this last unwillingness on Wright's part to comply with any of the Martins' requests for changes to the Martin House that proved to be the final straw.

33   Wright proposed the bailout scheme to Darwin Martin in a letter of November 21, 1926, SU-WMP: "I am trying to get ten friends to take over my collections and realty and underwrite my indebtedness to the bank so I can be free to sell and work my way out, in the hands of a trustee they may appoint. I have assets of nearly $360 at a conservative evaluation and over a total indebtedness of 475,000." Darwin offered to pay in one tenth, or $7,500, but doubled it within a year. Others involved included Mrs. Avery Coonley (who also took a double share), Alexander Woollcott, and Maginel Wright Barney (Wright's sister).

34 Dorothy Martin Foster, interview with the author, 14 November 1975. Both Martin children expressed a distaste for Wright in interviews, but this seems to have stemmed from Wright's behavior toward Isabelle Martin in the decade following Darwin's death, when Isabelle was nearly destitute and Wright ignored her.

In point of fact, Dorothy Martin Foster did not tear up Wright's drawings for her house; her brother appropriated them, and they surfaced on the market in the 1980s.

35 DDM to FLW, 24 March 1932, SU-WMP.

36 Olgivanna (née Lazovich) Wright, the architect's third wife, was born to aristocratic parents in Cetinje, Montenegro, in 1898. She married Vlademir Hinzenberg, a Russian architect, in 1917, gave birth to a daughter, studied at Fontainebleau with the Russian mystic, G. I. Gurdjieff, in the early 1920s, and emigrated to the United States, following her husband, in 1922. Olgivanna met Wright, who was recently separated from his second wife, Miriam Noel, in 1924, and began to live with him at Taliesin in 1925. In December 1925 she gave birth to a daughter, Iovanna, but owing to legal battles with Miriam Noel, Hinzenberg, and others, Wright and Olgivanna were not married until 1928.

37 *Buffalo Evening News*, 18 December 1935.

38 A substantial amount of the original Wright-designed furniture was purchased from the Martin children at that time and returned to the house.

ILLUSTRATION CREDITS

Architectural Record (March 1908), figs. 45, 54; (January 1928), fig. 93

Brackett, Carolyn Mann, fig. 19

Buffalo and Erie County Historical Society, Buffalo, New York, figs. 35, 106

Canadian Centre for Architecture/Centre Canadien d'Architecture, Montreal, figs. 50, 61–63, 78, 83, 85–88, 95–97, 102, 105, 118

Carr, Doug, figs. 89, 112–15

Jean Castex, *Le Printempts de la Prairie House* (Liege and Brussels: Pierre Mardaga Editeur, 1985), fig. 51

Deutsches Architekturmuseum, Frankfurt, fig. 67

Frank Lloyd Wright Foundation, Inc., figs. 2, 5, 9, 10, 22, 23, 27, 40–44, 47–49, 64–66, 84, 91, 99, 103, 110, 117

Giedion, Sigfried, *Space, Time and Architecture* (Cambridge, Mass.: Harvard University Press, 1971), fig. 15

Henrich, Biff, Keystone Film Productions, fig. 98

Historic American Buildings Survey, Washington, D.C., figs. 25, 26, 108

Hitchcock, Henry-Russell, *In the Nature of Materials* (Duell, Sloan and Pearce, New York, 1942), figs. 33, 34, 109

Illinois Historic Preservation Agency, Dana–Thomas House, fig. 111

Ladies' Home Journal, figs. 7, 8, 30–32

Larkin, Daniel I., fig. 12

Lewis, Arnold and Keith Morgan, *Victorian Houses* (New York: Dover Publications, 1983), fig. 11

Mangione, Steve, fig. 76

Manson, Grant C., *Frank Lloyd Wright to 1910* (New York: Reinhold, 1958), figs. 36–38

O'Hara, Michael, delineator HHL, figs. 53, 55, 79, 94, 101

Quinan, Jack, figs. 3, 14, 69–73, 92, 100

Richard W. Bock Museum, Greenville College, Greenville, Illinois, figs. 107, 116

Sharma, Bhavna, figs. 24, 39

State University of New York at Buffalo Archives, figs. 4, 13, 16–18, 20, 21, 28, 29, 52, 56–60, 68, 74, 75, 77, 80–82, 119–23

Wright, Frank Lloyd, *Ausgeführte Bauten und Entwürfe von Frank Lloyd Wright* (Berlin: Ernst Wasmuth Verlag, 1910), figs. 1, 6, 46, 90

The drawings of Frank Lloyd Wright ©2002 The Frank Lloyd Wright Archives, Scottsdale, AZ

INDEX